The Writings of
Henry D. Thoreau

*Early Essays and
Miscellanies*

HENRY D. THOREAU

Early Essays and Miscellanies

EDITED BY JOSEPH J. MOLDENHAUER
AND EDWIN MOSER,
WITH ALEXANDER C. KERN

PRINCETON, NEW JERSEY
PRINCETON UNIVERSITY PRESS
MCMLXXV

Editorial expenses for this volume have been met in part
by grants from the National Endowment for the Humanities
administered through the Center for Editions of
American Authors of the Modern Language Association

Contents

Early Essays

1828-1829?

The Seasons.

> Why do the Seasons change? and why
> Does Winter's stormy brow appear?
> It is the word of him on high,
> Who rules the changing varied year.

THERE are four Seasons in a year, Spring, Summer, Autumn, and Winter. I will begin with Spring. Now we see the ice beginning to thaw, and the trees to bud. Now the Winter wears away, and the ground begins to look green with the new born grass. The birds which have lately been to more southern countries return again to cheer us with their morning song.

Next comes Summer. Now we see a beautiful sight. The trees and flowers are in bloom.—Now is the pleasantest part of the year. Now the fruit begins to form on the trees, and all things look beautiful.

In Autumn we see the trees loaded with fruit. Now the farmers begin to lay in their Winter's store, and the markets abound with fruit. The trees are partly stripped of their leaves. The birds which visited us in Spring are now retiring to warmer countries, as they know that Winter is coming.

Next comes Winter. Now we see the ground covered with snow, and the trees are bare. The cold is so intense that the rivers and brooks are frozen.— There is nothing green to be seen. We have no birds to cheer us with their morning song. We hear only the sound of the sleigh bells.

> Give your idea of the anxieties and Delights of a Discoverer of whatever class, Columbus, Herschel, Newton.

IT almost invariably happens, that the lives of most distinguished characters are chequered with trials and disappointments, and that their eminence has been attained by years of toil and anxiety. But this seems particularly to be the case with the Discoverer. With him all is uncertainty; chance may crown him with the highest honors, and chance may expose him to the ridicule and contempt of his fellow men; fortune may flatter him when all hope has vanished, and desert him when success seems near. Indeed, to the fall of an apple could Newton trace his famous discovery of the laws of universal gravitation. Perhaps one succeeds, and makes a discovery which will immortalize his name; still his work is not finished; he has the prejudices of the whole world to combat; he is satisfied in his own mind, but others are yet to be persuaded; the burden of proof lies on his side; and many are there who have sunk under it; who have met with more difficulty in gaining proselytes, than in establishing the fact to their own satisfaction. A dismal picture this. Of their Delight we may judge, by taking an example; Columbus for instance.

He conceives a project of sailing to the Indies by a bold and unusual route; this proposal, promising to make his native shores the centre of opulence and power, is rejected by the Genoese as chimerical. Stung with indignation and disappointment, he retires from his own country to lay his scheme before the court of France, where his reception is still more mortifying; nothing daunted he presses onward, urged forward with irresistible ardor: is France averse to his project, England is his next resort; if one hill is not lofty enough to afford him a prospect of his El Dorado he mounts another. In fact his whole soul is wrapped up in his undertaking. Neglected by Portugal, Spain is his only resource; and there, after eight years of anxiety and toil, he succeeds, through the interest of queen Isabella, in obtaining three small ships. Trials still await him; an alteration of the compass spreads terror through his crew: threatened with mutiny he still pursues his course at the hazard of his life. A glorious discovery awaits him, the dazzling splendor of which casts into the shade all his previous trials and difficulties. What must have been his reflections on finding himself the discoverer of a new world? Did he ever regret his perseverance? Did he ever repent of having set himself up as the laughing stock of Europe? Nay, did not rather a sense of what he had endured serve to heighten the enjoyment of his success?

December 20, 1834

The different ideas we form of men whose pursuit is money, power, distinction, domestic happiness, public good.

EACH one is, for the most part, under the influence of some ruling passion, and almost invariably possesses a taste for some particular pursuit. This pursuit, this object of all one's wishes, and end of all his endeav-

ours, has great influence with his fellow men in de-
termining his character; so that many, when possessed
of this seemingly slight knowledge, think to fathom
one's very thoughts and feelings. When we hear it
said of a man, that money is the idol which he wor-
ships, that his whole soul is wrapped up in the pursuit
of wealth, we figure to ourselves one who is continually striving after something which he is destined
never to obtain, and who does not enjoy life as it
passes, but lives upon expectation; in short one who
has painted to himself an imaginary Elysium, towards
which no step in his progress brings him nearer; in
other words, we imagine him one, who is never satisfied with the wealth already amassed, but expects that
when arrived at a certain pitch, every thing desirable
will be within his reach: but alas! when he has
reached the summit of one peak, he is only enabled
the more fully to realize the immense height of the
next in succession. That every one is ashamed to
acknowledge the pursuit in question as his own, is a
fact which seems sufficiently to prove its baseness.

Aristocrats may say what they please, liberty and
equal rights are and ever will be grateful, till nature
herself shall change; and he who is ambitious to exercise authority over his fellow beings, with no view to
their benefit or injury, is to be regarded as actuated
by peculiarly selfish motives. Self-gratification must be
his sole object. Perhaps he is desirous that his name
may be handed down to posterity, that in after ages
something more may be said of him, than that he
lived, and died. He may be influenced by still baser
motives; he may take delight in the enjoyment of
power merely, and feel a kind of satisfaction at the
thought, that he can command and be obeyed. It is
evident then, that he, who thus influenced, attains at
last the summit of his wishes, will be a curse upon

mankind. His deeds may never be forgotten; but is this greatness? If so, may I pass through life unheeded and unknown.

> "But grant that those can conquer; these
> can cheat;
> 'Tis phrase absurd to call a villain great."

Small, very small, is the number of those who labour for the public good. There appears to be something noble, something exalted, in giving up one's own interest for that of his fellow beings, which excites in us feelings of admiration, and respect. He is a true patriot, who casting aside all selfish thoughts, and not suffering his benevolent intentions to be polluted by thinking of the fame he is acquiring, presses forward in the great work which he has undertaken with unremitted zeal; who is as one pursuing his way through a garden abounding with fruits of every description, without turning aside, or regarding the brambles which impede his progress, but pressing onward with his eyes fixed upon the golden fruit before him. He is worthy of all praise: his is indeed true greatness. He is satisfied with himself, and all around him, nor is he troubled with *his* stings of conscience, whose memory lives, with the smart which he leaves, but

> "One self-approving hour whole years outweighs
> Of stupid starers, and of loud huzzas."

January 17, 1835

Of keeping a private journal or record of our thoughts, feelings, studies, and daily experience,—containing abstracts of books, and the opinions we formed of them on first reading them.

As THOSE pieces which the painter sketches for his own amusement in his leisure hours, are often superior to his most elaborate productions, so it is that ideas often suggest themselves to us spontaneously, as it were, far surpassing in beauty those which arise in the mind upon applying ourselves to any particular subject. Hence, could a machine be invented which would instantaneously arrange on paper each idea as it occurs to us, without any exertion on our part, how extremely useful would it be considered! The relation between this and the practice of keeping a journal is obvious. But yet, the preservation of our scattered thoughts is to be considered an object but of minor importance.

Every one can think, but comparatively few can write, can express their thoughts. Indeed, how often do we hear one complain of his inability to express what he feels! How many have occasion to make the following remark, "I am sensible that I understand this perfectly, but am not able to find words to convey my idea to others".

But if each one would employ a certain portion of each day in looking back upon the time which has passed, and in writing down his thoughts and feelings, in reckoning up his daily gains, that he may be able to detect whatever false coins have crept into his coffers, and, as it were, in settling accounts with his mind, not only would his daily experience be greatly increased, since his feelings and ideas would thus be more clearly defined, but he would be ready to turn over a new leaf, having carefully perused the preceding one, and would not continue to glance carelessly over the same page, without being able to distinguish it from a new one.

Most of us are apt to neglect the study of our own characters, thoughts, and feelings, and for the purpose of forming our own minds, look to others, who should merely be considered as different editions of the same great work. To be sure, it would be well for us to examine the various copies, that we might detect any errors, but yet, it would be foolish for one to borrow a work which he possessed himself, but had not perused.

In fine, if we endeavoured more to improve ourselves by reflection, by making a business of thinking, and giving our thoughts form and expression, we should be led to "read not to contradict and confute, nor to believe and take for granted, nor to find talk and discourse, but to weigh and consider".

January 31, 1835

> "We are apt to become what others, (however erroneously) think us to be; hence another motive to guard against the power of others' unfavourable opinion."

WE FIND, on looking around us, even within the small circle of our acquaintances, many who, though not at all deficient in understanding, cannot muster resolution enough to commence any undertaking, even the most trifling, without consulting a friend; who are too diffident of their ability to judge for themselves, and who eventually, after a certain degree of solicitation, after the requisite number of arguments has been brought forward, almost invariably yield, though, perhaps, their good sense tells them better. I would not, by any means, have it understood that we are to neglect the advice of our friends, and ask another's opinion, as many do, merely to refute it, without considering that it is given at our own request, and that therefore we are to consider it a favour; but the majority of mankind are too easily induced to follow any course which accords with the opinion of the world: nine out of ten will tell you, in answer to the question, "How shall you act with regard to this matter", "I haven't concluded. What do you think best"? or something similar. They seem to be tossed about in the rapid current of human life at the mercy of the waves; the voyage may be prosperous, they may eventually drift into a calm and secure haven, but, on the other hand, it is much more likely that shipwreck will overtake them, or, as they are drifted along by the foaming torrent, thinking themselves secure from the innumerable enemies who crowd the shores on either side, they may be dashed down the cataract, which, while meditating on which shore they shall land, to which party they shall surrender, had escaped their notice. Thus are their actions principally the result of chance, and they become mere tools in the hands of others, since they are little qualified by nature to depend upon their own strength and powers.

One principal cause of this, is a false shame which many feel lest they be considered singular or eccentric, and therefore they run into the opposite extreme, become all things to all men, and conform to existing customs and rules, whether good or bad: this grows into a habit, and thus an entire change takes place in the disposition and character of the man.

February 14, 1835

> On what grounds may the forms, ceremonies, and restraints of polite society be objected to?
> Speak of some of them.
> What purposes are they intended to answer?

IN A primitive state of society, where man is buried in ignorance, and the arts and refinements of civilized life neglected, or rather unknown, but few forms or ceremonies exist; while on the other hand, as civilization advances and the pursuits and studies of mankind assume a nobler and more elevated character, in that proportion does man in his intercourse with his fellows comply with certain rules, which serve in a measure to preserve a just balance between the different classes of society.

I say in a measure only, for most are apt to go to excess in this particular; if one wishes to obtain their good opinion, he must go through a long catalogue of useless forms, and sacrifice truth, sincerity, and candor to politeness.

A friend is invited to dine,—each dish is excellent,—the very dinner he could have desired,—neither too rare, nor overdone; are the contents of his neighbour's glass unluckily transferred to his dress,—Oh 'tis of no consequence! he has already determined to send it to the die-house, and moreover had previously fixed upon the very color which will conceal its present defect. Thus are these petty evils beauties in his eyes, (those which for the time he uses,) and himself perhaps, in the eyes of his host, what is still more estimable, a perfect gentleman,—truly a pattern of politeness.

After much bowing and scraping, he is released,— yes released, for during the last hour or two he has been under a certain restraint, and is now as glad to be liberated as the prisoner when his term has expired. Perhaps on his way home he meets his friend G,—there is no escape,—the road is straight,—he must therefore summon up courage, and press onward,— "How do you do! I am heartily glad to see you; have been penned up at my friend R's these three hours; hope you will honor me with a call immediately,— (aside) fortunately I am about to leave town."

This is carried too far; it is beneath the dignity of a true gentleman to be tied down by such restraints. To be sure, ceremony may serve as a barrier against impertinence, but it also hides a multitude of sins. Far from estimating a man's character by the degree of attention he bestows upon this point, you may rest assured that the more extensive the outworks, the wider, and deeper the moat, the more insignificant is the garrison within. Like the Romans who, half famished with hunger, in order to deceive their enemy, cast forth that bread which was so scarce; so do the ceremonious deceive those around them, with regard to their true characters, by an occasional display of that wisdom which they so much need.

To conclude, "ceremony" as an eminent writer has remarked "is the superstition of good-breeding, as well as of religion; but yet, being an outwork to both, should not be absolutely demolished". It must, to a certain degree, be complied with, though by itself considered a very silly thing.

> Explain the phrases,—a man of business, a
> man of pleasure, a man of the world.

To SAY of one that he is a man of business, according to the general acceptation of the phrase, seems
not merely to imply that he is engaged in business,
but also that he is an energetic persevering man, one
who is always on the lookout, ever awake to his interest,—well calculated to get along in the world.

A man may be an excellent calculator, he may form
the best of plans, but fail in the execution of them;
and, on the other hand, many who have no fixed
plans, who are incapable of looking far into futurity,
and of forming or abiding by any fixed rules of conduct, may in the end succeed better than the former.
Nothing can be of more advantage in business than a
habit of despatch, and what contributes more to this
than method? In fine, let one possess method and
perseverance, industry and activity, united with pru-
dence and foresight, and a competent knowledge of
human nature, and you may justly call him a man of
business.

A large portion of mankind are wrapped up in the
pursuit of what they imagine to be pleasure, which,
like their own shadows, is always within a certain
distance, but which no efforts on their part can bring
nearer, so that their only real enjoyment lies in the
anticipation of pleasure.

The fault seems to lie not so much in the object as
in the means employed; they have a false idea of
pleasure; with them as far as a thing is useful, so
far is it devoid of pleasure; hence they "forsake what
may instruct, for what may please."

> "Whom call we gay? That honour has been
>   long
> The boast of mere pretenders to the name.
> The innocent are gay—"

Hence we perceive that the phrase a man of pleasure is generally applied to those who in fact enjoy the least.

Avoid a man of the world, as you would a viper, for like the viper in the fable he will sting the hand which has nourished him.

Sheridan has observed with regard to this class, that they have become so polished and refined, that their Maker's inscription is worn from them, and when he calls in his coin he will not know them for his own. This man is your friend as long as it serves his interest: he is well acquainted with men and manners, and by means of his art, passes perhaps for a true gentleman, for an honourable and benevolent man; but in truth his honor and morality are regulated by the fashion of the times. His principal object is to turn every thing to his advantage, and for this purpose he endeavours to gain the respect or good will of all around him.

Musings. April 20th 1835.

'Twas always my delight to monopolize the little Gothic window, which overlooked the kitchen garden, particularly of a Sabbath afternoon, when all around was quiet and nature herself was taking her afternoon nap, when the last peal of the bell in

> "the neighboring steeple,
> "Swinging slow with sullen roar," had
> "Left the vale to *solitude and me*,"

and the very air scarcely dared breathe lest it should disturb the universal calm. Then did I use with eyes upturned to gaze upon the clouds, and, allowing my imagination to wander, search for flaws in their rich drapery that I might get a peep at that world beyond which they seem intended to veil from our view. Now is my attention engaged by a truant hawk, as, like a messenger from those ethereal regions, he issues from the bosom of a cloud, and, at first a mere speck in the distance, comes circling onward exploring every seeming creek and rounding every jutting precipice. And now, his mission ended, what can be more majestic than his stately flight, as he wheels around some towering pine, enveloped in a cloud of smaller birds that have united to expel him from their premises.

Fair Haven. In the freshness of the dawn my brother and I were ever ready to enjoy a stroll to a certain cliff, distant a mile or more, where we were wont to climb to the highest peak, and, seating ourselves on some rocky platform, catch the first ray of the morning sun as it gleamed upon the smooth still river wandering in sullen silence far below. The approach to the precipice is by no means calculated to prepare one for the glorious dénouement at hand; after following for some time a delightful path that winds through the woods, occasionally crossing a rippling brook, and not forgetting to visit a sylvan dell whose solitude is made audible by the unwearied tinkling of a crystal spring—you suddenly emerge from the trees upon a flat and mossy rock which forms the summit of a beetling crag. The feelings which come over one on first beholding this freak of nature are indescribable. The giddy height, the iron-bound rock, the boundless horizon open around, and the beautiful river at your feet, with its green and sloping banks fringed with trees and shrubs of every description are calculated to excite in the beholder

as in its effects. Hence are we so often surprised by hearing of the decision of character, perseverance and success, of those whom we always considered weak, irresolute, and totally unfitted to succeed in life. This surprise in part arises from our not having accustomed ourselves to behold this quality in all its forms. Some are easily excited, of a sanguine temper, ready for every undertaking, and for a time wholly absorbed in the prosecution of their designs. They aim to accomplish everything by the suddenness of their decisions, and the rapidity of their movements; but, as some one has justly observed, zeal and enthusiasm are never very accurate calculators. Their energy is of an inconstant kind, it is not accompanied by calmness and deliberation; so that their success, if they meet with any, is not so much the effect of their own exertions, as the work of chance. They are bold to decide, and though not easily overcome by obstacles, (for these have the effect of arousing them to action,) still they are too ready to abandon a project, not through discouragement, but want of interest. Others again differ from the former in this respect only, that they are no less constant and determined in carrying through their undertakings, than hasty to decide; they are resolved not to relinquish a design once adopted be it good or bad, and thus their energy amounts to rashness or foolishness as the case may be, and they are apt to employ it to little or no purpose.

That description of this quality which Philip Van Artevelde possessed in so high a degree, appears by far the most desirable. Here judgment is called upon to give her sanction or veto to the course proposed; her subjects armed with her consent, together with that of her counsellors calmness and caution, are prepared for every emergency,—they have but one end in view, which is, the execution of her projects. Energy here holds a subordinate station, she composes the bone and muscle of the state, but Judgment and Deliberation are invested with the reins of government, and have the sole direction of affairs.

I know of no more suitable examples, by which to illustrate these two descriptions, than the characters of Francis 1st and Charles Vth, who, rivals for a period of twenty eight years—each possessing uncommon talents, were as different in their temperaments, as their abilities and the advantages they enjoyed. The former was sudden to adopt his resolutions, and ardent in carrying them through;—he exhibited the most daring courage in forming as well as executing his plans, but was however too apt to relinquish them through impatience or disgust.

Charles was long in coming to a decision, and cool and collected on every occasion—having once adopted a design, no obstacles could turn him from the prosecution of it.

Francis, by the rapidity of his motions and the impetuosity of his career, often baffled his rival's best laid schemes. Like the mountain torrent swollen by a freshet, which in its rapid and irresistible course sweeps all before it, he often fell upon his enemy in a defenceless state with a shock so violent as to drive him from the field at once; but in a few days this mighty torrent dwindles to a rippling brook, which, not being able to reach the ocean, ends its course in some stagnant pool. Charles, on the other hand, resembled a broad but calm river, which, steady though rapid in its progress, flows onward to the ocean, disdaining to be swallowed up by any inland sea, or to contribute its portion to a sister stream. It would doubtless have been well had Charles possessed a little of Francis' ardor and enterprise, but as it was, energy such as his was by far the most effective. The enlightened and cultivated mind—it is folly for him whose intellect has not been trained to study and meditation, to look for pleasure here; to him the path is dark and dreary, barren and desolate. "This art of meditation" says an author "is the power of withdrawing ourselves from the world, to view that world moving within ourselves, while we are in repose; as the artist by an optical instrument concentrates the boundless landscape around him, and patiently traces all nature in that small space." Innocent and easily procurable pleasures constitute man's most lasting happiness: these are such as literature and imagination are both able and willing to afford. That undefinable misery—that insupportable tediousness, the curse of those who have nothing to do, is inconsistent with this relish for literature and science, which is a source of continual gratification to the mind. He who is dependent upon himself alone for his enjoyments,—who finds all he wants within himself, is really independent; for to look to others for that which is the object of every man's pursuit, is to live in a state of perpetual trust and reliance. Happy the man who is furnished with all the advantages to relish solitude; he is never alone, and yet may be retired in the midst of a crowd; he holds sweet converse with the sages of antiquity, and gathers wisdom from their discourse —he enjoys the fruit of their labors—their knowledge is his knowledge—their wisdom his inheritance. It is knowledge that creates the difference between man and man—that raises one man above another—it is the soul of man—the mind that is filled with this valuable furniture is a "magazine richly furnished"—a storehouse of the wisdom of ages, from which Reflection, who is door-keeper, and has charge of the keys, draws forth from time to time sublime truths, as the mind, the proprietor, has need of them. The sentiments of such a mind are of a pure and noble cast; rising

above what is ignoble and mean, they breathe truth—
the "essence of good": thus, inspired with a presenti-
ment of virtue, man "is led to look through nature up
to nature's God."

September, 1835

The comparative moral policy of severe and
mild punishments.

THE end of all punishment is the welfare of the state,—
the good of community at large,—not the suffering of
an individual. It matters not to the lawgiver what a
man deserves, for to say nothing of the impossibility
of settling this point, it would be absurd to pass laws
against prodigality, want of charity, and many other
faults of the same nature, as if a man was to be fright-
ened into a virtuous life, though these in a great
measure constitute a vicious one. We leave this to a
higher tribunal. So far only as public interest is concerned, is punishment justifiable—if we overstep this
bound our own conduct becomes criminal. Let us
observe in the first place the effects of severity.

Does the rigor of the punishment increase the dread
operating upon the mind to dissuade us from the act?
It certainly does if it be unavoidable. But where death
is a general punishment, though some advantage may
seem to arise from the severity, yet this will invariably be more than counterbalanced by the uncertainty attending the execution of the law. We find
that in England, for instance, where, in Blackstone's
day, 160 offences were considered capital, between
the years 1805 and 1817 of 655 who were indicted for
stealing, 113 being capitally convicted, not one was

executed: and yet no blame could attach to the conduct of the juries, the fault was in the law. Had death, on the other-hand, been certain, the law could have existed but a very short time. Feelings of natural justice, together with public sentiment, would have concurred to abolish it altogether. In fact wherever those crimes which are made capital form a numerous class, and petty thefts and forgeries are raised to a level with murder, burglary and the like, the law seems to defeat its own ends. The injured influenced, perhaps, by compassion, forbear to prosecute, and thus are numerous frauds allowed to escape with impunity, for want of a penalty proportionate to the offence. Juries too, actuated by the same motives, adopt the course pointed out by their feelings. As long as one crime is more heinous and more offensive than another, it is absolutely necessary that a corresponding distinction be made in punishing them. Otherwise, if the penalty be the same, men will come to regard the guilt as equal in each case.

It is enough that the evil attending conviction exceed the expected advantage. This I say is sufficient, provided the consequences be certain, and the expected benefit be not obtained. For it is that hope of escaping punishment—a hope which never deserts the rogue as long as life itself remains, that renders him blind to the consequences, and enables him to look despair in the face. Take from him this hope, and you will find that certainty is more effectual than severity of punishment. No man will deliberately cut his own fingers. The vicious are often led on from one crime to another still more atrocious by the very fault of the law, the penalty being no greater, but the certainty of escaping detection being very much increased. In this case they act up to the old saying, that "one may as well be hung for stealing an old sheep as a lamb." Some have asked, "cannot reward be substituted for punishment? Is hope a less powerful incentive to action than fear? When a political pharmacopoeia has the command of both ingredients, wherefore employ the bitter instead of the sweet?" This reasoning is absurd. Does a man deserve to be rewarded for refraining from murder? Is the greatest virtue merely negative, or does it rather consist in the performance of a thousand everyday duties, hidden from the eye of the world? Would it be good policy to make the most exalted virtue even, a subject of reward here? Nevertheless, I question whether a pardon has not a more salutary effect, on the minds of those not immediately affected by it, vicious as well as honest, than a public execution.

It would seem then, that the welfare of society calls for a certain degree of severity; but this degree must bear some proportion to the offence. If this distinction be lost sight of punishment becomes unjust as well as useless—we are not to act upon the principle, that crime is to be prevented at any rate, cost what it may; this is obviously erroneous.

October 16, 1835

Popular Feeling &c.

What is meant by *popular feeling*? How are we to know what it is on any subject? Is it less likely to be safe and just than that of the *few*? Does it cause more harm when left to take its own course than when interfered with?

⟨. . .⟩ find another, perhaps no better satisfied than ourselves, whose opinion coincides with our own. Thus, leaning upon each other, we feel more confident, and seem determined not to be outdone, but to go all lengths in our belief.

If then we find a certain Few standing aloof from the multitude—not allowing themselves to be carried along by the current of Popular feeling, we may fairly conclude that they have good reason for so doing— that they have looked farther into the subject than others—so far, at least, as to discover what has escaped the notice of the rabble. Those in the stream are not aware of the cataract at hand, but those on the bank have it in full view. Whose is the wisest and safest course?

Those opinions which are most strenuously opposed are generally most firmly rooted. I have got the notion, for instance, that this or that effect will follow from certain causes: does any one contradict me, I look around for arguments, that I may seem consistent. If I do not convince him, I convince myself—my notion has grown into an opinion. So much the more difficult is it to stay the tide of Popular feeling, as it is easier to reason with a single individual than a host blinded by sympathy and party spirit. Opposition but "adds fuel to the flame". Dam up the torrent and it will deluge the country.

November 27, 1835

> The ways in which a man's style may be said
> to offend against simplicity.

IF WE would aim at perfection in any thing, simplicity must not be overlooked. If the author would acquire literary fame, let him be careful to suggest such thoughts as are simple and obvious, and to express his meaning distinctly and in good language. To do this, he must in the first place, omit all superfluous ornament; which, though very proper in its place, if indeed it can be said to have any in good composition, tends rather to confuse and distract the mind, than to render a passage more clear and striking, or an idea more distinct. I do not pretend to say that whatever adds to the grace, detracts from the simplicity of one's style. The ancient robe is the plainest dress imaginable, yet where will you find one more truly beautiful? It is equally so to the half naked savage, and to the foppish devotee of fashion.

Another very common fault is that of using uncommon words—words which neither render our meaning more obvious, nor our composition more elegant. In this case, the reader's attention is withdrawn from the subject, and is wholly employed upon the rare, and for that reason, offensive expression—offensive too, because it argues study and premeditation in the author. Obscurity may properly be called the opposite of simplicity. Hence whatever contributes to this, as far fetched metaphors and images, in fact, all that kind of ornament that forms the characteristic of the florid style, is not merely superfluous, but absolutely incompatible with excellence.

The style in question does not seem to be peculiar to such topics as are common and familiar, as some have affirmed, for the most sublime and noblest precepts may be conveyed in a plain and simple strain. The Scriptures afford abundant proof of this. What images can be more natural, what sentiments of greater weight, and at the same time more noble and exalted, than those with which they abound? They possess no local or relative ornament which may be lost in a translation; clothed in whatever dress they still retain their peculiar beauties. Here is simplicity itself. Every one allows this, every one admires it, yet how few attain to it! What hosts of writers, hourly contending for popularity, depend for success on their superior simplicity of style alone! Shakspeare, they say, has acquired immortal fame, and this is the distinguishing trait in his writings.

The union of wisdom and simplicity is plainly hinted at in the following lines by Milton.

> Suspicion sleeps
> At wisdom's gate, and to *Simplicity*
> Resigns her charge.

March 31, 1836

The Book of the Seasons; or The Calendar of Nature,

BY WILLIAM HOWITT.

WE HAVE here a book calculated to do all that books can do to excite a spirit of attachment to Nature—one expressly adapted to the climate and customs of England, but none the less acceptable to the lovers of natural scenery of whatever clime or nation—neither too scientific, nor too much abounding in technical terms and phrases to be comprehended by the general reader, nor yet of too miscellaneous and catch-penny a stamp for the would-be literati or bluestockings. "My plan has been" says the author, "to furnish an original article on the general appearances of Nature in each month, drawn entirely from my own regular observation through many seasons;

oil to solace him, an inhabitant of snow and ice, not of earth, crawls into a snow-bank, and yet his heart is not so frozen but that he feels at home. The tanned and dusky African realizes the delights of "de dear native land" in dancing a jig on (not under) the equator. We find that no region is so barren or so desolate as not to afford some human being a home. But Nature's home is everywhere, and in whatever clime, her devotee is at home with her. The attachment to his country which is manifested by the mariner, as he loses sight of "the blue line of his native land," (as Irving has beautifully expressed it,) and which is at no time more strongly felt than when, on some distant strand, his thoughts revert to some well-known steeple, the most conspicuous object in a country village, the slowly-winding stream, which flows at the foot of the hill where he nutted in Autumn and coasted in Winter, the cart path that leads down to the great meadows where the grapes were as thick as blackberries and cranberries were to be had for the picking, this attachment, I say, this love of natural scenery, (for they are equivalent—which explains the truth of the observation, that no one is more fond of home than the traveller,) is so interwoven with the best feelings of our nature that it would seem absurd to suppose it associated with meaner and baser sentiments, or vice in any shape. The great and good of every age and nation have felt its influence. Poetry, from Chaucer's to the present time has teemed with it. The loss of his sight did not shut out Nature from the view of Milton; the rich store-house of his mind was a source of serene and elevated pleasure in his hours of darkness—the inmost recesses of the Garden of Eden were as plainly visible to him as the light of day could have made them. "Between the poet and nature," says Schlegel, "no less than between the poet and man, there is a sympathy of feeling. Not only in the song of the Nightingale, or in the melodies to which all men listen, but even in the roar of the stream, and the rushing of the forest, the poet thinks that he hears a kindred voice of sorrow or of gladness; as if spirits and feelings like our own were calling to us from afar, or seeking to sympathize and communicate with us from the utmost nearness to which their Natures will allow them to approach us. It is for the purpose of listening to these tones, and of holding mysterious converse with the soul of nature, that every great poet is a lover of solitude!"

So much for Germany; with how much more truth would these remarks apply to America; "America," in the words of the Novelist, "with her beautiful and stupendous scenes of nature; her immense lakes; her broad and sweeping rivers; her climes melting into all the varieties of the globe; her cataracts shaking the earth; her mountains kissing the heavens; her solitudes and forests, yet hushed in primeval silence."

January is derived from the Latin, Janus, door-keeper of heaven, and God of peace. Under this head is described a great storm which will serve as a specimen of the author's style. "Frost—keen biting frost is in the ground, and in the air, a bitter scythe-edged, perforating wind from the north; or what is worse, the north-east, sweeps the descending snow along, whirling it from the open fields, and driving it against whatever opposes its course. People who are obliged to be passing to and fro muffle up their faces, and bow their heads to the blast. There is no loitering, no street-gossiping, no stopping to make recognition of each other; they shuffle along the most winterly objects of the scene, bearing on their fronts the tokens of the storm. Against every house, rock or bank the snow-drift accumulates. It curls over the tops of walls and hedges in fantastic wildness, forming often the most perfect curves, resembling the scrolls of Ionic capitals, and showing beneath romantic caves and canopies".

February is so called from the Roman custom of burning expiatory sacrifices, Februalia. "Nothing can perhaps illustrate so livingly our idea of a spirit," says Howitt, "as a mighty wind—present in its amazing power and Sublimity, yet seen only in its effects. We are whirled along with its careering torrent with ir-resistible power."

Who can stand on the verge of the forest, at the approach of night-fall, on the eve of a tempest, and hear it as it comes rushing and roaring in its mad career, without being influenced by overwhelming ideas of majesty, grandeur, and the awful power of the elements?

March, the first month in antiquity, was named so after Mars the god of war, because he was the father of their first prince. All Nature is now reviving; the earth throws off her snowy mantle and puts on the garb of Spring; the squirrel comes forth from his sub-terranean abode to snuff the fresh air, and commence his sprightly gambols along the walls and hedges, or skip from tree to tree, seemingly in mere sport. The air is still too chilly for the feathered race, though the shrill and doleful note of the jay is heard in the orchards.

April is so called from the Latin, Aprilis, which is derived from Aperire, to open. The allusion is obvious.

> "April showers
> Bring forth May-flowers,"

is one of these old sayings which possess no intrinsic merit of their own, but derive all their interest from the association of ideas, as Stewart would say.

May is so called from the Goddess Maia. This is, perhaps, the pleasantest month of the 12. The Botanist may now commence his rambles without much fear of suffocating heat or intense cold. Now also commences the harvest of death, and wo be unto the unlucky squirrel, bob-lincoln, or black bird that ventures to approach the haunts of man, or sit within the range of an old French-piece or horse-pistol! Every strippling that can shoulder a musket, or can hold up one end while the other rests on a rail, or can muster courage to touch-off a wooden cannon without shutting his eyes is up and stirring betimes.

And then what a rattling of ramrods! what a demand for wadding paper with which to stuff the pockets of the ragged troop that you may see assembled around the instrument of death, ready to counsel and assist, nay, even to take charge of the weapon itself should the absence of its present proprietor make it necessary. And now if some stray sparrow should have the imprudence to perch upon a neighboring post, tree, or rock, or if a bob-lincoln holding in utter contempt the marksmanship of the musket-bearer, should approach within gun-shot, then what a *scatteration* takes place; some are seen to ensconce themselves behind a tree, others fall flat upon the ground, while some favored 2 or 3 boldly accompany their leader to the work of death. The barrel is slowly raised, the now diminished group satisfy themselves that the right angle of elevation is attained, and then the hero of the day, with the rest to back him pulls the trigger. Tick, goes the lock, and now succeeds a hissing noise which proves the success of the experiment, showing that the powder is subjected to the process of ignition; endued with the patience of Job our hero abides the result. The passer-by will not probably have proceeded many rods, before he is startled by the report, which, reverberating through the surrounding forest produces a startling effect upon myriads of the smaller birds and quadrupeds, and, perhaps, disturbs, for a moment, the calm, unruffled serenity of the victim. Then for the hurry, bustle, and confusion of the motley crew who are hastening to be in at the death. The victim is finally transmitted to the hands of the executioner as completely bare and destitute of feathers, as the callow young who are piping anything but melody in the deserted nest.

June, probably from Juno, in honor of whom a festival was held at the beginning of this month. "June," says Howitt, "is the very carnival of Nature, and she is prodigal of her luxuries. It is luxury to walk abroad indulging every sense with sweetness, loveliness, and harmony. It is luxury to stand beneath the forest side, when all is still and basking at noon; and to see the landscape suddenly darken, the black and tumultuous clouds assemble as at a signal; to hear the awful thunder crash upon the listening air; and then to mark the glorious bow rise on the lurid rear of the tempest, the sun laugh jocundly abroad, and

> Every bathed leaf and blossom fair
> Pour out its soul to the delicious air.

It is luxury to plunge into the cool river; and, if ever we are tempted to turn anglers, it must be now. To steal away into a quiet valley, by a winding stream, buried, completely buried, in fresh grass; the foam-like flower of the meadow-sweet, the crimson loose-strife, and the large blue geranium nodding beside us; the dragon-fly, the ephemera, and the king-fisher glancing to and fro; the trees above casting their flickering shadows on the stream; and one of our 10,000 volumes of delightful literature in our pockets—then indeed might one be a most patient angler though taking not a single fin".

July, from J. Caesar. "Now is the general season of hay-making. There is a sound of tinkling teams and waggons rolling along lanes and fields the whole country over, ay, even at midnight, till at length, the fragrant ricks rise in the farm-yard, and the pale, smooth-shaven fields are left in solitary beauty."

Honest old Izaak Walton has done much in his quaint style, to impart an interest to quiet haunts and streams—to cool and shady banks, which if they are ever interesting are peculiarly so this month. Nature has spread her flowery carpet over the earth, and a thousand ripening berries invite the wanderer to prolong his walks.

August, from Augustus. The grand feature of this month is Corn Harvest. Berries of almost every description are now perfectly ripe; the sportsman may be seen, drenched with the morning dew, rambling about the fields, or reconnoitering the hedges, in search of game; the orchards assume a rosy tint, which is a sign that the season for commencing depredations has already set in. A walk in any direction is delightful, but a quiet cart-path leading through the woods to some sylvan dell, some well known spot, a "Sleepy Hollow" for instance, is preferable. Sept. It is the height of enjoyment, reclined at length upon the turf, in the shade of a noble tree, to give reins to the imagination—to hearken to the audible silence that prevails around—the hum of 10000 insects with which the air is filled—the materials it would seem, of which the atmosphere is composed. It is at such times that man realizes that he is indeed the Lord of Creation.

What can be more majestic than a stately oak, presiding with parental care over the surrounding fields, with arms out-stretched, as it were, to protect the traveller! What an idea of independence it suggests! there it stands, and there it has stood for ages; generation after generation has passed away, and still we talk of the oak; from year to year the birds have built their nests and carolled in its branches, and the squirrel frisked from bough to bough; the tired Indian, perchance, in times gone by, has sought shelter and refreshment in its shade. To use the words of a novelist, for novelists sometimes speak the truth, "The fruit of an insignificant seed, you were planted by accident, and grew in neglect; and now you appear flinging abroad your branches to heaven, striking your roots deep into the earth, bending and groaning sometimes beneath the storm, but never yielding to its fury; and towering above the surrounding woods, till the remote revolutions of time and nature shall lay your lofty honors in the dust." Oct. Nothing can be more pleasing to the eye than the appearance of the woods at this season. Green is allowed by most oculists to be the color which the eye may dwell upon with the least injury, as it is certainly that to which it is most accustomed. The trees have now thrown off their green costume and assumed a variegated dress of orange, red, brown, and yellow, a yellowish brown predominating. The waving surface of the forest, as from some height the eye runs over the sea of colors, invites the beholder to come down and stalk at large over the undulating, but seemingly compact plane, to explore each nook and cranny, the haunts of hawks and ravens.

Nov. "There is nothing melancholy in Nature". If there is, where is it? Is it in the op'ning bud of Spring —youthful, buoyant Spring,—in the blooming flower of Summer, or the yellow harvest of Autumn? To the eye of the dyspeptic, to be sure, all is stamped with melancholy. Let him walk out into the fields—take no exercise, but get as much as he can—let him look at the butterfly pursuing its zigzag course from flower to flower, and from field to field, and then talk of Dyspepsia: why it would puzzle the Blue Devils to follow suite. Do you think they would feel at home by the side of its gaudy pinions? Oh no! they would 'vanish into thin air'. But some, in a doleful tone, will remind you of the fall of the leaf.

Every tree sends forth its thousands—away they go, flying hither and thither, up and down, in search of a resting place. Behold dame Partlet sailing up the avenue with feathers all erect, urged by rude Boreas to an unwonted pace; or see how familiarly that North-wester plays with the coat-flaps of the traveller, or sends him over stone walls and rail-fences to fish his beaver out of a pond-hole. This is indeed melancholy.

The following are the words of one possessed of what he calls the golden abundance and profuse beauty of this magnificent globe, one who is ready to resign the true riches of this world to the uncivilized savage, and the poverty-stricken peasant.

"Those luscious ever-green valleys, those luxuriant hills, those rich slopes, clothed with the most gorgeous fruits and the tenderest and deepest verdure, and more than all, those gentle and transparent skies, seem beneficently designed for man in his more uncivilized state, or for the poor." The so-called rich may *enjoy* all the honors that titled rank can confer, they may revel in luxury and dissipation, and count their wealth by thousands and tens of thousands,—but if they reject or are denied those gifts which Nature alone can bestow—they are poor indeed.

Is it poverty to breathe the free air of heaven, to satisfy the cravings of hunger with the simple fruits of the soil, to quench the natural thirst from the running waters of the brook, or to seek refreshment for the wearied limbs on the lap of our common mother Earth? Is it wealth to monopolize the confined air of a pleasure carriage, to wage continual war with Nature, to pore over the hues of a few home-sick and stinted exotics to gratify the least intellectual of the 5 senses? Does it consist in the possession of one half this 'snug little farm the Earth' without enjoying a foot, or in the putting in jeopardy the health and spirits by swallowing the earliest green cucumber?

December. Nature is left in undisturbed possession of the country, while man resorts to his burrow the City.

April 7, 1836
Sir Henry Vane

⟨. . .⟩ The fact that he was no party man, the leader of no sect, but equally to be feared by the foes of freedom and religion every where, explains the circumstance of his being passed over, with little if any notice, by the historians of the day. The age in which he lived was not worthy of him, his cotemporaries knew not how to appreciate his talents or his motives to action, the principles which he advanced, the great truths which he foretold were soon to shake the civilized world to its very centre, and before which the bulwarks of tyranny and oppression were to crumble away, were to them absolutely unintelligible, unmean-

ing nonsense,—opposed to that "clearness of ratiocina-
tion", which even Clarendon allowed him to possess
in conversation.

It was peculiarly the duty of America to brush away
the dust of ages that had collected around his name—
to clear off the cobwebs that prejudice and calumny
had spun ⟨. . . . .

. . . .⟩
of argument in defence of liberty religious and political, were the captives that adorned his triumph—assembled multitudes formed the procession—the talent,
wealth, and nobility of the kingdom were collected
around his chariot, to wonder and admire. Thus fell
Vane,

> "Than whom", in the words of a kindred spirit,
>   "a better senator ne'er held
> "The helm of Rome, when gowns, not arms,
>   repelled"
> "The fierce Epirot, and the African bold,"
> "Whether to settle peace, or to unfold"
> "The drift of hollow states hard to be
>   spelled."
> On whose "firm hand Religion leans"
> "In peace, and reckons"—him—"her eldest
>   son".

Equally the terror of evil-doers, and the praise of
those who did well wherever and whoever they might
be.

April 14, 1836

Literary Digressions

⟨. . .⟩ author may chance, here and there, to throw
out, upon the characters and actions of his person-

ages, and which are regarded by the majority of his readers as interrupting to the course of the narrative, and are generally passed over with little if any notice, for wherein, I would ask, do these differ from the admonitions and exhortations of the express moral teacher? Perhaps his interest in the work, like an accompanying sweet, may induce the reader to swallow the bitter potion. Physiologists, however, would say, "let the draught be swallowed voluntarily if you would expect it to produce its full effect!" With regard to the 'exemplification' business, it reminds me of the fable of the lion and the painter;—if lions had been painters it would have been otherwise. Examples may be divided into good and bad.

April, 1836

Advantages and disadvantages of foreign influence on American Literature.

THE nations of the old world have each a literature peculiarly its own. Theirs is the growth of centuries; successive ages have contributed to form its character and mould its features. They may be said to have grown up, and become matured; the early centuries of our era presided over their infancy, and, in some instances, their origin may be traced back far into the fabulous ages that preceded the foundation of Rome. Spain is the land of romance, the character of her literature may be seen in that of almost every century of her history; her youth was passed in deeds of chivalry, or dozed away in the luxurious halls of the Alhambra. The taste for knight errantry, for adventure, and song, which forms the characteristic of her maturer years, is but a spice of the Moorish character.

France has had her troubadours, and her vintager still sings his evening hymn. The advancement of her literary interests was made a public concern as early as 1634, when Cardinal de Richelieu, the founder of the French Academy, reigned with despotic sway, not only over the king, court, and people, but also over the language. We of New England are a peculiar people, we whistle, to be sure, our national tune; but the character of our literature is not yet established, ours is still in the gristle, and is yet receiving those impressions from the parent literature of the mother Country, which are to mould its character. Utility is the rallying word with us; we are a nation of speculators, stock-holders, and money-changers; we do every thing by steam, because it is most expeditious, and cheapest in the long run; we are continually racking our brains to invent a quicker way or a cheaper method of doing this and that. The question with us is whether a book will take—will sell well, not whether it is worth taking, or worth selling; the purchaser asks the price, looks at the binding, the paper, or the plates, without learning the contents. The press is daily sending forth its thousands and tens of thousands, for the publisher says 'tis profitable. To judge from appearances rather than facts, to mistake the profitable for the useful, are errors incident to youth; but we are fast hardening into the bone of manhood; our literature though now dependent, in some measure, on that of the mother Country, must soon go alone; its future eminence must depend upon its bringing-up, upon the impressions it now receives, and the principles it imbibes; how important then that these impressions and these principles be of a manly and independent character!

We are, as it were, but colonies. True, we have declared our independence, and gained our liberty, but we have dissolved only the political bands which connected us with Great Britain; though we have rejected her tea she still supplies us with food for the mind. Milton and Shakspeare, Cowper and Johnson, with their kindred spirits, have done and are still doing as much for the advancement of literature, and the establishment of a pure and nervous language, on this as on the other side of the water; they are as much venerated, and their works are as highly prized by us as by our English brethren; and who will say that the influence they have exerted has been prejudicial to our literary interests?

Our national pride has been roused by the perusal of sundry journals and books of travels, purporting to contain faithful descriptions of men and manners in America; the remarks of English and Scotch reviewers have, in various instances, induced us to be more careful in the use of language, and to discard much that is superfluous or provincial in our vocabulary. We are not totally indifferent with regard to the notice which the soi-disant critics of Europe have condescended to take of our literature, and though we may affect to overlook their cutting remarks, or regard them as the sallies of envy and calumny, still we feel that they are not entirely without foundation. The more cuffs and hard knocks we sustain, the more robust and manly we grow. Each successive defeat afforded the Carthaginians new lessons in the art of war, till, at length, Rome herself trembled at their progress.

Our respect for what is foreign has a tendency, on the other hand, to render us blind to native merit, and lead us into a servile adoration of imported genius. We afford but little encouragement to that which is of domestic manufacture, but prefer to send out our raw material, that it may pass through a foreign mill. The aspirant to fame must breathe the atmosphere of foreign parts, and learn to talk about things which the home-bred student never dreamed of, if he would have his talents appreciated, or his opinion regarded, by his Countrymen; then will they dwell on every word he utters, watch the cut of his coat, the cock of his hat, ape his pronunciation and manners, and, perhaps, honor him with a public dinner.

Ours are authors of the day, they bid fair to outlive their works; they are too fashionable to write for posterity; what the public seizes upon to-day with avidity ceases to interest it to-morrow when the charm of novelty has worn off. Particular styles and subjects have each in their turn engaged the attention of the literati. How much ink has been shed, how much paper wasted, in imitations of Ossian, while the productions of Macpherson lie neglected on our shelves!

The devotee of literary fashion is no stranger to our shores; true, there are some amongst us who can contemplate the bubbling brook without, in imagination, polluting its waters with a mill-wheel, but even they are prone to sing of skylarks and nightingales, perched on hedges, to the neglect of the homely robin-red-breast, and the straggling rail-fences of their own native land.

May 3, 1836

Some account of the Life and Works of Sir W. Scott.

BY ALLAN CUNNINGHAM.

Familiar anecdotes of Sir W. Scott.

BY JAMES HOGG.

With a sketch of the life of the Shepherd

BY S. DEWITT BLOODGOOD.

OUR Literature is uncommonly rich in Biography. No sooner has a passing meteor, whose brilliancy and length of train arrests the attention of the gaping multitudes of this nether world, sunk below the horizon, than the literary astronomers of the day set about tracing its orbit, and soon crowd a ponderous tome with the phenomena it presented. This is all very well so far as it goes, but, for my part, I am not satisfied with being acquainted with a man's actions merely. I want to be introduced to the man himself. "Biography", says Fuseli, "however useful to man, or dear to art, is the unequivocal homage of inferiority offered to the majesty of genius." This is not the character of the works before us; we here behold Scott in the capacity of a friend, and patron, free from all restraint.

Divested of all the mystery in which genius is usually enveloped, he appears for the moment to have put on mortality, he is no longer the "Author of Waverly" the eighth wonder of the world. While we imagine him snugly ensconced in his antique armchair, poring over the pages of a huge black-letter folio containing the marvellous deeds of some Sir Tristram or Sir Guy who figured in border warfare, or performing a pilgrimage à la Terre Sainte, we find him, perchance, "leistering kippers in Tweed", or seated on the river's brink, while Rob Fletcher is gone after another fiery peat, singing Hogg's ballad of "Gilman's-cleuch". The account of the Life and Works of Scott is written in a frank and impartial style, though the author appears to be a little vain of his intimacy with Sir Walter. The same may be said of Hogg. The former winds up with these words, "No other genius ever exercised over the world so wide a rule: no one, perhaps, ever united so many great—almost godlike qualities, and employed them so generously for the benefit of the living. It is not to us alone that he has spoken: his voice will delight thousands of generations unborn, and charm his country while wood grows and water runs."

The Ettrick Shepherd was the second son of Robert Hogg and Margaret Laidlaw, and was born on the 25th of Jan'y, 1772, the anniversary of Burns' birth, who was born 1759. When 6 years of age he attended for a short time a neighboring school, and learned to read the Proverbs of Solomon and the Shorter Catechism, but at the age of 7 went to service as a cowherd, receiving for half a year's service, "a ewe lamb and a pair of shoes."

It was in his 18th year that he first saw the "Life and Adventures of Sir W. Wallace", and Ramsay's "Gentle Shepherd". It was in 1796 that he first felt the inspiration of the Muse; he now for the first time had access to a valuable library, and his genius shone forth so conspicuously, that he was known as "Jamie the Poeter." He could compose, but he could not write "and he wept to think, however fancy and inspiration might impart their influence, he could not 'catch their shadows as they passed'." The song commencing,

"My name it is Donald McDonald,"

written at the time England was threatened with invasion by Napoleon, was the first he published.

The following is a list of his works.

> The Queen's Wake.
> Pilgrims of the Sun.
> The Hunting of Badlewe.
> Mador of the Moor.
> Poetic Mirror.
> Dramatic Tales.
> Brownie of Bodsbeck.
> Winter Evening Tales
> Sacred Melodies.
> Border Garland.
> Jacobite Relics of Scotland
> The Spy.
> Queen Hynde.
> The Three Perils of Man.
> The Three do. of Women.
> Confessions of a Sinner.
> The Shepherd's Calendar.
> A Selection of Songs.
> The Queer Book.
> The Royal Jubilee.
> The Mountain Bard.
> The Forest Minstrel.
> The Altrive Tales.

Now living, 1834.

September 30, 1836

> The Love of stories, real or fabulous, in young and old. Account for it, and show what good use it may serve.

ONE thing can hardly be called more curious than another, yet all are not equally the objects of our curiosity. The earth we tread upon is as curious as the stars we gaze upon. "To the thinking mind", says Irving, "the whole world is enveloped in mystery, and everything is full of type and portent." *We* are curiously and wonderfully made, yet how few, comparatively, see anything to admire in the structure of their own bodies. How then shall we account for this indifference to what is common—this appetite for the novel? By accident, through the medium of the senses first, the child is made acquainted with some new truth. The acquisition of knowledge, he finds, taking the term in its widest sense, is attended, in this first instance, by a pleasurable emotion. The wisdom of which provision is obvious. Having experienced the pleasure, and noted, whether voluntarily or otherwise, the cause, he delights to examine whatever new objects may fall in his way, and thus familiar things, or such as he has already taken notice of, come to lose their attractions, and grow in a measure disgusting to him. Hence that love of novelty—that passion for what is strange, or as the phrase goes *remarkable*, whose influence may be discerned in almost every act of our lives.

But it by no means follows that those topics most replete with instruction will afford us the greatest pleasure. The love of novelty grows with our growth. Not satisfied with the world around us, we delight to revel in an imaginary one of our own creation. The ideas afforded by sensation and reflection are seized upon with avidity by the imagination, and so combined and arranged as to form new wholes of surpassing beauty, awfulness, or sublimity, as the case may be. It is in the exercise of this divine faculty that age finds its readiest solace, and youth its supreme delight. A mutual inter-change of imaginings serves not a little to enlarge the field of our enjoyment. Tired of our own creations, too indolent to rear our own castles, the tale well told,

> —"with many a winding bout
> "Of linked sweetness long drawn out,"

casts a luxurious—a delicious twilight, over the rugged scenes of life—reconciles us to the world—our friends —ourselves.

As this appetite is insatiable, so are the sources whence it may be gratified inexhaustible. When youth has ripened into manhood, and care has stamped the brow, though the lay may have lost its charm, which tells of curious things,

> "How wise men three of Gotham, in a bowl"
> "Did venture out to sea"—
> "And darkly hints their awful fate,"

though this be an old story, the page of history is never closed, the Castalian spring is never dry, the volume of nature is ever open, the story of the world never ceases to interest. The child enchanted by the melodies of Mother Goose, the scholar pondering the Tale of Troy Divine, and the historian breathing the atmosphere of past ages, all manifest the same passion—are alike the creatures of curiosity. In fine, the same passion for the novel, somewhat modified to be sure, that is manifested in our early days, leads us, in after life, when the sprightliness and credulity of youth have given way to the reserve and skepticism of manhood, to the more serious, though scarcely less wonderful, annals of the world. Whatever is said or done, seen or heard, is in any way taken cognizance of by the senses or the understanding, produces its effect—contributes its mite towards the formation of the character. Every sentence that is framed, every word that is uttered, is framed or uttered for good or for evil, nothing is lost. No auld wife's story is so trivial, or so barren, as to lack a moral; nor is the impression it makes as transitory as the "tale that is told." These trifling but oft recurring contributions, are, so to speak, the principles of our principles, the underpropping of that moral edifice, whose spire pierces the clouds, and points the way to that glorious Elysium beyond, the blessed habitation of the immortals.

The Love of Stories and of Story-telling, cherishes a purity of heart, a frankness and candor of disposition, a respect for what is generous and elevated, a contempt for what is mean and dishonorable, a proper regard *for*, and independence *of*, the petty trials of life, & tends to multiply merry companions and never-failing friends.

September, 1836

Whether the Cultivation of the Imagination Conduce to the Happiness of the Individual.

MAN is an intellectual being. Without the least hesitation, as well as from the most careful investigation, if, indeed, there be any question about it, we are led to conclude that this intellect is to be cultivated. Indeed, the doubt, if any exist, cannot be solved, without the exercise, and, consequently, the cultivation, of the intellectual faculties. We could not, if we would, entirely and effectually put a stop to their gradual expansion and developement, without offering violence to the organs through which they act. It would obviously be inconsistent with the design of the Creator, as observed in the works of creation, that man, made capable of comprehending the object of his existence, and of understanding the relation on which he stands to its author, should so far neglect the culture of his peculiar *faculties* as to lose his peculiar *privileges* as a free agent. The wisdom of the Creator has ever been the theme of the Christian's admiration and praise; shall, then, "Wisdom for a Man's Self" be rejected? In supplying his physical wants man but obeys the dictates of nature's law. Shall the intellectual be disregarded?

If reason was given us for any one purpose more than any other, it was, that we might so regulate our conduct as to ensure our eternal happiness. The cultivation of the mind, then, is conducive to our happiness. But this cultivation consists in the cultivation of its several faculties. What we call the Imagination is one of these, hence does its culture, in a measure, conduce to the happiness of the individual.

The Imagination, says Stewart, "is the power that gives birth to the productions of the poet and the painter", whose province it is, says another, "to select the parts of different conceptions, or objects of memory, to form a whole more pleasing, more terrible, or more awful, than has ever been presented in the ordinary course of nature;" a power by no means peculiar to the poet or the painter. Whatever the senses perceive, or the mind takes cognizance of, affords food for the Imagination. In whatever situation a man may be placed, to whatever straits he may be reduced, this faculty is ever busy. Its province is unbounded, its flights are not confined to space, the past and the future, time and eternity, all come within the sphere of its range. This power, almost coeval with reason itself, is a fruitful source of terror to the child. This it is that suggests to his mind the idea of an invisible monster lying in wait to carry him off in the obscurity of the night. Whether acquired or not, it is obviously susceptible of a high degree of cultivation. This fact, too, goes to prove what was already so evident. In fact there are the same objections to the cultivation of any other faculty of the intellect, that there are to the cultivation of the one in question. The Mind itself should receive only its due share of attention; but should the physical powers be entirely neglected, the fault would rather be a negative than a positive one. So too the mind *alone* must be well balanced, no one power should be cultivated to the neglect of any other power. It is no objection to the study of Mathematics to say, that an exclusive devotion to that branch is sure to render one unfit for the duties of life: properly speaking, a faculty of the mind cannot be cultivated to excess; the fault lies in the neglect of some other power. The arm of the smith is not too strong for his body, he would do wrong to lay aside the hammer, and relax the muscles, lest the right arm outstrip the left. There is one other consideration which seems to affect this question. Unlike most other pleasures, those of the Imagination are not momentary and evanescent, its powers are rather increased than worn out by exercise; the old, no less than the young, find their supreme delight in the building of cob-houses and air castles out of these fragments of different conceptions. It is not so with the pleasures of sense.

magic lantern, without any connection with the being and feelings of the Speaker or the Poet impressed upon them; we look *at* them, but cannot for a moment feel *for*, or *with* them.

In the second, the images are transfigured; their colors and shapes are modified; one master passion pervades and quickens them; and in them all it is the wild and heart-stricken Father-king that speaks alone. —Fancy collects materials from the visible world, and arranges them for exhibition, but it imparts to them no touch of human interest; Imagination takes and moulds the objects of nature at the same moment; it makes them all speak the language of man, and renders them instinct with the inspired breath of human passion." One of the peculiar features of the poetry of the Greeks and Romans may be traced to the influences of a national Mythology, differing materially from that system of Polytheism which obtained among the more Northern tribes. The former inhabiting a luxurious clime, breathing a balmy and fragrant air, accustomed to the wildest profusion and riotous abundance, passing their time, mostly, in the open air, now stretched at length by the mossy fount and lulled asleep by its murmurings, now whiling away the hour in amorous lays that find an echo in the neighboring grove, the creatures of Imagination, saw in the spring which slaked their thirst some gentle nymph or Naiad. A Pan or Satyr had a hand in every sound that broke upon the stillness of the glade. Wanting a visible type, a sensible figure to which to direct his prayers and before which to offer up the firstlings of the flock or the first fruits of the harvest, the Southern hind had recourse to symbolical images. This tendency to what has been called Anthropomorphism, this appetite for visible images is a peculiar feature in the character of the Southerns at the present day, as the violent opposition to the famous Iconoclasts can testify. In the nations of Scandinavian or Teutonic descent a different tendency may be noticed. The scenery that surrounded them was stern and rugged, the face of nature presented little that was attractive, little to charm the eye; the towering peak, the awful sublimity of a Northern tempest, their dark and craggy dells, their boundless and almost impenetrable forests, cast a shade of awe and mystery over the beholder. Their conceptions were as subtle and unapproachable as their own mountain mists, every retired glen, every beetling crag, every dark unfathomable abyss, had its peculiar spirit; the open air was the temple of their divinity, no human structure, no tangible symbol, was compatible with their mystical conceptions of an over-ruling power. It is this neglect of the material, this fondness for the dark and mysterious, this propensity to the spiritual, that marks every page of Milton and his kindred spirits. We *see* with Dante but we *feel* with Milton.

The conception and expression of the passion of Love form another distinguishing feature in the poetry of old and modern times.

Our author concludes his "General Introduction" with the following apostrophe. "Greek—the shrine of the genius of the old world; as universal as our race, as individual as ourselves; of infinite flexibility, of indefatigable strength, with the complication and the distinctness of nature herself; to which nothing was vulgar, from which nothing was excluded; speaking to the ear like Italian, speaking to the mind like English; with words like pictures, with words like the gossamer film of the summer; at once the variety and picturesqueness of Homer, the gloom and the intensity of AEschylus; not compressed to the closest by Thucydides, not fathomed to the bottom by Plato, not sounding with all its thunders, nor lit up with all its ardors even under the Promethean touch of Demosthenes! And Latin—the voice of empire and of war, of law and of the state; inferior to its half-parent and rival in the embodying of passion and in the distinguishing of thought, but equal to it in sustaining the measured march of history, and superior to it in the indignant declamation of moral satire; stamped with the mark of an imperial and despotizing republic; rigid in its construction, parsimonious in its synonymes; reluctantly yielding to the flowery yoke of Horace, although opening glimpses of Greek-like splendor in the occasional inspirations of Lucretius; proved, indeed, to the uttermost by Cicero, and by *him* found wanting; yet majestic in its bareness, impressive in its conciseness; the true language of History, instinct with the spirit of nations, and not with the passions of individuals; breathing the maxims of the world, and not the tenets of the schools; one and uniform in its air and spirit, whether touched by the stern and haughty Sallust, by the open and discursive Livy, by the reserved and thoughtful Tacitus". &c.

It is not a matter of perfect indifference to us how or by whom the supposed works of Homer were really composed. The personal existence of Homer, as the author of the Iliad, was first questioned about the close of the 17th century, by 2 Frenchmen, Hedelin and Perrault, who were the first to suggest the outlines of a theory, which has since been developed by Heyne. According to this theory the Iliad was not the composition of a single individual, but is a compilation, methodized and arranged by successive editors. Hedelin maintains that the Iliad was made up "ex tragoediis et variis canticis de trivio, mendicorum et circulatorum, à la manière des chansons du Pontneuf." Wolf believed it to have been made by one

Ponticus, AElian, and Plutarch. But the better founded account is, that Pisistratus with the help of many
of the most celebrated poets of his age, first made a
regular collection of the different Rhapsodies which
passed under Homer's name, and arranged them very
much in the series in which we now possess them.
(The division into books corresponding with the letters of the alphabet, our author supposes to have been
the work of the Alexandrian critics many centuries
later.) Some of the authorities for this account are
Cicero, Pausanias, AElian, Libanius, Eustathius, and
the Scholiast. Hipparchus is supposed to have completed the work which Solon had begun, and Pisistratus had principally executed. This will embrace about
80 years from the date of Solon's law, B. C. 594, to
the death of Hipparchus the son of Pisistratus, B. C.
513. In his summary our author observes that there
are 3 points of view in which this collection may be
placed;—1. "That Homer wrote the Iliad in its present
form—that by means of the desultory recitations of
parts only by the itinerant Rhapsodists, its original
unity of form was lost in Western Greece—and that P.
and his son did no more than collect all those parts
and re-arrange them in their primitive order:—2. That
Homer wrote the existing verses constituting the Iliad
in such short songs or rhapsodies as he, himself an
itinerant rhapsodist, could sing or recite separately,
and that these songs were *for the first time* put into
one body, and disposed in their Epic form, by Pisistratus, as aforesaid:—3. That *several* Rhapsodists originally composed the songs out of which, or with
which, the Iliad as *a* Poem was compiled." "The first
is the common opinion, and is supported by Mr. Gran-
ville Penn, in his 'Primary Argument of the Iliad:' the
second is Wolf's and Bentley's; the last is Heyne's,
and was, I believe, the opinion of the late Dr. Parr,

resolving to abandon Smyrna, made a proclamation, that whoever wished to follow them should go out of the city, and that thereupon Melesigenes said he would *follow* or *accompany* them (ὁμηρεῖν). Another derivation is from ὁ μὴ ὁρῶν. Another from ὁ μηρός, because he had some mark on his thigh to denote his illegitimacy. Proclus says that the Poet was delivered up by the people of Smyrna to Chios as a hostage (ὅμηρος). The derivation that favors the theories both of Wolf and Heyne is from ὁμοῦ εἴρειν—to speak together, or ὁμηρεῖν—assemble together.

But these are mere conjectures. Mr. C. thinks that the Iliad is, with the exception of the Pentateuch and some other books of the Old Testament, the most ancient composition known. According to Wood, Haller, and Mitford, H. lived about the middle of the 9th century before Christ. That the Odyssey is not of the same age, or by the same hands as the Iliad, is one of the positions of the German theory, which has been countenanced by many great scholars as probable, if not absolutely demonstrated. Their arguments are chiefly drawn from internal evidence.

The Margites, a satire upon some strenuous blockhead, which does not now exist, is also attributed to H. The Batrachomyomachia, or the Battle of the Frogs and Mice, is a short mock-heroic poem of ancient date. The Homeric Hymns, which were discovered in the last century at Moscow, amount to 33; but, with the exception of those to Apollo, Mercury, Venus, and Ceres, are so short as not to consist of more than about 350 lines in all. Under the title of Epigrams are classed a few verses on different subjects chiefly addresses to cities or private individuals. In general, the songs in Shakspeare, Ben Jonson, Waller, and where he writes with simplicity, in Moore, give a better notion of the Greek Epigrams than any other species of modern composition. The subject of the Little Iliad was the continuation of the Trojan war from the death of Hector, but fragments only remain.

October 28, 1836

> What is the meaning of "Fate", in the ancient use of the word?
> What its popular signification now?

No LANGUAGE is so meagre, or so imperfect, as not to contain a term very nearly, if not exactly, synonymous with our word Fate. This proves the universality of the idea. But men, in different ages and under different circumstances, have attributed to various causes the same or similar phenomena; though the works of fate have ever been the same, yet fate itself has undergone an almost infinite variety of modifications; whereas we read that in old times a certain inexorable trio, called "Μοῖραι," commencing with the raw material, spun out and finally severed the thread of human life, in these days of innovation one is compelled to do the work of three.

I have said that the idea was an universal one. Though many deny that there is any such thing as fate, and others differ in the views they take of it, yet we all have a sufficiently clear idea of what it is to write about it—I say *about* it, if not *upon* it. Some would at once reject the term, while others would modify its signification to adapt it to their own opinion.

There appear to have been those of every age and nation, who have risen above the sensuous conceptions of the multitude—who, satisfied if they could search out the causes of things by the aid of the mental eye alone, have thus from time to time rescued small fragments of truth from the general wreck.

According to the belief of the mass of the Greeks, 3 sisters, Clotho, Lachesis, and Atropos, presided over the destinies of men. They were acquainted with the past, the present, and the future, and are represented with spindles which they keep constantly in motion, spinning the thread of human life, and singing the fate of mortals. The Romans had their Parcae and the Northerns their Nornen.

These sisters were either regarded as independent powers—the originators as well as executors of certain inevitable, though not immutable, laws, or, as some supposed, were the daughters of Jupiter, and as such acted in obedience to his commands.

Plato's views appear to have been more correct. "All things," says he, "are in fate; i.e. within its sphere or scheme, but all things are not fated: it is not in fate that one man shall do so and so, and another suffer so and so, for that would be the destruction of our free agency and liberty: but if any one should choose such a life, and do such or such things, then it is in fate that such or such consequences shall ensue upon it." That Socrates did not adopt the popular opinion is evident from those words of Cicero, "esse divinum quoddam, quod Socrates demonium appellat, cui semper ipse paruerit, nunquam impellenti, saepe revocanti."

It is difficult to say whether, in the popular use of the word at the present day, any peculiar or even precise meaning is attached to the word "Fate"; many, however, employ it to signify the necessary and inevitable operations of certain fixed laws, which were originally imposed by the Deity. This definition corresponds to what has been termed Physical Fate.

The ancients never lost sight of an invisible agent or power, independent of the laws of nature.—The point at issue among the moderns is, whether the Deity fore-ordained or merely fore-knew before the world was created, what was to happen to his creatures—whether man is a free agent.

Such was "effatum," and is therefore unavoidable; said the ancients.

Though fated, it was by no means unavoidable; say we.

Whatever is "effatum" is fated; said they.—Everything or nothing is fated, yet nothing is "effatum"; say we.

October, 1836

> Whether the Government ought to educate the children of those parents, who refuse to do it themselves.

I MAINTAIN that the Government ought to provide for the education of all children who would otherwise be brought up, or rather grow up, in ignorance.

In the first place the welfare of the individual, and in the second that of the community, demand it. It is as much the duty of the parent to educate, as it is to feed and clothe, the child. For on what, I would ask, depends this last duty? Why is the child to be fed and clothed, if not to enable him to receive and make a proper use of—an education? an education which he is no better able to obtain for himself, than he is to supply his physical wants. Indeed the culture of the physical is important only so far as it is subservient to that of the intellectual man. No one disputes this. Should then poverty or neglect threaten to rob the child of this right—a right more dear and more worthy to be cherished and defended than any he can enjoy— in such a case, it appears to me to be the duty of that neighbor whose circumstances will allow of it, to *take* the part of the child, and *act* the part of a parent. The duty in this instance amounts to a moral obligation, and is as much a duty as it is a duty to preserve the life of the infant whose unnatural parents would suffer it to starve by the road-side. What can it profit a man that he hath enough to eat and to drink, and the wherewithal he may be clothed, provided he lose his own soul?

But as these wealthy neighbors can accomplish more good by acting in concert, can more effectually relieve the unfortunate by a community of good offices, it is their duty, or, in other words, the duty of the community, so to do. Thus much for the welfare of the child.

That such a course, in the second place, is consistent with, nay, is necessary to, the greatest good of the community, scarcely admits of a doubt.

I shall not undertake to prove that the community ought to do what is for its own good; this is entirely unnecessary; since the welfare of posterity is certainly to be consulted.

November 11, 1836

Travellers & Inhabitants

State some of the causes of differing and imperfect accounts of countries given by Travellers and by native authors.

⟨. . .⟩ and imposing temple.

The travelling author lands on our shores with all the prejudices of the old country fresh in his mind, prepared to criticise our manners, our customs, and our country—or in other words, to compare them with those paragons which he has left at home. Fully impressed, as every honest citizen should be, with the superiority of his own country, and the preeminent perfection of her government and institutions, to say nothing of her children, he judges of what is right and wrong, good and bad, for these are but relative terms, by a comparison with those fixed and faultless standards, to mistrust which is to him more than sacrilege, as he gives his countrymen the height of our mountains or breadth of our rivers by referring them to their particular measures—their miles, leagues, or versts, as the case may be. Be he ever so free from prejudice, ever so liberal, a cosmopolite in the broadest sense of the word, the professed journalist and travelling bachelor, is too tender of the bantling in his hands, that is soon to astonish the natives in the shape of a respectable (I speak of the externals,) duodecimo, containing hints to travellers, or gleanings during a 3 weeks' tour in the Valley of the Mississippi, too solicitous is he for the popularity of his book, swindling bard, to withhold the "sugared cates" so temptingly offered at every turn, or when he has done, to administer the needed cathartic. Preferring infamy to oblivion—in despair of acquiring a vigorous and healthy fame, he is fain to content himself with a short-lived and bloated reputation, though at the expense of truth. Not so with the native author; he feels that he is writing the biography of a family of which he is himself a member; it is the broad and flourishing homestead that he describes; the faults and blemishes in the picture he has never attended to, or the whim-whams and oddities of his brothers and sisters have become so familiar to him as no longer to seem such; he remarks in them those peculiarities alone from which he is free, and which, in the eyes of a stranger, have nothing in common with those peculiar habits of mind which are said to run in the family.

The one, in fine, knows too much, and the other too little, of the country he would describe, and the manners he pretends to portray. The former aims not to establish premises and draw conclusions, but generously offers to the public those results to ⟨. . .⟩

ca. October-November, 1836

The History of the Progress and Termination of the Roman Republic,

BY ADAM FERGUSON, LL. D. F. R. S. E.

OUR author compares his labor to that of a limner, "who," says he, "attempting to restore the portrait of a person deceased, is furnished only with fragments of sculpture, or shreds of canvass, bearing the form and outline of some feature, the tint of complexion, or color of eyes and hair, and who is reduced, where the original is wanting, to put up with a copy though by an inferior hand; fortunate, if in all these taken together, the features and character he is in search of can be made to appear." But in this instance the features are of so striking a cast, and have been moulded by such masterly hands, that the merest dauber may restore the portrait, though fragments of sculpture, or shreds of canvass alone remain.

The casual observer will be charmed with the brilliancy of the coloring, and if the laws of perspective are carefully observed, and life and expression given to the portrait, he is satisfied; he scans with no small degree of interest the venerable busts, the soiled and dusty paintings that adorn our libraries and museums—the random efforts of departed genius, but cares not who the artist was, or under what circumstances the piece was painted. Not so with the virtuoso; if the portrait is a restored one, he must know what remained to guide the painter, what was the character of the individual represented, that he may judge of the merits of the piece.

Now I shall follow this last example, and endeavor to present a concise view of the authorities on which a history of the Roman Republic must be founded.

The earliest memorials of what passed at Rome, still extant, are to be found in the compilations of Dionysius of Halicarnassus, Livy, Plutarch, and others, who lived after the Republic itself was no more. Dionysius was a Greek, who visited Rome soon after the sovereignty of the Empire devolved on Octavius, and remaining there 20 yrs., wrote no less than 20 vols., continuing his narration from the earliest tradition of any Roman story, down to the first Punic war. Of these, but 11 ending with the expulsion of the Decemvirs, about the close of the 4th century of Rome, have survived the revolutions of time and nature. Livy, whose work is a detail of what was reported from the first ages of Rome, was a native of Padua; and being retained in the family of Livia, as tutor to Claudius, who was afterwards emperor, must have had access to every source of information the times could afford. Of 140 books composed by him, only 35 have yet been recovered. These consist of the first 10, down to the 5th century; 25 also, from the beginning of the second Punic War to the reduction of Macedonia, about the year 580 U. C. These however, compared to what must have followed, are to be regarded as but the meaner and less authentic part of his Work. Plutarch, who was a Greek, lived at Rome in the reign of Trajan, about a century later than Livy. In his biography of distinguished men he probably borrowed from Livy and Dionysius. The writings of Florus, who is supposed to have lived in the reign of Trajan; of Eutropius, who served under Julian, in his expedition to Parthia; and of Velleius Paterculus, an officer of high rank under Tiberius; but, particularly, those of Polybius, Plutarch, Dion Cassius, and Appian, serve to supply the defects which might arise from the loss of Sallust's General History and a large portion of Livy. Of the works of Sallust, who is justly distinguished by the energy of his style, the war with Jugurtha, the conspiracy of Cataline, and a few fragments, are all that remain. We next come upon the ground of Caesar's Commentaries; with the Correspondence, and other works of Cicero; the Lives of the Caesars, by Suetonius; the Annals of Tacitus, respecting the latter times of Augustus, the reign of Tiberius, and the accession of Caius. We must often avail ourselves of the remarks of numerous other authors, not professing to write history; as Strabo the Geographer, who lived in the reign of Augustus; Pliny, the Natural Historian; A. Gellius, a Grammarian, or as we say, a man of letters, who lived under Hadrian, and wrote a collection called the Attic Nights; Asconius Paedianus and Festus—Introductions to the Orations of Cicero by the

spoke as he thought, and thought before he spoke—
who realized it, and felt it to be, as it were, literally
true. It has a deeper meaning, and admits of a wider
application than is generally allowed. The various
bundles which we label, French, English, and Scotch-
men, differ only in this, that while the first is made
up of gay, showy, and fashionable habits,—the second
is crowded with those of a more sombre hue, bearing
the stamp of utility and comfort,—and the contents of
the third, it may be, are as rugged and unyielding as
their very envelope. The color and texture of these
contents vary with different bundles, but the material
is uniformly the same.

Man is an abstract and general term, it denotes the
genus; French, English, Scotch, &c. are but the dif-
ferentiae. It is with the genus alone that the philosopher and poet have to do. Where then shall they study
it? As well here as there, surely, if it be every where
the same; one may as well view the moon from mount
AEtna as the Andes, her phenomena will be equally
obvious, his map equally correct, whatever the point
from whence he observes her. But he must look
through a national glass. It may be desirable, indeed,
to see clearly with the naked eye; we should then
need no astronomers; yet the same glass, since a glass
we must use, will afford us an equally accurate view,
whatever station we choose. If our view be affected at
all by the quality of the instrument, the effect will
be constant and uniform, though our observatories be
rolled about upon wheels. It would seem then, that an
author's nationality may be equally obvious, and yet
full justice be done to his subject, whether that subject be an ancient or modern, domestic or foreign one.
By full justice I mean, he may do all he intended to,
or that any one can reasonably expect or require. Nay
further, his nationality may be even more striking in

treating of a foreign than a domestic subject, since what is peculiar and national in the writer, by the side of what is real history and matter-of-fact in the description, will be made the more manifest by the contrast. What is peculiar in the French character will sooner appear in a book of travels than a domestic diary; in his descriptions of foreign scenes and customs the Frenchman himself will be the most conspicuous object. Suppose him to weave these materials into a novel or poem—to introduce his innkeeper or postillion, he is fully adequate to his task—he has only to learn particulars—his must be an inductive method—the phenomena he observes are to be referred to a general law. Is human nature our study, the humanity of the Romans for instance, we ourselves—our friends—the community—are our text book. We wish to paint, perhaps, the old Roman courtier; so far as we know anything of him, we know him as a man, as possessing the same faults and virtues that we observe in men of modern times; does he possess different ones, he is a sealed book to us—he is no longer one of us—we can no more conceive of him—describe him—class him—than the naturalist can class or conceive of—he knows not what, an animal it may be, but he neither walks, swims, nor flies—eats, drinks, nor sleeps,—and yet lives.

I come now to speak of that peculiar structure and bent of mind which distinguishes an individual from his nation. Much that has already been said will apply equally well to this part of our subject. In a play or poem the author's individual genius is distinguished by the points of character he seizes upon, and the features most fondly dwelt upon, as well as the peculiar combinations which he delights in, and the general effect of his picture. Into his idea of his fellow enters one half himself—he views his subject only through himself, and strange indeed would it be did not the portrait betray the medium through which the original was observed. As the astronomer must use his own eyes, though he looks through a national glass, not only are we to consider the quality of the lens, but also the condition of the observer's visual organs. A defect in his sight will not be made up for by distance—will be equally evident, whether it be the instrument itself or the star to which it points, that is subjected to his scrutiny. To read history with advantage one must possess, we are told, a vivid imagination, that he may, in a measure, realize and enter into the spirit of the story, so as to make himself familiar with the scenes and characters there described. Every one is differently impressed, and each impression bears the stamp of the individual's taste and genius; one seizes greedily upon circumstances which another neglects—one associates with an event those scenes which witnessed it—one grasps the ludicrous, another the marvellous,—and thus, when the taste and judgment come to weave these conceptions into poetry their identity is not lost. Here then, surely, one's individual genius is fully manifested.

The original 'Sweet Auburn' has been ascertained to be Lishoy, in the county of Westmeath, Ireland. Though Goldsmith intended to represent an English village "he took from Lishoy," as his biographer truly observes, "only such traits and characteristics as might be applied to village-life in England, and modified them accordingly. He took what belonged to human nature in rustic life, and adapted it to the allotted scene. In the same way a painter takes his models from real life around him, even when he would paint a foreign or a classic group." We may suppose Goldsmith to have written this justly celebrated poem in the Irish village above named, where he passed his youth. Many of his observations apply rather, in their full extent, to an Irish than an English village—but this is a difference not in kind, but degree. The desolation which is the subject of these verses was by no means confined to his native country.

> "Ill fares the land, to hastening ills a prey,
> Where wealth accumulates, and men decay,"

is, alas! a truth but too universal in its application. Has not the author done full justice to his subject? Let the popularity of his poem answer. Goldsmith is visible in every line. As to his nationality, I will only add, that the hypercritical have discovered that many of his descriptions "savor more of the rural scenery and rustic life of an English than an Irish village", which is proof enough that what is national makes no mean figure in the poem. D'Israeli, speaking of Dante, observes, that "every great genius is influenced by the objects and feelings which occupy his own times, only differing from the race of his brothers by the magical force of his developments; the light he sends forth over the world he often catches from the faint and unobserved spark which would die away and turn to nothing, in another hand." So confident were his commentators that his 'Inferno' was but an earthly hell after all, that the poem had no sooner appeared than they set about tracing its original, which, satisfactorily to their own minds, they have finally discovered. His biographer relates that in the year 1304, among the novel and diverse sports on an occasion of public rejoicing, one was the representation of the Infernal regions, upon a stage of boats on the Arno, at Florence. This, he adds, was the occasion of the 'Inferno'. The poet himself has remarked, "I found the original of my hell in the world which we inhabit."

Shakspeare is justly styled the 'poet of nature'—
here is the secret of his popularity—his was no ideal
standard—man was his hobby. It was one of the characteristics of his genius that it adapted itself to the
reality of things, and was on familiar terms with our
feelings. His characters are men—though historically
faulty, yet *humanly* true—domesticated at once—they
are English in everything but the name. Now this
characteristic is capable of being made equally manifest, whether his genius be employed upon an ancient
or modern, foreign or domestic subject—he is as much
the poet of nature in the one case as the other, in
describing a Roman as a London mob, in Antony's
speech over the dead body of Caesar as the character
of Falstaff. Were Antony Percy and Percy Antony,

> —"there were an Antony
> Would ruffle up your spirits"—

and exert, perhaps, as magical an influence upon the
wounds of Caesar, and the stones of Rome, as the true
Roman orator. We are told by one author that "Invention is one of the grand characteristics of Shakspeare". "Yet" he asks,

> " 'What can we reason but from what we know?' "

This separating Invention from Imagination, as he
does, seems altogether unnecessary, as another remarks, "seems to be merely dividing the included
from the including term". It may be, as Johnson has
observed, that "Shakspeare's adherence to the real
story, and to the Roman manners has impeded the
natural vigor of his genius"—he may have been confined, but he was no less Shakspeare—though chained
he was not tamed. We are not to compare Shakspeare
chained with Shakspeare at liberty, but Shakspeare in
chains with others in the same condition. A caravan

is made up of animals as distinct in their nature and habits as their fellows of the forest.

I question, in the next place, whether our poet's powers of Imagination are less manifest when employed upon an ancient or foreign subject. Take, for instance, one of the most powerful passages of his 'Julius Caesar,' beginning

> "But yesterday the word of Caesar might
> Have stood against the world;" &c.

What is there foreign in the sentiment?—to be sure, the word Caesar occurs thrice, Cassius and Brutus each once; but they were no impediment, no more so, at least, than Hotspur or Macbeth would have been. The individual is merged in the man. Is it answered that, in the latter case, the character will be well known, and that therefore, the poet will feel more easy—more at home, and under less restraint? I answer, this very familiarity, though a desideratum with the biographer, may prove a hinderance to the former; facts are so many guide-boards, which confine him to a beaten track, leaving no room for Imagination. Some talk as if this faculty, wearied by its flight to so distant a scene, would be unable to exhibit its accustomed fertility and vigor, or, among so many strange scenes and faces being overcome by feelings of homesickness and loneliness, would lose a great portion of its energy and creative power. But this objection is far from applying to Shakspeare—he was, as we say, never less alone than when alone. Fortunately, his familiarity with Roman history was not so remarkable as to multiply guideboards to a troublesome degree, or supersede the necessity of his judging for himself, or hazarding a conjecture now and then.

Shakspeare is Shakspeare, whether at home or abroad.

L'Allegro & Il Penseroso

⟨. . .⟩ college ⟨. . .⟩ bright spot in the student's history, a cloud by day, a pillar of fire by night, shedding a grateful lustre over long years of toil, and cheering him onward to the end of his pilgrimage. Immured within the dank but classic walls of a Stoughton or Hollis his wearied and ⟨. . . . .
. . . .⟩

The precise date of these poems is not known, they were probably, however, together with his Comus and Lycidas, the fruit of those five years of literary leisure, from 1632 to 1637, which our author is known to have spent at Horton, in Buckinghamshire. Surely ⟨. .
. . . .⟩
so faithfully the spirit of its divine Author? They were first published in 1645, but for nearly a century obtained but little notice from the lovers of polite literature, the Addisons and Popes of the day. They are thought, by Dr. Warton, to have been originally indebted to Handel's music for whatever notice they at last obtained.

L'Allegro is not an *effort* of Genius, but rather an out-pouring of poetic feeling. We have here a succession of pleasing and striking images, which are dwelt upon just long enough. ⟨. . .⟩ at ⟨. . . . .
. . . .⟩
never been heard of since the days of Robinhood.

The metre of these verses is admirably adapted to the subject. The reader can hardly believe that he is not one of the party, tripping it over hill and dale "on the light fantastic toe".

A verse of poetry should strike the reader, as it did

the poet, as a whole, not so much as the sign of an idea as that idea itself.

> —As Imagination bodies forth
> The forms of things unknown, the Poet's pen
> Turns them to shapes—

⟨. . .⟩ to which they are already ⟨. . . . .
. . . .⟩ in every respect, so as to satisfy its aerial occupant, it is enough, whatever may be the order of architecture. Thus was it with our architect.

But the parts and members of his verses are equally appropriate and striking. With the idea comes the very word, if its sense is not wanted, its sound is.

But lo! the sun is up, the hounds are out, the ploughman has already driven his team afield, and as he gaily treads the fragrant furrow, his merry whistle "is heard the *fields* around," responsive to the milkmaid's song, who now repairs with pail on head, and quick elastic step, to her humble stool. The mower, too, has commenced his labors in the meadow at hand,

> And every shepherd tells his tale
> Under the hawthorne in the dale.

Such a picture of rural felicity as is presented in these and the following lines, is rarely to be met with even in poetry. Fancy has her hands full, a thousand images are flitting before her, bringing with them a crowd of delightful associations, and she is forced, in spite of herself, to join the revel and thread the mazes of the dance. And then for

> the spicy nut-brown ale,
> With stories told of many a feat—

there are the "delights", the "recreations and jolly pastimes that will fetch the day about from sun to sun, and rock the tedious year as in a delightful

dream". The poet leaves not a single chord untouched
if the reader will but yield himself up to his influence.
This whole poem is to be regarded rather as a "sweet
digression" than an elaborate effort, as an effusion
rather than a production.

Johnson has well observed, in his biographical notice of Milton, "No mirth can indeed be found in his
melancholy; but I am afraid that I always meet some
melancholy in his mirth." His mirth wears a pensive
hue, his melancholy is but a pleasing contemplative
mood. The transition from L'Allegro to Il Penseroso
is by no means abrupt, the vain deluding joys which
are referred to in the commencement of the latter, are
not those unreproved pleasures which the poet has
just recounted, for they are by no means inconsistent
with that soft melancholy which he paints, but rather,
the fickle pensioners of that Euphrosyne whose sister
graces are Meat and Drink, a very different crew from
that which waits upon the "daughter fair" of Zephyr
and Aurora. The latter are content with daylight and
a moderate portion of the night—when tales are done

> —"to bed they creep,
> By whispering winds soon lulled asleep."

but the others proceed to evening amusements, and
even to the London theatres, and the "well-trod stage,"
—but only

> "If Jonson's learned sock be on,
> Or sweetest Shakspeare, Fancy's child,
> Warble his native wood-notes wild."

Beginning with the warning to idle joys, that they
depart and leave the poet to "divinest Melancholy,"
we soon come to that picture of her, perhaps, the
finest in the whole poem.

A sable stole thrown over her decent shoulders,
with slow and measured steps, and looks that hold

"sweet converse" with the skies, reflecting a portion of their own placidness, she gradually draws near. But lo! the "cherub contemplation" delays her lingering steps, her eyes upraised to heaven, the earth is for a space forgot—time loiters in his course, were it for but a moment—past—present—future—mingle as one. ⟨. . .
. . . .⟩

The picture of Morning in "Il Penseroso" differs greatly from that in "L'Allegro," and introduces that mention of the storm-wind in a cloudy day,—

"When rocking winds are piping loud,"—

a very poetic touch. A later poet, Thomson, attributes its sighing to the "sad Genius of the coming storm," Gray too, seems to have been equally affected by it. "Did you never observe" he writes, "that pause, as the gust is recollecting itself, and rising upon the ear in a shrill and plaintive tone, like the swell of an Æolian harp? I do assure you there is nothing in the world so like the voice of a spirit."

We are told, that it was while exposed to a violent storm of wind and rain, attended by frequent flashes of lightening, among the wilds of Glen-Ken, in Galloway, that Burns composed his far-famed song, the "Scots wha hae wi' Wallace bled". Ossian was the child of the storm, its music was ever grateful to his ear. Hence his poetry breathes throughout a tempestuous spirit—when read, as it should be, at the still hour of night, the very rustling of a leaf stirred by the impatient reader, seems to his excited imagination the fitful moanings of the wind, or sighings of the breeze.

But if Milton's winds rock they pipe also, even the monotony of a summer shower is relieved by the cheerful pattering of 'minute drops from off the eaves', and if the heavens are for a few moments overcast, the splendor of the succeeding sunshine is heightened by contrast.

It is amusing to know that Milton was a performer on the bass-viol. He is said even to have been a composer, though nothing remains to prove the assertion. It was his practice, say his biographers, when he had dined to play on some musical instrument, and either sing himself or make his wife sing, who, he said, had a good voice but no ear. This partiality for the sister muse is no where more manifest than in these poems; whether in a mirthful or a pensive mood, the "linked sweetness" of "soft Lydian airs", "the pealing organ", or 'the full-voiced quire', 'dissolve him into ecstasies.'

These poems are to be valued, if for no other reason, on account of the assistance they afford us in forming our estimate of the *man* Milton. They place him in an entirely new, and extremely pleasing, light to the reader who was previously familiar with him as the author of the Paradise Lost alone. If before he venerated, he may now admire and love him. The immortal Milton seems for a space to have put on mortality, to have snatched a moment from the weightier cares of heaven and hell, to wander for awhile among the sons of men. But we mistake; though his wings, as he tells us, were already sprouted, he was as yet content to linger awhile, with childlike affection, amid the scenes of his native earth.

The tenor of these verses is in keeping with the poet's early life; he was, as he confesses, a reader of romances, an occasional frequenter of the playhouse, and not at all averse to spending a cheerful evening, now and then, with some kindred spirits about town. We see nothing here of the Puritan. The "storied windows" which were afterwards an abomination in his eyes, admit a welcome, though sombre, light. The learning of Jonson, and the wild notes of Shakspeare, are among the last resources of the mirthful L'Allegro.

The student of Milton will ever turn with satisfaction from contemplating the stern and consistent nonconformist, and bold defender of civil and religious liberty, engaged, but not involved, in a tedious and virulent controversy,

> With darkness and with dangers compassed
> round,

his dearest hopes disappointed, and himself shut out from the cheering light of day, to these fruits of his earlier and brighter years; though of the earth, yet the flights of one who was contemplating to soar 'Above the Aonian mount', a heavenward and unattempted course.

I have not undertaken to write a critique, I have dwelt upon the poet's beauties and not so much as glanced at his blemishes. This may be the result of pure selfishness; Poetry is but a recreation. A pleasing image, or a fine sentiment, loses none of its charms, though Burton, or Beaumont and Fletcher, or Marlowe, or Sir Walter Raleigh, may have written something very similar; or even, in another connexion, have used the identical word whose aptness we so much admire. It always appeared to me that that contemptible kind of criticism which can deliberately, and in cold blood, dissect the sublimest passage, and take pleasure in the detection of slight verbal incongruities, was, when applied to Milton, little better than sacrilege, and that those critics who condescended to practice it, were to be ranked with the parish officers who, prompted by a profane and mercenary spirit, tore from their grave and exposed for sale, what were imagined to be the remains of Milton.

January 15, 1837
All Men Are Mad

It is my candid belief, that all men are mad. Either madness never existed, or it is universal. It is a difference in degree, not in kind. We are all mad in each other's eyes—but who is mad in his own eyes?

What greater folly than presumptuousness?—yet who more presumptuous than the sane man? He presumes upon the madness of his neighbor, and *madly* clings to reason. Define Reason, then, and not till then, assert thy own title to it. Analyze Instinct, and when thou hast done, despise the brute, and thank God that *thou* wast born a *reasonable* being. Let thy crucibles be filled with madness—thine alembics o'erflow with folly—distill its essence—produce its elements—report. Choose *Wisdom* for thine inheritance, and leave folly for a patrimony to fools.

In fine, the poet—that 'arch chymic'—who says ' 'tis madness—to defer'—has afforded us by far the most satisfactory definition that I have hitherto met with.

January 20, 1837

Point out particulars in the speeches of Moloch & the rest, P. L. II, which appear to you characteristic.

> "After short silence then,
> And summons read, the great consult
> began."

Satan, Moloch, Belial, Mammon, and Beëlzebub,—'the flower of Heaven once', but now the pride of Hell,—

successively harangue the assembly. First Satan, 'author of all ill,' takes it upon himself to comfort his mates and followers, by assuring them that all is not lost, that Heaven may yet be regained. Fit ruler of such a host. By showing them how good has already come out of evil, refraining to dwell on their misfortunes, and appearing solicitous only to restore them to their former condition, though, in reality, preferring 'to reign in Hell, rather than serve in Heaven', he effectually revives their drooping energies, and proves himself the master spirit of the host.

From the contents of the preceding book, we should expect to observe in Satan's speech, ambition aided by matchless cunning; the former it was, that first suggested the revolt, and what but the latter could have so far carried his plans into execution? The poet has not failed to do his character justice in the present instance; his speech is marked throughout by superior subtlety, and when at last, the 'devilish counsel, first proposed—and in part devised', by himself, is adopted, the spirit of revenge which first prompted the undertaking, retires before self-interest, and gives place, for a while, to ambition. Proud, as it were, of this new responsibility, he declares that 'none shall partake with him the enterprise', and while they 'seek to render Hell more tolerable', reserves to himself the glory of their deliverance; thus proving himself, both cunning to devise, and prompt to execute.

What a contrast does Satan afford to the exasperated Moloch. Here is no dissimulation, no hellish craft, no nice calculation of chances, no ambition to shine; self interest is swallowed up in revenge. Urged by despair, he counsels to scale the walls of Heaven, and oppose 'infernal thunder' to the Almighty's engines. Danger he sees none,—

'but perhaps
The way seems difficult and steep to scale'.

The difficulty is, to get at the enemy. He is 'a plain blunt *devil*,' who 'only speaks right on—no orator as *Satan* is', easily exasperated, but not so easily pacified —the creature of impulse. Next rose Belial, second to none in dissimulation, 'nor yet behind in hate'. With a fair outside all is false and hollow within. As is often the case, his faint heart suggests a wise and prudent course; but he is none the less a devil, though a timid one. Difficulties and dangers innumerable beset his path, he deals in hypotheses and conjectures, counts what is lost, and thanks his stars that so much yet remains,—dwells upon the evils to be apprehended from obstinately persevering in rebellion, and closing, touches upon the effect of submission to appease the victor.

Next, Mammon proves himself the same cool and deliberate calculator, who engrosses so large a share of man's homage at the present day. War has no charms for him. Deficient neither in courage nor cunning, he is for adopting the readier and surer way to counteract the Almighty's vengeance, by seeking to 'compose the present evils—dismissing quite all thoughts of war'. 'Cui bono'? is his motto. Though he looks only upon the dark side of the picture, when he speaks of the project to 'dethrone the King of Heaven', it is the effect, not of fear or despair, but a worldly, or rather hellish, policy.

Beëlzebub resembles in many respects his infernal master. His harangue breathes throughout a true Pandemonian spirit. The most consummate skill, the fiercest hate, and a determined spirit of revenge, mark him the devil of devils. He is the cool, the deliberate, the accomplished, villain. Mischief is his element,—he loves it for its own sake.

The skill with which Milton has adapted every part, and especially the opening, of each harangue, to the character of the speaker, is deserving of notice. Indeed, the first two or three lines, are, in each case, entirely characteristic of the individual—a perfect sample of the whole speech. This may have been the work of chance, but it certainly looks like design.

Satan begins his address in a formal and courtier-like manner.

> 'Powers and dominions, deities of Heaven;
> For since no deep' &c.

Here is a set speech, cut and dried, as it were, for the occasion. The commencement of the second line betrays a hidden purpose, some proposition to be made, or project to be unfolded. The very indirectness with which the subject is introduced is a proof of design, a warning of craft to be used in the pursuit of a favorite object.—

> 'My sentence is for open war: of wiles,
> More unexpert, I boast not:'—

Here is evident a straight-forwardness and singleness of purpose, a contempt of ornament and art. The first three words argue a mind made up. The indicative *is* simply declares his resolution; as if it only remained to make known what was already resolved.

How different the following.

> 'I *should* be much for open war, O Peers,
> As not behind in hate; *if*' &c.

A *should* and an *if* to begin with. The second word *should* implies hesitation; the *if*, in the next line, is a harbinger of fear and irresolution. Indeed, the whole speech is one string of interrogatories, plentifully sprinkled with words expressive of doubt and uncertainty, such as could, would, should, yet, and or. Timidity is the mother of inquisitiveness.

> 'Either to disenthrone the King of Heaven
> We war, if war be best, or to regain
> Our own right lost:'—

These words, it is true, express uncertainty as to the course to be pursued, but it is the uncertainty, not of fear or despair, but self-interest. The second line will not admit of any other interpretation. The manner in which the all-absorbing subject war is introduced, gives promise of a ready support in case war should be declared. Beëlzebub's elaborate exordium would by no means disgrace his Satanic majesty.

> 'Thrones and imperial powers, offspring of Heaven,
> Ethereal virtues:'—

He has evidently followed some such rule as that laid down by Cicero, "not to compose the Introduction first, but to consider first the main argument, and let that suggest the Exordium." Even in these few lines, his resemblance to Satan, his ambitious master and superior, is sufficiently obvious.

February 17, 1837

> Speak of the characteristics which, either humorously or reproachfully, we are in the habit of ascribing to the people of different sections of our own country.

A NATIONALITY is not necessarily, nor strictly speaking, an aggregate of individualities, any further than words are concerned. A people, to be sure, may be peculiarly industrious,—distinguished in that respect from their neighbors, in the same manner that an individual is, but usually, when we reckon industry among the characteristics of a people, we refer not to any peculiarity in that industry, but to its prevalence. When, on the other hand, we say of an individual, that he is a shrewd man, no peculiarity is implied; so that, unless we coin an epithet for the occasion, we are fain to call him a *peculiarly* shrewd man.

This may teach us how far the knowledge of a nation's characteristics should influence our judgment of individuals. In the first place, we are to consider that the individual before us may be one of the few, who, constituting but a small item of the national character, were not taken into the account, and, in the second place, that if of the majority, not a single individual peculiarity can be embraced or implied. Add to this the fact, that such characteristics may generally be traced to the journal of some traveller, who has taken a hasty and partial survey of but one section of a country, and are often the mere echo of previous prejudices, and we shall be able to judge how slight the probability is, that the so called characteristics of a people have any foundation in truth.

It is not a little curious to observe how man, the boasted Lord of creation, is the slave of a name—a mere sound. Cassius was not the first to note this. The distinction of classes in a college affords an instance of it. If a multitude be collected from all quarters, and of every condition, and a common name be given them, a powerful sympathy will immediately spring up, which in time will generate a community of interests. In this light, man is properly enough called a gregarious animal, but it appears to me the common epithet is as often the connecting link, as it is the result of such a union.

Rome had never been mistress of the world had not the distinction of allies been merged in the title of Roman citizens. They were Romans who conquered the world; so many Latins, Apulians, and Campanians, had they stood, in other respects, in precisely the same relative situations, would sooner have gone to war with each other. How much mischief have those magical words, North, South, East, and West, caused. Could we rest satisfied with one mighty, all-embracing West, leaving the other three cardinal points to the old world, methinks we should not have cause for so much apprehension about the preservation of the Union. When, in addition to these natural distinctions, descriptive and characteristic epithets are applied, by their own countrymen, to the people of different sections of the country, though in a careless and bantering manner, the patriot may well tremble for the Union.

A sound and impartial judgment is less to be esteemed for the evident good consequences it leads to, than prejudice is to be feared for the incalculable evil it engenders. It is easier to convince a man's reason, than to warp or regulate his feelings. There are certain principles implanted in us, which, independently of the will, teach us the consistency and inconsistency of things, when viewed in certain relations. By operating upon these principles, through the medium of certain definite propositions, corresponding invariable results, in the mind of each one, of necessity follow. That these conclusions as invariably affect the conduct, I do not pretend. The feelings, on the other hand, are not at the mercy of any such definite law, which regulates and disposes them. The eloquence which, at one time, causes to vibrate all the chords of human sympathy, and raises almost to a pitch of phrensy the rapt and excited multitude, at another, perhaps, falls powerless and ineffectual, or excites those very feelings it was its object to soothe and allay.

There is the same difficulty in dissipating those prejudices already formed;—the sober truth may be recognised, the false judgment admitted, but a crowd of associations has so confounded error with the most palpable truths, that the evil can be but partially, if ever, eradicated. What once floated harmlessly upon the surface, in time commingles with, and becomes a part of the mighty element, which at first barely afforded it a resting place.

March 3, 1837

> Compare some of the Methods of gaining or exercising public Influence: as,
> Lectures, the Pulpit, Associations, the Press, Political Office.

INVETERATE custom, as well as the respect with which most men regard his sacred office, secure to the preacher a certain, though limited, degree of influence. He is the shepherd of a flock—the infallible guide and arbiter in spiritual affairs. His parish is his kingdom, where he rules with an almost despotic sway; the young, even from the cradle, are taught to value his approving smile, and tremble at his frown; the aged despise not his teachings, nor are the vicious backward to respect those virtues which they yet fail to imitate. At church, he can depend upon an orderly,

if not attentive, audience; the great truths and principles which are there expounded, equally concern
the highest interests of all. Criticism has no place
there,—the peculiarities and failings of the preacher
are overlooked, or, if noticed, are willingly pardoned
by his indulgent hearers. The character of the day, as
well as the sanctity of the place, are the sources of a
thousand associations, which impart a degree of so-
lemnity and weight to his words, scarcely to be attained by the most labored style, aided by all the arts
of eloquence.

> "Truth from his lips *prevails* with double
>   sway,"
> "And fools, who came to scoff, *remain* to
>   pray."

Yet the sphere of the preacher's influence is, comparatively, narrow and circumscribed. His own little
flock alone acknowledge his sway; the village spire
overlooks his puny territories, while the sound of the
"church-going bell" is heard in their remotest corner.

To respect his teachings, and venerate his person,
from a duty degenerates into a habit, which, from
the very nature of its origin, too often opposes an
insuperable barrier to a further increase of his authority.

He, on the other hand, who addresses his fellow
men through the medium of the press, is so far a
stranger to the mass of his readers, as not to be exposed to the effects of those prejudices which a personal acquaintance would be inevitably attended by.
His field of labor is the universe. The influ- ⟨. . .⟩ The
thousands of newspapers that circulate throughout
the United States develope different sorts of editors.
One sort gives his readers conclusions at which he
had previously arrived, without troubling them with a
formidable list of propositions and connecting links;

here are the facts,—let them "pepper and dish as they choose." Another editor is by far more sophistical; in his articles not a single term, premise or mode but is subjected to the severest scrutiny. He goes on very well till he comes to the inference: but then, alas! after all this display, he is wont to draw his inference by main force from some other quarter. One editor is disposed to show all he knows, if not to know all he shows. Another is so overwhelmed with particulars that he is unable to wield them all. His inference may be so unwieldy that he is unable to start it. Another takes but a partial view of things, and is very much in the situation of one who looks through a microscope, and thus obtains a correct idea of the minute parts of an object; but is apt to lose sight of its outward bulk and more obvious qualities.

March 17, 1837

> Name, and speak of, Titles of Books, either as pertinent to the matter, or merely ingenious and attractive.

WHEN at length, after infinite toil and anxiety, an author has fairly completed his work, the next, and by far the most important concern that demands his attention, is the christening. He is about to send forth his bantling to seek its fortune in the world, and he feels a kind of parental interest in its welfare, prompting him to look about for some expressive and euphonic Title, which, at least, will secure it a civil treatment from mankind, and may, perchance, serve as an introduction to their sincere esteem and regard.

A Title may either be characteristic, consisting of a single expressive word or pithy sentence, or ingenious and amusing, so as to catch the fancy, or excite the curiosity. Some, such as "Ivanhoe", for instance, though familiarity with the contents may impart to them an interest not their own, or other associations render them pleasing to the ear, seem to have been adopted as merely, or chiefly, distinctive, without any attempt to enlighten the reader upon the nature of the subject, or to deceive him into a perusal of the volume.

In the infancy of a nation's literature, when books, like angels' visits, are "few and far between", their very rarity seems to require that they should be distinguished by Titles equally rare, and not unusually does it happen, that these prove so exceedingly attractive, as to cast quite into the shade the humble volume which they were intended merely to usher into notice. The character of the contents is often quite overlooked in the desire to make a favorable first impression, and the author's whole ingenuity is exerted in the framing of some fanciful or dignified Title, which will at once recommend his book to the favor of the reading public. As some fond parents, in the lower walks of life, are accustomed to ransack the long list of departed worthies for sonorous and well-tried names, or, from the cast-off spoils of the novel heroine, seek to swell the scanty portion which fortune may have allotted to their offspring.

What can be more alluring than the following tempting, and somewhat luxurious display of verbal delicacies—"Paradise of Dainty Devices"? What may be the nature of these "Dainty Devices" is left to be imagined by the reader, it being safer to leave him to his own vague conjectures, than to tell the plain truth at once.

Robert Langland, a contemporary of Chaucer, taught the fundamental doctrines of Christianity in a voluminous poetical work, entitled "Pierce the Ploughman's Crede". One William is overtaken by sleep, among the Malvern hills, and in a dream, beholds the different classes of society pursuing their respective avocations, upon a spacious plain before him. He is addressed by various allegorical personages, among whom True Religion and Reason are the most conspicuous. By "Piers Ploughman" is sometimes meant the "true and universal church", at others, he is a mysterious personage, who undertakes to guide mankind to the abode of Truth, declaring that he himself has long been 'his' faithful and devoted follower. Where the uninitiated reader would expect a rude pastoral, or rural ditty, or perhaps an essay on husbandry, nothing is found to repay him for the trouble of a perusal, but obscure and interminable allegories,

> "In notes, with many a winding bout
> Of linked *dulness* long drawn out."

Southwell's "Funeral Tears" is another of the same description.

The following give one a slight insight into the subject. "Abuses Stript and Whipt", being a volume of satirical essays; in later times, "Heliconia", a "selection of English Poetry of the Elizabethan age"; and "Archaica", a "reprint of scarce Old English Prose Tracts", by Sir Egerton Brydges.

"Davy's Salmonia", which is also of this description, must have puzzled many.

Our early literature abounds in such conceited Titles as the following; "The Ladder of Perfection"; "A Looking Glass for London and England"; "A Fan to drive away Flies"; and "Matches lighted by the divine Fire." One author, through an excess of modesty or squeamishness, calls a discourse upon the life and death of an individual, an "Epitaph"; another has packed off a quarto with the inexplicable, and therefore attractive, Title, "Prayse of the Red Herring".

Our ancestors were fond of regarding their works as so many different centres, from which diverged rays of various hues, carrying light and heat to every quarter—as choice repositories of learning, or perennial fountains of amusement, and therefore, overlooking their general character, gave them collective Titles, taken, for the most part, from the analogy of matter. Some such have already been mentioned. Painter's "Palace of Pleasure", "The Temple of Memory", "Coryat's Crudities", &c. are other instances. We may also add "The Mirour for Magistrates", a rather odd Title for a chronicle history, written during the reign of queen Mary, and embracing "the lives and untimely falles" of "unfortunate Princes and men of note" from Brutus down.

Not even sober philological and grammatical works have escaped the absurdity of unintelligible and affected Titles. Horne Tooke's "Diversions of Purley" must have disappointed many a desultory reader in search of amusement. The difficulty is not removed by the addition of the poetical expletive "Epea Pteroenta". The student has heard of this celebrated treatise, and he feels a desire to examine it; he has recourse, perhaps, to the catalogue of some library, which informs him merely, that John Horne Tooke was the author of a book called "Diversions of Purley". He is somewhat astonished that so learned a philologist as Mr. Tooke should have condescended to dabble in light literature, or have sacrificed a moment in amusements or diversions of any kind.

It cannot be that he is mistaken, Mr. Tooke was certainly the author of the work he is in quest of;

perhaps those ill-starred "Diversions", however, may
contain a biographical notice of their author, which
will throw some light upon the subject. He examines
and is undeceived.

Instead of a Dictionary of Sports, or a Panegyric on
the Delights of Rural Life, he finds a critical treatise
on the English language, displaying no small degree
of philological learning.

No people have been more prone to these extrava-
gances than the Persians. Mohammed Eben Emir
Chowand Shah, who flourished in 1741, was the author of a voluminous historical work, entitled "Hortus
Puritatis, in Historia Prophetarum, Regum, et Chali-
farum". A Persian-Turkish dictionary bears the Title
of "Naëmet Allah", or "Delight of Gods". "The Gulistan", or "Flower-Garden", a collection of moral fables
and apophthegms, by Shaikh Sadī of Shiraz, being
written in an excessively florid style, may aptly
enough be compared to a garden of flowers, or a parcel of nosegays. We next come upon the ground of
the "Lebtarik", or "Marrow of History", by the immortal, so far as his name is concerned, Al Emir
Yahia Ebn Abdollatif al Kazwini. Abu Said wrote a
universal history, from Adam to his own time, under
the Title of "Historical Pearl Necklace."

Revolutions have not been confined to political institutions and forms of government; not even Old
Books nor Old Clothes have escaped the all-grasping
hand of reform. Men have learned that "all is not
gold that glisters." Books have cast off their gaudy
and cumbrous court dresses, and appear, in these
days, in a plain Republican garb. The works of the
philosopher, the poet, and the statesman, carry no
recommendation upon their backs, nor does a dis-
couraging array of clasps compel the faint-hearted
reader to rely upon outward appearances. Indeed,

their Titles, should a perusal warrant it, are concealed by an every-day dress of paper, while their contents are equally accessible to all.

It is not a little remarkable that so few really valuable works have anything to recommend them in their externals.

March 31, 1837

> "The thunder's roar, the Lightning's flash, the billows' roar, the earthquake's shock, all derive their dread sublimity from Death."
>
> "The Inheritance." chapter 56.

Examine this theory.

"WHATEVER," says Burke, "is fitted in any sort to excite the ideas of pain, and danger, that is to say, whatever is in any sort terrible, or is conversant about terrible objects, or operates in a manner analogous to terror, is a source of the sublime."–"Indeed terror is in all cases whatsoever, either more openly or latently, the ruling principle of the sublime." Hence Obscurity, Solitude, Power, and the like, in so far as they are fitted to excite terror, are sources of the sublime. This is a theory far more satisfactory than that which we are about to examine. He does not make death the source of terror, but rather pain, using the word in its broadest sense.

Death itself is sublime. It has all the attributes of sublimity–Mystery, Power, Silence–a sublimity which no one can resist, which may be heightened, but cannot be equalled, by the thunder's roar, or the cannon's peal. But yet, though incomparably more awful, this is the same sublimity that we ascribe to the tumult of the troubled ocean, the same in kind, though different in degree, depending for its effect upon the same principles of our nature, though affecting us more powerfully and universally. To attribute the two to different principles, is not only unphilosophical, but manifestly unnecessary.

We shrink with horror from attributing emotions so exalted and unearthly, and withal so flattering to our nature, to an abject fear of death. We would fain believe that the immortals, who know no fear, nor ever taste of death, can sympathize with us poor worldlings in our reverence for the sublime,—that they listen to the thunder's roar, and behold the lightning's flash, with emotions similar to our own. We do believe it; we have so represented it. The sublimity of the conflict on the plains of Heaven, between the rebel angels and the Almighty's loyal bands, as described by Milton, was not lost upon the *spirits* engaged in it. Raphaël, who recounts the particulars of the fight to our forefather Adam, describes the Messiah as riding *sublime* "on the wings of cherub,"

> "On the crystalline sky, in sapphire thron'd,
> Illustrious far and wide;"—

Nor could he have been entirely unconscious of the emotion in question, when he compared the combat between Satan and Michael, to the meeting of two planets. "As if", to use his own expression,

> "Among the constellations war were sprung,
> "Two planets, rushing from aspect malign
> "Of fiercest opposition, in mid sky
> "Should combat, and their jarring spheres
>   confound."

—Who can contemplate the hour of his birth, or reflect upon the obscurity and darkness from which he then emerged into a still more mysterious existence, without being powerfully impressed with the idea of sublimity? Shall we derive this sublimity from death? Nay, further, can anything be conceived more sublime than that second birth, the resurrection? It is a subject which we approach with a kind of reverential awe. It has inspired the sublimest efforts of the poet and the painter. The trump which shall awake the dead is the creation of poetry; but, to follow out the idea, will its sound excite in us no emotion, or will the blessed, whom it shall summon to forsake the mouldering relics of mortality, and wing their way to brighter and happier worlds, listen with terror, or indifference? Shall he, who is acknowledged while on earth to have a *soul* for the sublime and beautiful in nature, hereafter, when he shall be all soul, lose this divine privilege? Shall we be indebted to the body for emotions which would adorn heaven? And yet there are some, who will refer you to the casting off of this "mortal coil", as the origin, and, I may add, the consummation of all this.

We can hardly say that fear is a source of the sublime; it may be indispensable, it is true, that a certain degree of awe should enter into the astonishment or admiration with which we listen to the billow's roar, or the howlings of the storm. We do not tremble with fright, but the calm which comes over the soul, is like that which precedes the earthquake. It is a pleasure of the highest kind, to behold a mighty river, rolling impetuously, and, as it were, blindly onward to the edge of the precipice, where, for successive ages, it plunges headlong to the bottom, roaring and foaming, in its mad career, and shaking the solid earth by its fall, but it is not joy that we experience, it is pleasure, mingled with reverence, and tempered with humility. Burke has said, that "terror is in all cases whatsoever, either more openly or latently, the ruling principle of the sublime," Alison says as much, and Stewart advances a very different theory. The first would trace the emotion in question to the influence of pain, and terror, which is but an apprehension of pain. I would make an inherent respect, or reverence, which certain objects are fitted to demand, that ruling principle; which reverence, as it is altogether distinct from, so shall it outlive, that terror to which he refers, and operate to exalt and distinguish us, when fear shall be no more.

Whatever is grand, wonderful, or mysterious, *may* be a source of the sublime. Terror inevitably injures, and, if excessive, may entirely destroy its effect. To the coward, the cannon's peal, the din and confusion of the fight, are not sublime but rather terrible, the calm and self-collected alone, are conscious of their sublimity. Hence, indeed, are they inspired with courage to sustain the conflict. To fear is mortal, angels may reverence. The child manifests respect ere it has experienced terror. The Deity would be reverenced, not feared.

Hence is it, that the emotion in question is so often attended by a consciousness of our own littleness; we are accustomed to admire what seemeth difficult, or beyond our attainment. But to feel conscious of our own weakness, is not positively unpleasant, unless we compare ourselves with what is incapable of commanding our respect, or reverence, and consequently, is not a source of the sublime.

Grandeur, of some kind or other, must ever enter into our idea of the sublime. Niagara would still retain her sublimity, though her fall should be reduced many feet, but the puny mountain stream must make up in depth of fall, for what it lacks in volume. What is more grand than mystery? The darker it is, the grander it grows. We habitually call it great. Burke has well remarked, that the divisibility of matter is sublime, its very infinity makes it so. Infinity is the essence of sublimity.

Whatever demands our admiration or respect, is, in a degree, sublime. It is true, nothing could originally demand our respect, which was not, at the same time, *capable*, in a greater or less degree, of exciting our fear, but this does not prove fear to be the source of that respect. Nothing, on the other hand, of which we stand in awe, is an object of our contempt, yet the source of that contempt is not, surely, indifference, or a feeling of security. It will be enough, merely to advert to the immense influence which the association of ideas exerts.

Burke's theory would extend those emotions which the sublime excites, to the brute creation. They suffer pain—they experience terror—they possess the faculty of memory, and philosophers have ascribed to them those of imagination and judgment. Why may not, then, the brute hearken with rapture to the thunder's peal, or, in the depths of the forest, enjoy the grandeur of the storm? Man's pride will not admit it. It savors of Immortality. But the brute knows not that peculiar reverence for what is grand, whether in nature, or in art, or in thought, or in action, which is the exclusive birthright of the lord of creation. There is an infinity in the mystery, the power, and grandeur, which concur in the sublime, the abstract nature of which is barely recognised, though not comprehended, by the human mind itself. Philosophers, it is true, have ascribed to brutes "devotion, or respect for superiors", but, so to speak, this is a respect grounded on experience, it is practical or habitual, not the fruit of abstract reflection, nor does it amount to the recognition of any moral superiority.

But to some it may appear, that this reverence for the grand, if I may so style it, is not an original principle of our nature,—that it originates in fear. I answer, *if* this is not, neither is fear. Nay more, the former is a principle more universal in its operation, more exalting and ennobling in its influence, and is, besides, so superior to, and at variance with, fear, that we cannot, for a moment, derive it from the latter.

The philosopher sees cause for wonder and astonishment in everything, in himself, and in all around him, he has only to reflect, that he may admire. Terror avoids reflection, though reflection alone can restore to calmness and equanimity. How regard, respect, reverence, can grow out of fear, is, I must confess, incomprehensible.

We reverence greatness, moral and intellectual, the giant intellect is no sooner recognised, than it demands our homage. Moral greatness calls for the admiration of the depraved even.

The emotion excited by the sublime is the most unearthly and godlike we mortals experience. It depends for the peculiar strength, with which it takes hold on, and occupies, the mind, upon a principle which lies at the foundation of that worship, which we pay to the Creator himself. And is fear the foundation of that worship? is fear the ruling principle of our religion? Is it not rather the mother of superstition? Yes, that principle which prompts us to pay an involuntary homage to the infinite, the incomprehensible, the sublime, forms the very basis of our religion. It is a principle implanted in us by our Maker, a part of our very selves, we cannot eradicate it, we cannot resist it; fear may be overcome, death may be despised, but the infinite, the sublime, seize upon the soul and disarm it. We may overlook them, or rather fall short of them, we may pass them by, but so sure as we meet them face to face, we yield.

April 28, 1837

> The opinions of Dymond and Mrs. Opie respecting the general obligation *to tell the truth*; are they sound and applicable?
>
> Vide Dymond's "Essays on Morality" and Mrs. Opie's "Illustrations of Lying."

I shall confine myself to the examination of Mr. Dymond's opinions without pretending to offer any of my own. He defines a lie to be "uttering what is not true when the speaker professes to utter truth, or when he knows it is expected by the hearer." We are to bear in mind that whether the term is to be understood in a good or a bad sense, must depend upon the definition assigned it. As here used, it is altogether arbitrary. Mr. Dymond does not tell us that this or that is a lie, but finds it necessary first to define the term—to inform us what, in the following essay, is to be understood by the term lie.

This being premised, let us inquire first, whether a man may, under any conceivable circumstances, tell a lie without the infraction of the moral law. May we not lie to a robber, in order to preserve our property? Our author thinks not. If we may lie to preserve our property, says he, we may murder, and as it would be

wrong to murder in such a case, so would it be wrong
to lie. But this reasoning is by no means conclusive,
for who can say what constitutes a lie. Dymond applies the term arbitrarily to certain forms of speech;
suppose we do the same. To lie, we will say, is to
"utter what is *true* when the speaker professes to
utter truth, or when he knows it is expected by the
hearer."

To lie then, in this sense, would be immoral, because to murder, with the same view, would be immoral. It is the similarity of purpose, and not of
means, which constitutes the immorality in this case.
This method of reasoning amounts, in fact, to a
manifest petitio principii.

But further, may we not "tell a falsehood to a mad-
man for his own advantage"? Dymond's answer
amounts to this. It would not be for his advantage,
and hence would it be morally wrong to commit so
egregious a blunder. Indeed, this is the only sign of
an argument adduced to prove this particular point.
This surely is founding the guilt of lying upon its ill
effects, which procedure our author condemned in
the outset.

In the second place, are those untruths sometimes
amounting to lies, in the sense in which Dymond uses
the term, which custom has sanctioned, in any way
defensible? We must here have some regard to the
effects of the practice, the motives and expectations
of the parties being unknown. If these are not lies
they are evidently gratuitous, for where is the use of
telling an untruth to one who receives it as such, if
it be not a fiction calculated to please or instruct?
Might not one as well remain silent? But what is useless is never harmless. If, on the other hand, these are
lies, if the speaker "utters what is untrue when he

profess to utter truth, or when he knows it is expected by the hearer," his conduct is certainly to be condemned.

As for those cases in which it is impossible to be deceived—the compliments which bring up the rear in a dedication or epistle,—we can at best say no good of them. To excuse them because they are taken for what they are worth, would be like pardoning the vices of a dangerous member of society, because his character is properly estimated—the very fact of its being understood implying its condemnation.

May 5, 1837

> Paley in his Nat. Theology, Chap. 23—speaks of minds utterly averse to "the *flatness* of being content with common reasons"—and considers the highest minds "most liable to this repugnancy."
>
> See the passage, and explain the moral or intellectual defect.

TURGOT has said, "He that has never doubted the existence of matter, may be assured he has no aptitude for metaphysical inquiries." It would seem as if doubt and uncertainty grew with the growth of the intellect, and strengthened with its strength. The giant intellect, it is true, is for a season borne along with the tide, the opinions and prejudices of the mass are silently acquiesced in, the senses are, for awhile, the supreme arbiters from whose decisions there is no appeal—mystery is yet afar off, it is but a cloud in the

distance, whose shadow, as it flits across the landscape, gives a pleasing variety to the scene. But as the
perfect day approaches, its morning light discovers
the dark and straggling clouds, which at first skirted
the horizon, assembling as at a signal, and, as they
expand and multiply, rolling slowly onward to the
zenith, till at last the whole heavens, if we except a
faint glimmering in the east, are overshadowed. The
earth was once firm beneath the feet, but it now affords but a frail support,—its solid surface is as yielding and elastic as air. The grass grew and the water
ran, and who so blind as to question their reality? A
feeling of loneliness comes over the soul, for these
things are of the past.

This is the season of probation, but the time approaches, and is now at hand, when the glorious bow
shall "rise on the lurid rear of the tempest, the sun
laugh jocundly abroad, and

> Every bathed leaf and blossom fair
> Pour out its soul to the delicious air."

The embryo philosopher seeks the sunny side of
the hill, or the grateful coolness of the grove—he in-
stinctively bares his bosom to the zephyr, that he may
with the less inconvenience discuss the reality of outward existences. No proposition is so self-evident as
to escape his suspicion, nor yet so obscure as to with-
stand his scrutiny. He acknowledges but two distinct
existences, Nature and Spirit; all things else which
his obstinate and self-willed senses present to him,
are plainly, though unaccountably, absurd. He laughs
through his tears at the very mention of a mathematical demonstration. There is a flatness about what
is common that at once excites his ridicule or disgust.
He goes abroad into the world, and hears men assert
and deny in positive terms, and he is astounded—he

is shocked—he perceives no meaning in their words or their actions. He recognises no axioms, he smiles at reason and common sense, and sees truth only in the dreams and superstitions of mankind. And yet he but carries out principles which men practically admit every day of their lives. Most, nay all, acknowledge a few mysteries; some things, they admit, are hard to understand; but these are comparatively few, and could they but refer them back one link in the chain of causes and effects, the difficulty would at once be removed.

Our philosopher has a reasonable respect for the opinions of men, but this respect has not power to blind his judgment; taking as he does an original view of things, he innocently confounds the manifest with the mysterious.

That such is the common reason, was properly enough, in the first place, no recommendation with him, and is now a positive objection. What is more common than error? Some seeming truths he has clung to as the strongholds of certainty, till a closer investigation induced mistrust. His confidence in the infallibility of reason is shaken,—his very existence becomes problematical. He has been sadly deceived, and experience has taught him to doubt, to question even the most palpable truths. He feels that he is not secure till he has gone back to their primitive elements, and taken a fresh and unprejudiced view of things. He builds for himself, in fact, a new world.

The opinions of the few, the persecuted, the dreamers of this world, he has a peculiar respect for—he is prepossessed in their favor. Man does not wantonly rend the meanest tie that binds him to his fellow; he would not stand aloof, even in his prejudices, did not the stern demands of truth, backed by conviction, require it. He is ready enough to float with the tide, and when he does stem the current of popular opinion, sincerity, at least, must nerve his arm. He has not only the burden of proof, but that of reproof, to support. We may call him a fanatic—an enthusiast—but these are titles of honor, they signify the devotion and entire surrendering of himself to his cause. Where there is sincerity there is truth also. So far as my experience goes, man *never* seriously maintained an objectionable principle, doctrine, or theory. Error *never* had a sincere defender; her disciples were *never* enthusiasts.

This is strong language, I confess, but I do not rashly make use of it. We are told that "to err is human," but I would rather call it *in*human, if I may use the word in this sense. I speak not of those errors that have to do with facts and occurrences, but rather errors of judgment. Words, too, I would regard as mere signs of ideas.

That passage in the Vicar of Wakefield which Johnson pronounced fine, but which Goldsmith was wise enough to strike out, previous to publication, must be taken in a very limited sense. "When I was a young man", he writes, "I was perpetually starting new propositions; but I soon gave this over; *for I found that generally what was new was false*".

At best, we can but say of a common reason, that men do not dispute it. True, they defend it when attacked, for if *they* did not, Reason never would. This is well explained by Gray, when he undertakes to account for the popularity of Shaftesbury. "Men are very prone", says he, "to believe what they do not understand;—they will believe anything at all, provided they are under no obligation to believe it;—they love to take a new road even when that road leads nowhere."

May 19, 1837

> "The clock sends me to bed at ten, and makes me rise at eight. I go to bed awake, and arise asleep; but I have ever held conformity one of the best arts of life, and though I might choose my own hours, I think it proper to follow theirs."
>
> E. Montagu's Letters

Speak of the duty, inconvenience and dangers of *conformity,* in little things and great.

NEITHER natural nor revealed religion affords any rules by which we may determine the comparative enormity of different vices, or the comparative excellence of different virtues. The Hebrew code, which Christ came not to destroy but to fulfil, makes no such distinction—vice, under whatever form, is condemned in unqualified and positive terms. We are told, in our Savior's exposition of the law, that one jot or one tittle shall in no wise pass from the law, till all be fulfilled; —and whosoever shall break one of the least commandments, and shall teach men so, he shall be called the least in the kingdom of heaven. So far, too, as man has deduced a moral code from a philosophical study of the works of creation—their operation and design—our remark will hold good with respect to that also.

The idea appears to be a prevalent one, that duty consists in certain outward acts, whose performance is more or less obligatory under different circumstances, though it can never be entirely neglected with impunity; and, consequently, that one duty may interfere with another, and that there may be situations in which a man cannot possibly avoid the violation of duty. This arises, I think, from confining duty to the outward act, instead of making it consist in conformity to the dictates of an inward arbiter, in a measure independent of matter, and its relations, time and space.

Duty is one and invariable—it requires no impossibilities, nor can it ever be disregarded with impunity; so far as it exists, it is binding, and if all duties are binding, so as on no account to be neglected, how can one bind stronger than another?

So far then as duty is concerned, we may entirely neglect the distinction of little things and great.

Mere conformity to another's habits or customs is never, properly speaking, a duty, though it may follow as a natural consequence of the performance of duty.

The fact that such is the general practice of mankind does not affect a question of duty. I am required, it is true, to respect the feelings of my neighbor within the limits of his own estate, but the fear of displeasing the world ought not, in the least, to influence my actions; were it otherwise the principal avenue to reform would be closed.

May 26, 1837

Whether Moral Excellence tend directly to increase Intellectual Power?

FIRST, what is moral excellence? Not, surely, the mere acknowledgement of the divine origin of the Scriptures, and obedience to their dictates as such; nor yet an implicit compliance with the requisitions of what may be termed popular morality. It consists rather in allowing the religious sentiment to exercise a natural and proper influence over our lives and conduct—in acting from a sense of duty, or, as we say, from principle.

The morally excellent, then, are constantly striving to discover and pursue the right. This is their whole duty; for, in the inquiry what is right, reason alone can decide, and her dictates are ever identical with the dictates of duty. Here then is ample room for the exercise of the intellectual faculties.

What, in fact, is the end of all inquiry but the discovery of truth—of right? The man of the world, no less than the logician, though his objects of pursuit be unworthy a man, is still anxious only to learn the best way to attain them; the degraded and vicious have already discovered the *right* way to do wrong. Indeed no man ever proves so wholly false to his nature as not to worship truth under some form or other, none so lost to all sense of honesty, as not to contend for, and lay claim to, the right.

The morally right, or true, differs only from the worldly or temporal, in that it is the only real and universal right—that most worthy of man's inquiry and pursuit—the only right recognised by philosophy. As it is the most abstract, so is it the most practical of all, for it admits of universal application.

None, in fine, but the highest minds, can attain to moral excellence. With by far the greater part of mankind, religion is a habit, or rather, habit is religion, their views of things are illiberal and contracted, for the very reason that they possess not intellectual power sufficient to attain to moral excellence. However paradoxical it may seem, it appears to me that to reject *Religion* is the first step towards moral excellence; at least, no man ever attained to the highest degree of the latter by any other road. Byron's character is a favorite argument with those who maintain the opposite opinion; a better for my own purpose I could not have desired. He advanced just far enough on the road to excellence to depart from the religion of the vulgar, nay further, twelve lines, says Constant, (and he quotes them) of his poetry, contain more true religion than was ever possessed by any or all of his calumniators.

Could infidels but live double the number of years allotted to other mortals, they would become patterns of excellence. So too of all true poets—they would neglect the beautiful for the true.

So far, then, from impeding the developement of the Intellectual Powers, Moral Excellence is made the sole pursuit, and is attainable only, by the highest minds.

June 2, 1837

The mark or standard by which a nation is judged to be barbarous or civilized.

Barbarities of civilized states.

The justice of a nation's claim to be regarded as civilized, seems to depend, mainly, upon the degree in which Art has triumphed over Nature. The culture implied by the term Civilization is the influence of Art, and not Nature, on man. He mingles his own will with the unchanged essences around him, and becomes, in his turn, the creature of his own creations.

The end of life is education. An education is good or bad, according to the disposition or frame of mind it induces. If it tend to cherish and develope the religious sentiment—continually to remind man of his mysterious relation to God and Nature—and exalt him above the toil and drudgery of this matter-of-fact world, it is good. Civilization, we think, not only does not accomplish this, but is directly adverse to it. The civilized man is the slave of matter. Art paves the earth, lest he may soil the soles of his feet, it builds walls, that he may not see the heavens, year in, year out, the sun rises in vain to him, the rain falls and the wind blows, but they do not reach him. From his wigwam of brick and mortar he praises his Maker for the genial warmth of a sun he never saw, or the fruitfulness of an earth he disdains to tread upon. Who says this is not mockery?

So much for the influence of Art.

Our rude forefathers took liberal and enlarged views of things, rarely narrow or partial. They surrendered up themselves wholly to Nature—to contemplate her was a part of their daily food. Was she stupendous, so were their conceptions. The inhabitant of the mountain can hardly be brought to use a microscope, he is accustomed to embrace empires in a single glance. Nature is continually exerting a moral influence over man, she accommodates herself to the soul of man. Hence his conceptions are as gigantic as her mountains. We may see an instance of this if we will but turn our eyes to the strongholds of liberty, Scotland, Switzerland, and Wales.

What more stupendous can Art contrive than the Alps?—what more sublime than the thunder among the hills?

The savage is far sighted, his eye, like the Poet's,

"Doth glance from Heaven to Earth, from
    Earth to Heaven,"

he looks far into futurity, wandering as familiarly

through the land of spirits as the *civilized* man through his wood lot or pleasure grounds. His life is practical poetry—a perfect epic; the earth is his hunting ground—he lives suns and winters—the sun is his time-piece, he journeys to its rising or its setting, to the abode of winter or the land whence the summer comes. He never listens to the thunder but he is reminded of the Great Spirit—it is his voice. To him, the lightening is less terrible than it is sublime— the rainbow less beautiful than it is wonderful—the sun less warm than it is glorious.

The savage dies and is buried, he sleeps with his forefathers, & before many winters his dust returns to dust again, and his body is mingled with the elements. The civilized man can scarce sleep even in his grave. Not even there are the weary at rest, nor do the wicked cease from troubling. What with the hammering of stone, and the grating of bolts, the worms themselves are well-nigh deceived. Art rears his monument, learning contributes his epitaph, and interest adds the "Carey fecit," as a salutary check upon the unearthly emotions which a perusal might otherwise excite.

A nation may be ever so civilized and yet lack wisdom. Wisdom is the result of education, and education being the bringing out, or developement, of that which is in a man, by contact with the Not Me, is safer in the hands of Nature than of Art. The savage may be, and often is, a sage. Our Indian is more of a man than the inhabitant of a city. He lives as a man—he thinks as a man—he dies as a man. The latter, it is true, is more learned; Learning is Art's creature; but it is not essential to the perfect man—it cannot educate. A man may spend his days in the study of a single species of animalculae, invisible to the naked eye, and thus become the founder of a new branch of science, without having advanced the great object for which life was given him at all.

The naturalist, the chemist, or the mechanist, is no more a man for all his learning. Life is still as short as ever, death as inevitable, and the heavens are as far off.

The Indian journeys many suns to visit ⟨. . .⟩

June 30, 1837

T. Pomponius Atticus as an Example

ONE cannot safely imitate the actions, as such, even of the wise and good. Truth is not exalted, but rather degraded and soiled by contact with humanity. We may not conform ourselves to any mortal pattern, but should conform our every act and thought to Truth.

Truth is that whole of which Virtue, Justice, Benevolence and the like are the parts, the manifestations; she includes and runs through them all. She is continually revealing herself. Why, then, be satisfied with the mere reflection of her genial warmth and light? why dote upon her faint and fleeting echo, if we can bask in her sunshine, and hearken to her revelations when we will? No man is so situated that he may not, if he choose, find her out; and when he has discovered her, he may without fear go all lengths with her; but if he take her at second hand, it must be done cautiously; else she will not be pure and unmixed.

Wherever she manifests herself, whether in God, in man, or in nature, by herself considered, she is equally admirable, equally inviting; though to our view she seems, from her relations, now stern and repulsive, now mild and persuasive. We will then consider Truth by herself, so that we may the more heartily adore her, and more confidently follow her.

Next, how far was the life of Atticus a manifestation of Truth? According to Nepos, his Latin biographer: "He so carried himself as to seem level with the lowest, and yet equal to the highest. He never sued for any preferment in the State, because it was not to be obtained by fair and honorable means. He never went to law about anything. He never altered his manner of life, though his estate was greatly increased. His complaisance was not without a strict regard to truth."

Truth neither exalteth nor humbleth herself. She is not too high for the low, nor yet too low for the high. She never stoops to what is mean or dishonorable. She is persuasive, not litigious, leaving Conscience to decide. Circumstances do not affect her. She never sacrificeth her dignity that she may secure for herself a favorable reception. Thus far the example of Atticus may safely be followed. But we are told, on the other hand: "That, finding it impossible to live suitably to his dignity at Rome, without offending one party or the other, he withdrew to Athens. That he left Italy that he might not bear arms against Sylla. That he so *managed* by taking no active part, as to secure the good will of *both* Cæsar and Pompey. Finally, that he was careful to avoid even the appearance of crime."

It is not a characteristic of Truth to use men tenderly, nor is she over-anxious about appearances. The honest man, according to George Herbert,—is

"He that doth still and strongly good pursue,
To God, his neighbor and himself most true;
   Whom neither fear nor fawning can
Unpin, or wrench from giving all their due.
   Who rides his sure and even trot,
While the World now rides by, now lags behind.
   Who, when great trials come,
Nor seeks nor shuns them, but doth always stay
Till he the thing, and the example weigh;
   All being brought into a sum,
What place or person calls for, he doth pay."

Atticus seems to have well understood the maxim applied to him by his biographer,—"*Sui cuique mores fingunt fortunam.*" (Character shapes his lot for each of us.)

ca. June, 1837

Class Book Autobiography

DAVID HENRY THOREAU.

I AM of French extract, my ancestors having taken refuge in the isle of Jersey, on the revocation of the edict of Nantes, by Lewis 14th, in the year 1685. My grandfather came to this country about the year −73, "sans souci sans sous," in season to take an *active part* in the Revolution, as a sailor before the mast.

I first saw the light in the quiet village of Concord, of Revolutionary memory, July 12th, 1817.

I shall ever pride myself upon the place of my birth—may she never have cause to be ashamed of her sons. If I forget thee, O Concord, let my right hand forget her cunning. Thy name shall be my passport in foreign lands. To whatever quarter of the world I may wander, I shall deem it my good fortune that I hail from Concord North Bridge.

At the age of sixteen I turned my steps towards these venerable halls, bearing in mind, as I have ever since done, that I had two ears and but one tongue. I came—I saw—I conquered—but at the hardest, another such a victory and I had been undone. "One branch more", to use Mr. Quincy's own words, "and you had been turned by entirely. You have barely got in." However "A man's a man for a' that," I was in, and didn't stop to ask how I got there.

I see but two alternatives, a page or a volume. Spare me, and be thou spared, the latter.

Suffice it to say, that though bodily I have been a member of Harvard University, heart and soul I have been far away among the scenes of my boyhood. Those hours that should have been devoted to study, have been spent in scouring the woods, and exploring the lakes and streams of my native village. Oft could I sing with the poet,

> My heart's in the Highlands, my heart is
> 　　not here;
> 　My heart's in the Highlands a-chasing the
> 　　deer;
> Chasing the wild deer, and following the roe,
> My heart's in the Highlands wherever I go.

The occasional day-dream is a bright spot in the student's history, a cloud by day, a pillar of fire by night, shedding a grateful lustre over long years of toil, and cheering him onward to the end of his pilgrimage. Immured within the dank but classic walls of a Stoughton or Hollis, his wearied and care-worn spirit yearns for the sympathy of his old, and almost forgotten friend, Nature, but failing of this is fain to have recourse to Memory's perennial fount, lest her features, her teachings, and spirit-stirring revelations, be forever lost.

Think not that my Classmates have no place in my heart—but this is too sacred a matter even for a Class Book.

> "Friends! that parting tear reserve it,
> Tho' 'tis doubly dear to me!
> Could I think I did deserve it,
> How much happier would I be."

As to my intentions——enough for the day is the evil thereof.

August 30, 1837

> "The commercial spirit of modern times considered in its influence on the Political, Moral, and Literary character of a Nation."

THE history of the world, it has been justly observed, is the history of the progress of humanity; each epoch is characterized by some peculiar development; some element or principle is continually being evolved by the simultaneous, though unconscious and involuntary, workings and struggles of the human mind. Profound study and observation have discovered, that the characteristic of our epoch is perfect freedom—freedom of thought and action. The indignant Greek, the oppressed Pole, the jealous American, assert it. The skeptic no less than the believer, the heretic no less than the faithful child of the church, have begun to enjoy it. It has generated an unusual degree of energy and activity—it has generated the *commercial spirit*. Man thinks faster and freer than ever before. He moreover moves faster and freer. He is more restless, for the reason that he is more independent, than ever. The winds and the waves are not enough for him; he must needs ransack the bowels of the earth that he may make for himself a highway of iron over its surface.

Indeed, could one examine this beehive of ours from an observatory among the stars, he would perceive an unwonted degree of bustle in these later ages. There would be hammering and chipping, baking and brewing, in one quarter; buying and selling, money-changing and speech-making, in another. What impression would he receive from so general and impartial a survey? Would it appear to him that mankind used this world as not abusing it? Doubtless he would first be struck with the profuse beauty of our orb; he would never tire of admiring its varied zones and seasons, with their changes of livery. He could not but notice that restless animal for whose sake it was contrived, but where he found one to admire with him his fair dwelling place, the ninety and nine would be scraping together a little of the gilded dust upon its surface.

In considering the influence of the commercial spirit on the moral character of a nation, we have only to look at its ruling principle. We are to look chiefly for its origin, and the power that still cherishes and sustains it, in a blind and unmanly love of wealth. And is it seriously asked, whether the prevalence of such a spirit can be prejudicial to a community? Wherever it exists it is too sure to become the *ruling* spirit, and as a natural consequence, it infuses into all our thoughts and affections a degree of its own selfishness; we become selfish in our patriotism, selfish in our domestic relations, selfish in our religion.

Let men, true to their natures, cultivate the moral affections, lead manly and independent lives; let them make riches the means and not the end of existence, and we shall hear no more of the commercial spirit. The sea will not stagnate, the earth will be as green as ever, and the air as pure. This curious world which we inhabit is more wonderful than it is convenient, more beautiful than it is useful—it is more to be admired and enjoyed then, than used. The order of things should be somewhat reversed,— the seventh should be man's day of toil, wherein to earn his living by the sweat of his brow, and the other six his sabbath of the affections and the soul, in which to range this wide-spread garden, and drink in the soft influences and sublime revelations of Nature.

But the veriest slave of avarice, the most devoted and selfish worshipper of Mammon, is toiling and calculating to some other purpose than the mere acquisition of the good things of this world; he is preparing, gradually and unconsciously it may be, to lead a more intellectual and spiritual life. Man cannot if he will, however degraded or sensual his existence, escape Truth. She makes herself to be heard above the din and bustle of commerce, by the merchant at his desk, or the miser counting his gains, as well as in the retirement of the study, by her humble and patient follower.

Our subject has its bright as well as its dark side. The spirit we are considering is not altogether and without exception bad. We rejoice in it as one more indication of the entire and universal freedom which characterizes the age in which we live—as an indication that the human race is making one more advance in that infinite series of progressions which awaits it. We rejoice that the history of our epoch will not be a barren chapter in the annals of the world,—that the progress which it shall record bids fair to be general and decided. We glory in those very excesses which are a source of anxiety to the wise and good, as an evidence that man will not always be the slave of matter, but erelong, casting off those earth-born desires which identify him with the brute, shall pass the days of his sojourn in this his nether paradise as becomes the Lord of Creation.

Miscellanies

Died:

IN THIS town, on the 12th inst. Miss Anna Jones, aged 86.

When a fellow being departs for the land of spirits, whether that spirit take its flight from a hovel or a palace, we would fain know what was its demeanor in life—what of beautiful it lived.

We are happy to state, upon the testimony of those who knew her best, that the subject of this notice was an upright and exemplary woman, that her amiableness and benevolence were such as to win all hearts, and, to her praise be it spoken, that during a long life, she was never known to speak ill of any one. After a youth passed amid scenes of turmoil and war, she has lingered thus long amongst us a bright sample of the Revolutionary woman. She was as it were, a connecting link between the past and the present—a precious relic of days which the man and patriot would not willingly forget.

The religious sentiment was strongly developed in her. Of her last years it may truly be said, that they were passed in the society of the apostles and prophets; she lived as in their presence; their teachings were meat and drink to her. Poverty was her lot, but she possessed those virtues without which the rich are but poor. As her life had been, so was her death.

Aulus Persius Flaccus.

IF YOU have imagined what a divine work is spread out for the poet, and approach this author too, in the hope of finding the field at length fairly entered on, you will hardly dissent from the words of the prologue,

> "Ipse semipaganus
> Ad sacra Vatum carmen affero nostrum."

Here is none of the interior dignity of Virgil, nor the elegance and fire of Horace, nor will any Sibyl be needed to remind you, that from those older Greek poets, there is a sad descent to Persius. Scarcely can you distinguish one harmonious sound, amid this unmusical bickering with the follies of men.

One sees how music has its place in thought, but hardly as yet in language. When the Muse arrives, we wait for her to remould language, and impart to it her own rhythm. Hitherto the verse groans and labors with its load, but goes not forward blithely, singing by the way. The best ode may be parodied, indeed is itself a parody, and has a poor and trivial sound, like a man stepping on the rounds of a ladder. Homer, and Shakspeare, and Milton, and Marvell, and Wordsworth, are but the rustling of leaves and crackling of twigs in the forest, and not yet the sound of any bird. The Muse has never lifted up her voice to sing. Most of all satire will not be sung. A Juvenal or Persius do not marry music to their verse, but are measured fault-finders at best; stand but just outside the faults they condemn, and so are concerned rather about the monster they have escaped, than the fair prospect before them. Let them live on an age, not a secular one, and they will have travelled out of his shadow and harm's way, and found other objects to ponder.

As long as there is satire, the poet is, as it were, *particeps criminis*. One sees not but he had best let bad take care of itself, and have to do only with what is beyond suspicion. If you light on the least vestige of truth, and it is the weight of the whole body still which stamps the faintest trace, an eternity will not suffice to extol it, while no evil is so huge, but you grudge to bestow on it a moment of hate. Truth never turns to rebuke falsehood; her own straightforwardness is the severest correction. Horace would not have written satire so well, if he had not been inspired by it, as by a passion, and fondly cherished his vein. In his odes, the love always exceeds the hate, so that the severest satire still sings itself, and the poet is satisfied, though the folly be not corrected.

A sort of necessary order in the development of Genius is, first, Complaint; second, Plaint; third, Love. Complaint, which is the condition of Persius, lies not in the province of poetry. Ere long the enjoyment of a superior good would have changed his disgust into regret. We can never have much sympathy with the complainer; for after searching nature through, we conclude he must be both plaintiff and defendant too, and so had best come to a settlement without a hearing.

I know not but it would be truer to say, that the highest strain of the muse is essentially plaintive. The saint's are still *tears* of joy.

But the divinest poem, or the life of a great man, is the severest satire; as impersonal as nature herself, and like the sighs of her winds in the woods, which convey ever a slight reproof to the hearer. The greater the genius, the keener the edge of the satire.

Hence have we to do only with the rare and fragmentary traits, which least belong to Persius, or,
rather, are the properest utterance of his muse; since
that which he says best at any time is what he can
best say at all times. The Spectators and Ramblers
have not failed to cull some quotable sentences from
this garden too, so pleasant is it to meet even the
most familiar truth in a new dress, when, if our
neighbor had said it, we should have passed it by as
hackneyed. Out of these six satires, you may perhaps
select some twenty lines, which fit so well as many
thoughts, that they will recur to the scholar almost as
readily as a natural image; though when translated
into familiar language, they lose that insular emphasis, which fitted them for quotation. Such lines as the
following no translation can render commonplace.
Contrasting the man of true religion with those, that,
with jealous privacy, would fain carry on a secret
commerce with the gods, he says,—

> "Haud cuivis promptum est, murmurque humilesque
>   susurros
> Tollere de templis; et aperto vivere voto."

To the virtuous man, the universe is the only
sanctum sanctorum, and the penetralia of the temple
are the broad noon of his existence. Why should he
betake himself to a subterranean crypt, as if it were
the only holy ground in all the world he had left un-
profaned? The obedient soul would only the more
discover and familiarize things, and escape more and
more into light and air, as having henceforth done
with secrecy, so that the universe shall not seem
open enough for it. At length, it is neglectful even of
that silence which is consistent with true modesty,
but by its independence of all confidence in its dis-
closures, makes that which it imparts so private to

the hearer, that it becomes the care of the whole world that modesty be not infringed.

To the man who cherishes a secret in his breast, there is a still greater secret unexplored. Our most indifferent acts may be matter for secrecy, but whatever we do with the utmost truthfulness and integrity, by virtue of its pureness, must be transparent as light.

In the third satire he asks,

> "Est aliquid quò tendis, et in quod dirigis arcum?
> An passim sequeris corvos, testâve, lutove,
> Securus quò pes ferat, atque ex tempore vivis?"

Language seems not to have justice done it, but is obviously cramped and narrowed in its significance, when any meanness is described. The truest construction is not put upon it. What may readily be fashioned into a rule of wisdom, is here thrown in the teeth of the sluggard, and constitutes the front of his offence. Universally, the innocent man will come forth from the sharpest inquisition and lecturings, the combined din of reproof and commendation, with a faint sound of eulogy in his ears. Our vices lie ever in the direction of our virtues, and in their best estate are but plausible imitations of the latter. Falsehood never attains to the dignity of entire falseness, but is only an inferior sort of truth; if it were more thoroughly false, it would incur danger of becoming true.

> "Securus quò pes ferat, atque ex tempore *vivit*,"

is then the motto of a wise man. For first, as the subtle discernment of the language would have taught us, with all his negligence he is still secure; but the sluggard, notwithstanding his heedlessness, is insecure.

The life of a wise man is most of all extemporane-
ous, for he lives out of an eternity that includes all
time. He is a child each moment, and reflects wisdom.
The far darting thought of the child's mind tarries
not for the development of manhood; it lightens itself, and needs not draw down lightning from the
clouds. When we bask in a single ray from the mind
of Zoroaster, we see how all subsequent time has
been an idler, and has no apology for itself. But the
cunning mind travels farther back than Zoroaster
each instant, and comes quite down to the present
with its revelation. All the thrift and industry of
thinking give no man any stock in life; his credit
with the inner world is no better, his capital no
larger. He must try his fortune again to-day as yesterday. All questions rely on the present for their solu-
tion. Time measures nothing but itself. The word
that is written may be postponed, but not that on the
lip. If this is what the occasion says, let the occasion
say it. From a real sympathy, all the world is forward
to prompt him who gets up to live without his creed
in his pocket.

In the fifth satire, which is the best, I find,

> "Stat contrà ratio, et secretam garrit in aurem.
> Ne liceat facere id, quod quis vitiabit agendo."

Only they who do not see how anything might be
better done are forward to try their hand on it. Even
the master workman must be encouraged by the
reflection, that his awkwardness will be incompetent
to do that harm, to which his skill may fail to do
justice. Here is no apology for neglecting to do many
things from a sense of our incapacity,—for what deed
does not fall maimed and imperfect from our hands?
—but only a warning to bungle less.

The satires of Persius are the farthest possible from inspired; evidently a chosen, not imposed subject. Perhaps I have given him credit for more earnestness than is apparent; but certain it is, that that which alone we can call Persius, which is forever independent and consistent, was in earnest, and so sanctions the sober consideration of all. The artist and his work are not to be separated. The most wilfully foolish man cannot stand aloof from his folly, but the deed and the doer together make ever one sober fact. The buffoon may not bribe you to laugh always at his grimaces; they shall sculpture themselves in Egyptian granite, to stand heavy as the pyramids on the ground of his character.

The Laws of Menu.

[In pursuance of the design intimated in our Number for July, to give a series of ethnical scriptures, we subjoin our extracts from the Laws of Menu. We learn, from the preface of the translator, that "Vyasa, the son of Parasara, has decided that the Veda, with its Angas, or the six compositions deduced from it, the revealed system of medicine, the Puranas, or sacred histories, and the code of Menu, were four works of supreme authority, which ought never to be shaken by arguments merely human." The last, which is in blank verse, and is one of the oldest compositions extant, has been translated by Sir William Jones. It is believed by the Hindoos "to have been promulged in the beginning of time, by Menu, son or grandson of Brahma," and "first of created beings." Brahma is said to have "taught his laws to Menu in a hundred thousand verses, which Menu explained to the primitive world in the very words of the book now translated." Others affirm that they have undergone successive abridgments for the convenience of mortals, "while the gods of the lower heaven, and the band of celestial musicians, are engaged in studying the primary code."

"A number of glosses or comments on Menu were composed by the Munis, or old philosophers, whose treatises, together with that before us, constitute the Dherma Sastra, in a collective sense, or Body of Law." Culluca Bhatta* was one of the more modern of these.]

Custom.

"Immemorial custom is transcendent law."

"The roots of the law are the whole Veda, the ordinances and moral practices of such as perfectly un-

---

* In the following selections his gloss is for the most part omitted, but when retained is printed in Italics.

derstand it, the immemorial customs of good men, and self-satisfaction."

"Immemorial custom is a tradition among the four pure classes, in a country frequented by gods,—and at length is not to be distinguished from revelation."

TEMPERANCE.

"The resignation of all pleasures is far better than the attainment of them."

"The organs, being strongly attached to sensual delights, cannot so effectually be restrained by avoiding incentives to pleasure, as by a constant pursuit of divine knowledge."

"But, when one among all his [the Brahmin's] organs fails, by that single failure his knowledge of God passes away, as water flows through one hole in a leathern bottle."

"He must eat without distraction of mind."

"Let him honor all his food, and eat it without contempt; when he sees it, let him rejoice and be calm, and pray, that he may always obtain it."

"Food, eaten constantly with respect, gives muscular force and generative power; but, eaten irreverently, destroys them both."

"It is delivered as a rule of the gods, that meat must be swallowed only for the purpose of sacrifice; but it is a rule of gigantic demons, that it may be swallowed for any other purpose."

PURIFICATION AND SACRIFICE.

"By falsehood, the sacrifice becomes vain; by pride, the merit of devotion is lost; by insulting priests, life is diminished; and by proclaiming a largess, its fruit is destroyed."

"To a king, on the throne of magnanimity, the law

ascribes instant purification, because his throne was raised for the protection of his people, and the supply of their nourishment."

"The hand of an artist employed in his art is always pure."

"Bodies are cleansed by water; the mind is purified by truth; the vital spirit, by theology and devotion; the understanding, by clear knowledge."

"If thou be not at variance by speaking falsely with Yama the Subduer of all, with Vaivaswata the Punisher, with that great divinity who dwells in the breast, go not on a pilgrimage to the river Ganga, nor to the plains of Curu, for thou hast no need of expiation."

"Whoever cherishes not five orders of beings,—the deities, those who demand hospitality, those whom he ought by law to maintain, his departed forefathers, and himself,—that man lives not, even though he breathe."

"To all the gods assembled let him throw up his oblation in open air; by day, to the spirits who walk in light; and by night, to those who walk in darkness."

"Some, who well know the ordinances for those oblations, perform not always externally the five great sacraments, but continually make offerings in their own organs."

"Some constantly sacrifice their breath in their speech, *when they instruct others, or praise God aloud*, and their speech in their breath, *when they meditate in silence;* perceiving in their speech and breath, *thus employed*, the imperishable fruit of a sacrificial offering."

"The act of repeating his Holy Name is ten times better than the appointed sacrifice; a hundred times better, when it is heard by no man; and a thousand times better, when it is purely mental."

"Equally perceiving the supreme soul in all beings, and all beings in the supreme soul, he sacrifices his own spirit by fixing it on the spirit of God, and approaches the nature of that sole divinity, who shines by his own effulgence."

TEACHING.

"A Brahmin, who is the giver of spiritual birth, the teacher of prescribed duty, is by right the father of an old man, though himself be a child."

"Cavi, child of Angiras, taught his paternal uncles and cousins to read the Veda, and, excelling them in divine knowledge, said to them 'Little sons.'

"They, moved with resentment, asked the gods the meaning of that *expression;* and the gods, being assembled, answered them, 'The child has addressed you properly;'

"For an unlearned man is in truth a child; and he who teaches him the Veda is his father: holy sages have always said child to an ignorant man, and father to a teacher of scripture."

"Greatness is not conferred by years, not by gray hairs, not by wealth, not by powerful kindred; the divine sages have established this rule: 'Whoever has read the Vedas, and their Angas, he among us is great.' "

"The seniority of priests is from sacred learning; of warriors, from valor; of merchants, from abundance of grain; of the servile class, only from priority of birth."

"A man is not therefore aged, because his head is gray; him, surely, the gods considered as aged, who, though young in years, has read *and understands* the Veda."

"Let not a sensible teacher tell what he is not asked, nor what he is asked improperly; but let him, however intelligent, act in the multitude as if he were dumb."

"A teacher of the Veda should rather die with his learning, than sow it in sterile soil, even though he be in grievous distress for subsistence."

REWARD AND PUNISHMENT.

"Justice, being destroyed, will destroy; being preserved, will preserve; it must therefore never be violated. Beware, O judge, lest Justice, being overturned, overturn both us and thyself."

"The only firm friend, who follows men even after death, is Justice; all others are extinct with the body."

"The soul is its own witness; the soul itself is its own refuge: offend not thy conscious soul, the supreme internal witness of men."

"O friend to virtue, that supreme spirit, which thou believest one and the same with thyself, resides in thy bosom perpetually, and is an all-knowing inspector of thy goodness or of thy wickedness."

"Action, either mental, verbal, or corporeal, bears good or evil fruit, *as itself is good or evil;* and from the actions of men proceed their various transmigrations in the highest, the mean, and the lowest degree."

"Iniquity, committed in this world, produces not fruit immediately, *but*, like the earth, *in due season;* and, advancing by little and little, it eradicates the man who committed it."

"Yes; iniquity, once committed, fails not of producing fruit to him who wrought it; if not in his own person, yet in his sons; or, if not in his sons, yet in his grandsons."

"He grows rich for a while through unrighteousness; then he beholds good things; then it is, that he vanquishes his foes; but he perishes at length from his whole root upwards."

"If the vital spirit had practised virtue for the most part, and vice in a small degree, it enjoys delight in celestial abodes, clothed with a body formed of pure elementary particles."

"But, if it had generally been addicted to vice, and seldom attended to virtue, then shall it be deserted by those pure elements, and, *having a coarser body of sensible nerves*, it feels the pains to which Yama shall doom it."

"Souls, endued with goodness, attain always the state of deities; those filled with ambitious passions, the condition of men; and those immersed in darkness, the nature of beasts: this is the triple order of transmigration."

"Grass and earth to sit on, water to wash the feet, and affectionate speech, are at no time deficient in the mansions of the good."

THE KING.

"He, sure, must be the perfect essence of majesty, by whose favor Abundance rises on her lotos; in whose favor dwells conquest; in whose anger, death."

WOMEN AND MARRIAGE.

"The names of women should be agreeable, soft, clear, captivating the fancy, auspicious, ending in long vowels, resembling words of benediction."

In the second quarter of the Brahmin's life, when he has left his instructor, to commence house-keeping,—

"Let him choose for his wife a girl, whose form has no defect; who has an agreeable name; who walks *gracefully*, like a phenicopteros, or like a young elephant; whose hair and teeth are moderate respectively in quantity and in size; whose body has exquisite softness."

THE BRAHMIN.

"When a Brahmin springs to light, he is born above the world, the chief of all creatures, assigned to guard the treasury of duties religious and civil."

"Whatever exists in the universe, is all in effect the wealth of the Brahmin, since the Brahmin is entitled to it all by his primogeniture and eminence of birth."

"The Brahmin eats but his own food; wears but his own apparel; and bestows but his own in alms: through the benevolence of the Brahmin, indeed, other mortals enjoy life."

"Although Brahmins employ themselves in all sorts of mean occupation, they must invariably be honored; for they are something transcendently divine."

"He must avoid service for hire."

"He may either store up grain for three years, or garner up enough for one year, or collect what may last three days, or make no provision for the morrow."

"Let him never, for the sake of a subsistence, have recourse to popular conversation; let him live by the conduct of a priest, neither crooked, nor artful, nor blended *with the manners of the mercantile class.*"

"Let him not have nimble hands, restless feet, or voluble eyes; let him not be crooked in his ways; let him not be flippant in his speech, nor intelligent in doing mischief."

"He must not gain wealth by any art that pleases the sense; nor by any prohibited art; nor, whether he be rich or poor, indiscriminately."

"Though permitted to receive presents, let him avoid a habit of taking them; since, by taking many gifts, his divine light soon fades."

"A twice-born man, void of true devotion, and not having read the Veda, yet eager to take a gift, sinks down together with it, as with a boat of stone in deep water."

"A Brahmin should constantly shun worldly honor, as he would shun poison; and rather constantly seek disrespect, as he would seek nectar."

"For, though scorned, he may sleep with pleasure; with pleasure may he awake; with pleasure may he pass through this life: but the scorner utterly perishes."

"All that depends on another gives pain; all that depends on himself gives pleasure; let him know this to be in few words the definition of pleasure and of pain."

As for the Brahmin who keeps house,—

"Let him say what is true, but let him say what is pleasing; let him speak no disagreeable truth, nor let him speak agreeable falsehood: this is a primeval rule."

"Let him say 'well and good,' or let him say 'well' only; but let him not maintain fruitless enmity and altercation with any man."

"Giving no pain to any creature, let him collect virtue by degrees, for the sake of acquiring a companion to the next world, as the white ant by degrees builds his nest."

"For, in his passage to the next world, neither his father, nor his mother, nor his wife, nor his son, nor his kinsmen, will remain in his company: his virtue alone will adhere to him."

"Single is each man born; single he dies; single he receives the reward of his good, and single the punishment of his evil, deeds."

"When he leaves his corpse, like a log or a lump of clay, on the ground, his kindred retire with averted faces; but his virtue accompanies his soul."

"Continually, therefore, by degrees, let him collect virtue, for the sake of securing an inseparable companion; since, with virtue for his guide, he will traverse a gloom—how hard to be traversed!"

"Alone, in some solitary place, let him constantly meditate on the divine nature of the soul; for, by such meditation, he will attain happiness."

"When the father of a family perceives his muscles become flaccid, and his hair gray, and sees the child of his child, let him then seek refuge in a forest:"

"Then, having reposited his holy fires, as the law directs, in his mind, let him live without external fire, without a mansion, wholly silent, feeding on roots and fruit;"

"Not solicitous for the means of gratification, chaste as a student, sleeping on the bare earth, in the haunts of pious hermits, without one selfish affection, dwelling at the roots of trees;"

"—— for the purpose of uniting his soul with the divine spirit."

"Or, *if he has any incurable disease*, let him advance in a straight path, towards the invincible *north-eastern* point, feeding on water and air, till his mortal frame totally decay, and his soul become united with the Supreme."

"A Brahmin having shuffled off his body by any of those modes, which great sages practised; and becoming void of sorrow and fear, rises to exaltation in the divine essence."

"Departing from his house, taking with him pure implements, *his waterpot and staff*, keeping silence, unallured by desire of the objects near him, let him enter into the fourth order."

"Alone let him constantly dwell, for the sake of his own felicity; observing the happiness of a solitary man, who neither forsakes nor is forsaken, let him live without a companion."

"Let him have no culinary fire, no domicil: let him, when very hungry, go to the town for food; let him patiently bear disease; let his mind be firm: let him study to know God, and fix his attention on God alone."

"An earthen water-pot, the roots of large trees, coarse vesture, total solitude, equanimity toward all creatures, these are the characteristics of a Brahmin set free."

"Let him not wish for death; let him not wish for life; let him expect his appointed time, as a hired servant expects his wages."

Entirely withdrawn from the world,—"without any companion but his own soul, let him live in this world, seeking the bliss of the next."

"Late in the day let the Sannyasi beg food: for missing it, let him not be sorrowful; nor for gaining it let him be glad; let him care only for a sufficiency to support life, but let him not be anxious about his utensils."

"Let him reflect also, with exclusive application of mind, on the subtil, indivisible essence of the supreme spirit, and its complete existence in all beings, whether extremely high, or extremely low."

"Thus, having gradually abandoned all earthly attachments, and indifferent to all pairs of opposite things, *as honor, and dishonor, and the like*, he remains absorbed in the divine essence."

"A mansion with bones for its rafters and beams; with nerves and tendons for cords; with muscles and blood for mortar; with skin for its outward covering, filled with no sweet perfume, but loaded with fæces and urine;"

"A mansion infested by age and by sorrow; the seat of malady, harassed with pains, haunted with the quality of darkness, and incapable of standing long;

such a mansion of the vital soul, let its occupier always cheerfully quit."

"As a tree leaves the bank of a river, when it falls in, or as a bird leaves the branch of a tree at his pleasure, thus he, who leaves his body by necessity, or by legal choice, is delivered from the ravening shark, or crocodile, of the world."

GOD.

"Let every Brahmin with fixed attention consider all nature, both visible and invisible, as existing in the divine spirit; for, when he contemplates the boundless universe existing in the divine spirit, he cannot give his heart to iniquity:"

"The divine spirit is the whole assemblage of gods; all worlds are seated in the divine spirit; and the divine spirit, no doubt, produces the connected series of acts performed by embodied souls."

"He may contemplate the subtil ether in the cavities of his body; the air in his muscular motion and sensitive nerves; the supreme *solar and igneous* light, in his digestive heat and his visual organs; in his corporeal fluids, water; in the terrene parts of his fabric, earth;"

"In his heart, the moon; in his auditory nerves, the guardians of eight regions; in his progressive motion, Vishnu; in his muscular force, Hara; in his organs of speech, Agni; in excretion, Mitra; in procreation, Brahma:"

"But he must consider the supreme omnipresent intelligence as the sovereign lord of them all; a spirit which can only be conceived by a mind slumbering; but which he may imagine more subtil than the finest conceivable essence, and more bright than the purest gold."

"Him some adore as transcendently present in elementary fire; others in Menu, lord of creatures; some, as more distinctly present in Indra, *regent of the clouds and the atmosphere;* others, in pure air; others, as the most High Eternal Spirit."

"Thus the man, who perceives in his own soul the supreme soul present in all creatures, acquires equanimity towards them all, and shall be absorbed at last in the highest essence, even that of the Almighty himself."

DEVOTION.

"All the bliss of deities and of men is declared by sages who discern the sense of the Veda to have in devotion its cause, in devotion its continuance, in devotion its fulness."

"Devotion is equal to the performance of all duties; it is divine knowledge in a Brahmin; it is defence of the people in a Cshatriya; devotion is the business of trade and agriculture in a Vaisya; devotion is dutiful service in a Sudra."

"Perfect health, or unfailing medicine, divine learning, and the various mansions of deities are acquired by devotion alone; their efficient cause is devotion."

"Whatever is hard to be traversed, whatever is hard to be acquired, whatever is hard to be visited, whatever is hard to be performed, all this may be accomplished by true devotion; for the difficulty of devotion is the greatest of all."

Sayings of Confucius.

CHEE says, if in the morning I hear about the right way, and in the evening die, I can be happy.

A man's life is properly connected with virtue. The life of the evil man is preserved by mere good fortune.

Coarse rice for food, water to drink, and the bended arm for a pillow—happiness may be enjoyed even in these. Without virtue, riches and honor seem to me like a passing cloud.

A wise and good man was Hooi. A piece of bamboo was his dish, a cocoa-nut his cup, his dwelling a miserable shed. Men could not sustain the sight of his wretchedness; but Hooi did not change the serenity of his mind. A wise and good man was Hooi.

Chee-koong said, Were they discontented? The sage replies, They sought and attained complete virtue;—how then could they be discontented?

Chee says, Yaou is the man who, in torn clothes or common apparel, sits with those dressed in furred robes without feeling shame.

To worship at a temple not your own is mere flattery.

Chee says, grieve not that men know not you; grieve that you are ignorant of men.

How can a man remain concealed! How can a man remain concealed!

Have no friend unlike yourself.

Chee-Yaou enquired respecting filial piety. Chee says, the filial piety of the present day is esteemed merely ability to nourish a parent. This care is extended to a dog or a horse. Every domestic animal can obtain food. Beside veneration, what is the difference?

Chee entered the great temple, frequently enquiring about things. One said, who says that the son of the

Chou man understands propriety? In the great temple he is constantly asking questions. Chee heard and replied—"This is propriety."

Choy-ee slept in the afternoon. Chee says, rotten wood is unfit for carving: a dirty wall cannot receive a beautiful color. To Ee what advice can I give?

A man's transgression partakes of the nature of his company.

Having knowledge, to apply it; not having knowledge, to confess your ignorance; this is real knowledge.

Chee says, to sit in silence and recall past ideas, to study and feel no anxiety, to instruct men without weariness;—have I this ability within me?

In forming a mountain, were I to stop when one basket of earth is lacking, I actually stop; and in the same manner were I to add to the level ground though but one basket of earth daily, I really go forward.

A soldier of the kingdom of Ci lost his buckler; and having sought after it a long time in vain, he comforted himself with this reflection; 'A soldier has lost his buckler, but a soldier of our camp will find it; he will use it.'

The wise man never hastens, neither in his studies nor his words; he is sometimes, as it were, mute; but when it concerns him to act and practise virtue, he, as I may say, precipitates all.

The truly wise man speaks little; he is little eloquent. I see not that eloquence can be of very great use to him.

Silence is absolutely necessary to the wise man. Great speeches, elaborate discourses, pieces of eloquence, ought to be a language unknown to him; his actions ought to be his language. As for me, I would never speak more. Heaven speaks; but what language does it use to preach to men? That there is a sovereign principle from which all things depend; a sovereign principle which makes them to act and move. Its motion is its language; it reduces the seasons to their time; it agitates nature; it makes it produce. This silence is eloquent.

Dark Ages.

WE should read history as little critically as we consider the landscape, and be more interested by the atmospheric tints, and various lights and shades which the intervening spaces create, than by its groundwork and composition. It is the morning now turned evening and seen in the west,—the same sun, but a new light and atmosphere. Its beauty is like the sunset; not a fresco painting on a wall, flat and bounded, but atmospheric and roving or free. In reality history fluctuates as the face of the landscape from morning to evening. What is of moment is its hue and color. Time hides no treasures; we want not its *then* but its *now*. We do not complain that the mountains in the horizon are blue and indistinct; they are the more like the heavens.

Of what moment are facts that can be lost,—which need to be commemorated? The monument of death will outlast the memory of the dead. The pyramids do not tell the tale that was confided to them; the living fact commemorates itself. Why look in the dark for light? Strictly speaking, the historical societies have not recovered one fact from oblivion, but are themselves instead of the fact that is lost. The researcher is more memorable than the researched. The crowd stood admiring the mist, and the dim outlines of the trees seen through it, when one of their number advanced to explore the phenomenon, and with fresh admiration, all eyes were turned on his dimly retreating figure. It is astonishing with how little coöperation of the societies, the past is remembered. Its story has indeed had a different muse than has been assigned it. There is a good instance of the manner in

which all history began, in Alwákidi's Arabian Chronicle. "I was informed by *Ahmed Almatîn Aljorhami*,
who had it from *Rephâa Ebn Kais Alámiri*, who had
it from *Saiph Ebn Jabalah Alchátgami*, who had it
from *Thabet Ebn Alkamah*, who said he was present
at the action." These fathers of history were not anxious to preserve, but to learn the fact; and hence it
was not forgotten. Critical acumen is exerted in
vain to uncover the past; the *past* cannot be *presented;*
we cannot know what we are not. But one veil hangs
over past, present, and future, and it is the province
of the historian to find out not what was, but what is.
Where a battle has been fought, you will find nothing
but the bones of men and beasts; where a battle is
being fought there are hearts beating. We will sit on
a mound and muse, and not try to make these skeletons stand on their legs again. Does nature remember, think you, that they *were* men, or not rather that
they *are* bones?

Ancient history has an air of antiquity; it should
be more modern. It is written as if the spectator
should be thinking of the backside of the picture on
the wall, or as if the author expected the dead would
be his readers, and wished to detail to them their own
experience. Men seem anxious to accomplish an orderly retreat through the centuries, earnestly rebuild-
ing the works behind, as they are battered down by
the encroachments of time; but while they loiter, they
and their works both fall a prey to the arch enemy.
It has neither the venerableness of antiquity, nor the
freshness of the modern. It does as if it would go to
the beginning of things, which natural history might
with reason assume to do; but consider the Universal
History, and then tell us—when did burdock and plan-
tain sprout first? It has been so written for the most

part, that the times it describes are with remarkable propriety called *dark ages*. They are dark, as one has observed, because we are so in the dark about them. The sun rarely shines in history, what with the dust and confusion; and when we meet with any cheering fact which implies the presence of this luminary, we excerpt and modernize it. As when we read in the history of the Saxons, that Edwin of Northumbria "caused stakes to be fixed in the highways where he had seen a clear spring," and "brazen dishes were chained to them, to refresh the weary sojourner, whose fatigues Edwin had himself experienced." This is worth all Arthur's twelve battles.

But it is fit the past should be dark; though the darkness is not so much a quality of the past, as of tradition. It is not a distance of time but a distance of relation, which makes thus dusky its memorials. What is near to the heart of this generation is fair and bright still. Greece lies outspread fair and sunshiny in floods of light, for there is the sun and daylight in her literature and art. Homer does not allow us to forget that the sun shone—nor Phidias, nor the Parthenon. Yet no era has been wholly dark, nor will we too hastily submit to the historian, and congratulate ourselves on a blaze of light. If we could pierce the obscurity of those remote years we should find it light enough; only there is not our day.—Some creatures are made to see in the dark.—There has always been the same amount of light in the world. The new and missing stars, the comets and eclipses do not affect the general illumination, for only our glasses appreciate them. The eyes of the oldest fossil remains, they tell us, indicate that the same laws of light prevailed then as now. Always the laws of light are the same, but the modes and degrees of seeing vary. The

Chinese Four Books.

[PRELIMINARY NOTE. Since we printed a few selections from Dr. Marshman's translation of the sentences of Confucius, we have received a copy of "the Chinese Classical Work, commonly called the Four Books, translated and illustrated with notes by the late Rev. David Collie, Principal of the Anglo-Chinese College, Malacca. Printed at the Mission Press." This translation, which seems to have been undertaken and performed as an exercise in learning the language, is the most valuable contribution we have yet seen from the Chinese literature. That part of the work, which is new, is the Memoirs of Mencius in two books, the Shang Mung and Hea Mung, which is the production of Mung Tsze (or Mencius,) who flourished about a hundred years after Confucius. The subjoined extracts are chiefly taken from these books.]

ALL things are contained complete in ourselves. There is no greater joy than to turn round on ourselves and become perfect.

The human figure and color possess a divine nature, but it is only the sage who can fulfil what his figure promises.

The superior man's nature consists in this, that benevolence, justice, propriety, and wisdom, have their root in his heart, and are exhibited in his countenance. They shine forth in his face and go through to his back. They are manifested in his four members.

Wherever the superior man passes, renovation takes place. The divine spirit which he cherishes above and below, flows on equal in extent and influence with heaven and earth.

Tsze Kung says, The errors of the superior man are like the eclipses of the sun and moon. His errors all men see, and his reformation all men look for.

Mencius says, There is not anything but is decreed; accord with and keep to what is right. Hence he, who understands the decrees, will not stand under a falling wall. He, who dies in performing his duty to the utmost of his power, accords with the decrees of heaven. But he who dies for his crimes, accords not with the divine decree.

There is a proper rule by which we should seek, and whether we obtain what we seek or not, depends on the divine decree.

Put men to death by the principles which have for their object the preservation of life, and they will not grumble.

The Scholar.

Teen, son of the king of Tse, asked what the business of the scholar consists in? Mencius replied, In elevating his mind and inclination. What do you mean by elevating the mind? It consists merely in being benevolent and just. Where is the scholar's abode? In benevolence. Where is his road? Justice. To dwell in benevolence, and walk in justice, is the whole business of a great man.

Benevolence is man's heart, and justice is man's path. If a man lose his fowls or his dogs, he knows how to seek them. There are those who lose their hearts and know not how to seek them. The duty of the student is no other than to seek his lost heart.

He who employs his whole mind, will know his nature. He who knows his nature, knows heaven.

It were better to be without books than to believe all that they record.

The Taou.

Sincerity is the *Taou* or way of heaven. To aim at it is the way of man.

From inherent sincerity to have perfect intelligence, is to be a sage by nature; to attain sincerity by means of intelligence, is to be such by study. Where there is sincerity, there must be intelligence. Where intelligence is, it must lead to sincerity.

He who offends heaven, has none to whom he can pray.

Mencius said, To be benevolent is man. When man and benevolence are united, they are called *Taou*.

To be full of sincerity, is called beauty. To be so full of sincerity that it shines forth in the external conduct, is called greatness. When this greatness renovates others, it is called sageness. Holiness or sageness which is above comprehension, is called divine.

Perfection (or sincerity) is the way of heaven, and to wish for perfection is the duty of a man. It has never been the case that he who possessed genuine virtue in the highest degree, could not influence others, nor has it ever been the case that he who was not in the highest degree sincere could influence others.

There is a divine nobility and a human nobility. Benevolence, justice, fidelity, and truth, and to delight in virtue without weariness, constitute divine nobility. To be a prince, a prime minister, or a great officer of state constitute human nobility. The ancients adorned divine nobility, and human nobility followed it.

The men of the present day cultivate divine nobility in order that they may obtain human nobility; and when they once get human nobility, they throw away divine nobility. This is the height of delusion, and must end in the loss of both.

OF REFORM.

Taou is not far removed from man. If men suppose that it lies in something remote, then what they think of is not *Taou*. The ode says, "Cut hatchet handles." This means of doing it, is not remote; you have only to take hold of one handle, and use it to cut another. Yet if you look aslant at it, it will appear distant. Hence the superior man employs man, (that is, what is in man,) to reform man.

When Tsze Loo heard anything that he had not yet fully practised, he was afraid of hearing anything else.

The governor of Yih asked respecting government. Confucius replied, Make glad those who are near, and those who are at a distance will come.

The failing of men is that they neglect their own field, and dress that of others. They require much of others, but little of themselves.

War.

Mencius said, From this time and ever after I know the heavy consequences of killing a man's parents. If you kill a man's elder brother, he will kill your elder brother. Hence although you do not yourself kill them, you do nearly the same thing.

When man says, I know well how to draw up an army, I am skilled in fighting, he is a great criminal.

Politics.

Ke Kang asked Confucius respecting government. Confucius replied, Government is rectitude.

Ke Kang was harassed by robbers, and consulted Confucius on the subject. Confucius said, If you, sir, were not covetous, the people would not rob, even though you should hire them to do it.

Mencius said, Pih E's eye would not look on a bad color, nor would his ear listen to a bad sound. Unless a prince were of his own stamp, he would not serve him, and unless people were of his own stamp, he would not employ them. In times of good government, he went into office, and in times of confusion and bad government, he retired. Where disorderly government prevailed, or where disorderly people lived, he could not bear to dwell. He thought that to live with low men was as bad as to sit in the mud with his court robes and cap. In the time of Chou, he dwelt on the banks of the North Ka, watching till the Empire should be brought to peace and order. Hence, when the fame of Pih E is heard of, the stupid become intelligent, and the weak determined.

E Yin said, What of serving a prince not of one's own stamp! What of ruling a people which are not to your mind! In times of good government he went into office, and so did he in times of disorder. He said, heaven has given life to this people, and sent those who are first enlightened to enlighten those who are last, and has sent those who are first aroused to arouse those who are last. I am one of heaven's people who am first aroused. I will take these doctrines and arouse this people. He thought that if there was a single man or woman in the Empire, who was not benefited by the doctrines of Yaou and Shun, that he was guilty of pushing them into a ditch. He took the heavy responsibility of the Empire on himself.

Lew Hea Hooi was not ashamed of serving a dirty Prince, nor did he refuse an inferior office. He did not conceal the virtuous, and acted according to his principles. Although he lost his place, he grumbled not. In poverty he repined not. He lived in harmony with men of little worth, and could not bear to abandon them. He said, "You are you, and I am I; although you sit by my side with your body naked, how can you defile me?" Hence when the fame of Lew Hea Hooi is heard of, the mean man becomes liberal, and the miserly becomes generous.

VIRTUE.

Chung Kung asked, What is perfect virtue? Confucius said, What you do not wish others to do to you, do not to them.

Sze Ma Neu asked, What constitutes perfect virtue? Confucius replied; It is to find it difficult to speak. "To find it difficult to speak! Is that perfect virtue?" Confucius rejoined, What is difficult to practise, must it not be difficult to speak?

Confucius says, Virtue runs swifter than the royal postillions carry despatches.

The She King says, "Heaven created all men having their duties and the means or rules of performing them. It is the natural and constant disposition of men to love beautiful virtue." Confucius says, that he who wrote this ode knew right principles.

Confucius exclaimed, Is virtue far off? I only wish for virtue, and virtue comes.

Confucius said, I have not seen any one who loves virtue as we love beauty.

Confucius says, The superior man is not a machine which is fit for one thing only.

Tze Kung asked, Who is a superior man? Confucius replied, He who first practises his words, and then speaks accordingly.

The principles of great men illuminate the whole universe above and below. The principles of the superior man commence with the duties of common men and women, but in their highest extent they illuminate the universe.

Confucius said, Yew, permit me to tell you what is knowledge. What you are acquainted with, consider that you know it; what you do not understand, consider that you do not know it; this is knowledge.

Confucius exclaimed, How vast the influence of the

Kwei Shin (spirits or gods). If you look for them, you cannot see them; if you listen, you cannot hear them; they embody all things, and are what things cannot be separated from. When they cause mankind to fast, purify, and dress themselves, everything appears full of them. They seem to be at once above, and on the right, and on the left. The ode says, The descent of the gods cannot be comprehended; with what reverence should we conduct ourselves! Indeed that which is least, is clearly displayed. They cannot be concealed.

Homer. Ossian. Chaucer.

EXTRACTS FROM A LECTURE ON POETRY,
READ BEFORE THE CONCORD LYCEUM,
NOVEMBER 29, 1843, BY HENRY D. THOREAU.

HOMER.

The wisest definition of poetry the poet will instantly prove false by setting aside its requisitions. We can therefore publish only our advertisement of it.

There is no doubt that the loftiest written wisdom is rhymed or measured, is in form as well as substance poetry; and a volume, which should contain the condensed wisdom of mankind, need not have one rhythmless line. Yet poetry, though the last and finest result, is a natural fruit. As naturally as the oak bears an acorn, and the vine a gourd, man bears a poem, either spoken or done. It is the chief and most memorable success, for history is but a prose narrative of poetic deeds. What else have the Hindoos, the Persians, the Babylonians, the Egyptians, done, that can be told? It is the simplest relation of phenomena, and describes the commonest sensations with more truth than science does, and the latter at a distance slowly mimics its style and methods. The poet sings how the blood flows in his veins. He performs his functions, and is so well that he needs such stimulus to sing only as plants to put forth leaves and blossoms. He would strive in vain to modulate the remote and transient music which he sometimes hears, since his song is a vital function like breathing, and an integral result like weight. It is not the overflowing of life but its subsidence rather, and is drawn from under the feet of the poet. It is enough if Homer but say the sun sets. He is as serene as nature, and we can hardly detect the enthusiasm of the bard. It is as if nature spoke. He presents to us the simplest pictures of human life, so that childhood itself can understand them, and the man must not think twice to appreciate his naturalness. Each reader discovers for himself, that succeeding poets have done little else than copy his similes. His more memorable passages are as naturally bright, as gleams of sunlight in misty weather. Nature furnishes him not only with words, but with stereotyped lines and sentences from her mint.

"As from the clouds appears the full moon,
All shining, and then again it goes behind the shadowy
    clouds,
So Hector, at one time appeared among the foremost,
And at another in the rear, commanding; and all with
    brass
He shone, like to the lightning of ægis-bearing Zeus."

He conveys the least information, even the hour of the day, with such magnificence, and vast expense of natural imagery, as if it were a message from the gods.

"While it was dawn, and sacred day was advancing,
For that space the weapons of both flew fast, and
    the people fell;
But when now the woodcutter was preparing his
    morning meal
In the recesses of the mountain, and had wearied
    his hands
With cutting lofty trees, and satiety came to his mind,
And the desire of sweet food took possession of his
    thoughts;
Then the Danaans by their valor broke the phalanxes,
Shouting to their companions from rank to rank."

When the army of the Trojans passed the night under arms, keeping watch lest the enemy should re-embark under cover of the dark,

"They, thinking great things, upon the neutral ground
of war,
Sat all the night; and many fires burned for them.
As when in the heavens the stars round the bright
moon
Appear beautiful, and the air is without wind;
And all the heights, and the extreme summits,
And the shady valleys appear; and the shepherd
rejoices in his heart;
So between the ships and the streams of Xanthus
Appeared the fires of the Trojans before Ilium."

The "white-armed goddess Juno," sent by the Father of gods and men for Iris and Apollo,

"Went down the Idæan mountains to far Olympus,
As when the mind of a man, who has come over
much earth,
Sallies forth, and he reflects with rapid thoughts,
There was I, and there, and remembers many things;
So swiftly the august Juno hastening flew through
the air,
And came to high Olympus."

There are few books which are fit to be remembered in our wisest hours, but the Iliad is brightest in the serenest days, and imbodies still all the sunlight that fell on Asia Minor. No modern joy or ecstasy of ours can lower its height or dim its lustre; but there it lies in the east of literature, as it were the earliest, latest production of the mind. The ruins of Egypt oppress and stifle us with their dust, foulness preserved in cassia and pitch, and swathed in linen; the death of that which never lived. But the rays of Greek poetry struggle down to us, and mingle with the sunbeams of the recent day. The statue of Memnon is cast down, but the shaft of the Iliad still meets the sun in his rising.

So too, no doubt, Homer had his Homer, and Orpheus his Orpheus, in the dim antiquity which preceded them. The mythological system of the ancients, and it is still the only mythology of the moderns, the poem of mankind, interwoven so wonderfully with their astronomy, and matching in grandeur and harmony with the architecture of the Heavens themselves, seems to point to a time when a mightier genius inhabited the earth. But man is the great poet, and not Homer nor Shakspeare; and our language itself, and the common arts of life are his work. Poetry is so universally true and independent of experience, that it does not need any particular biography to illustrate it, but we refer it sooner or later to some Orpheus or Linus, and after ages to the genius of humanity, and the gods themselves.

OSSIAN.*

The genuine remains of Ossian, though of less fame and extent, are in many respects of the same stamp with the Iliad itself. He asserts the dignity of the bard no less than Homer, and in his era we hear of no other priest than he. It will not avail to call him a heathen because he personifies the sun and addresses it; and what if his heroes did "worship the ghosts of their fathers," their thin, airy, and unsubstantial forms? we but worship the ghosts of our fathers in more substantial forms. We cannot but respect the vigorous faith of those heathen, who sternly believed somewhat, and are inclined to say to the critics, who are offended by their superstitious rites, don't interrupt these men's prayers. As if we knew

* "The Genuine Remains of Ossian, Literally Translated, with a Preliminary Dissertation, by Patrick Macgregor. Published under the Patronage of the Highland Society of London. 1 vol. 12mo. London, 1841." We take pleasure in recommending this, the first literal English translation of the Gaelic originals of Ossian, which were left by Macpherson, and published agreeably to his intention, in 1807.

more about human life and a God, than the heathen and ancients. Does English theology contain the recent discoveries?

Ossian reminds us of the most refined and rudest eras, of Homer, Pindar, Isaiah, and the American Indian. In his poetry, as in Homer's, only the simplest and most enduring features of humanity are seen, such essential parts of a man as Stonehenge exhibits of a temple; we see the circles of stone, and the upright shaft alone. The phenomena of life acquire almost an unreal and gigantic size seen through his mists. Like all older and grander poetry, it is distinguished by the few elements in the lives of its heroes. They stand on the heath, between the stars and the earth, shrunk to the bones and sinews. The earth is a boundless plain for their deeds. They lead such a simple, dry, and everlasting life, as hardly needs depart with the flesh, but is transmitted entire from age to age. There are but few objects to distract their sight, and their life is as unincumbered as the course of the stars they gaze at.

> "The wrathful kings, on cairns apart,
> Look forward from behind their shields,
> And mark the wandering stars,
> That brilliant westward move."

It does not cost much for these heroes to live. They want not much furniture. They are such forms of men only as can be seen afar through the mist, and have no costume nor dialect, but for language there is the tongue itself, and for costume there are always the skins of beasts and the bark of trees to be had. They live out their years by the vigor of their constitutions. They survive storms and the spears of their foes, and perform a few heroic deeds, and then,

> "Mounds will answer questions of them,
> For many future years."

Blind and infirm, they spend the remnant of their days listening to the lays of the bards, and feeling the weapons which laid their enemies low, and when at length they die, by a convulsion of nature, the bard allows us a short misty glance into futurity, yet as clear, perchance, as their lives had been. When Mac-Roine was slain,

> "His soul departed to his warlike sires,
> To follow misty forms of boars,
> In tempestuous islands bleak."

The hero's cairn is erected, and the bard sings a brief significant strain, which will suffice for epitaph and biography.

> "The weak will find his bow in the dwelling,
> The feeble will attempt to bend it."

Compared with this simple, fibrous life, our civilized history appears the chronicle of debility, of fashion, and the arts of luxury. But the civilized man misses no real refinement in the poetry of the rudest era. It reminds him that civilization does but dress men. It makes shoes, but it does not toughen the soles of the feet. It makes cloth of finer texture, but it does not touch the skin. Inside the civilized man stands the savage still in the place of honor. We are those blue-eyed, yellow-haired Saxons, those slender, dark-haired Normans.

The profession of the bard attracted more respect in those days from the importance attached to fame. It was his province to record the deeds of heroes. When Ossian hears the traditions of inferior bards, he exclaims,

> "I straightway seize the unfutile tales,
> And send them down in faithful verse."

His philosophy of life is expressed in the opening of the third Duan of Ca-Lodin.

"Whence have sprung the things that are?
And whither roll the passing years?
Where does time conceal its two heads,
In dense impenetrable gloom,
Its surface marked with heroes' deeds alone?
I view the generations gone;
The past appears but dim;
As objects by the moon's faint beams,
Reflected from a distant lake.
I see, indeed, the thunder-bolts of war,
But there the unmighty joyless dwell,
All those who send not down their deeds
To far, succeeding times."

The ignoble warriors die and are forgotten;

"Strangers come to build a tower,
And throw their ashes overhand;
Some rusted swords appear in dust;
One, bending forward, says,
'The arms belonged to heroes gone;
We never heard their praise in song.' "

The grandeur of the similes is another feature which characterizes great poetry. Ossian seems to speak a gigantic and universal language. The images and pictures occupy even much space in the landscape, as if they could be seen only from the sides of mountains, and plains with a wide horizon, or across arms of the sea. The machinery is so massive that it cannot be less than natural. Oivana says to the spirit of her father, "Grey-haired Torkil of Torne," seen in the skies,

"Thou glidest away like receding ships."

So when the hosts of Fingal and Starne approach to battle,

"With murmurs loud, like rivers far,
The race of Torne hither moved."

And when compelled to retire,

> "dragging his spear behind,
> Cudulin sank in the distant wood,
> Like a fire upblazing ere it dies."

Nor did Fingal want a proper audience when he spoke;

> "A thousand orators inclined
> To hear the lay of Fingal."

The threats too would have deterred a man. Vengeance and terror were real. Trenmore threatens the young warrior, whom he meets on a foreign strand,

> "Thy mother shall find thee pale on the shore,
> While lessening on the waves she spies
> The sails of him who slew her son."

If Ossian's heroes weep, it is from excess of strength, and not from weakness, a sacrifice or libation of fertile natures, like the perspiration of stone in summer's heat. We hardly know that tears have been shed, and it seems as if weeping were proper only for babes and heroes. Their joy and their sorrow are made of one stuff, like rain and snow, the rainbow and the mist. When Fillan was worsted in fight, and ashamed in the presence of Fingal,

> "He strode away forthwith,
> And bent in grief above a stream,
> His cheeks bedewed with tears.
> From time to time the thistles gray
> He lopped with his inverted lance."

Crodar, blind and old, receives Ossian, son of Fingal, who comes to aid him in war,

> " 'My eyes have failed,' says he, 'Crodar is blind,
> Is thy strength like that of thy fathers?
> Stretch, Ossian, thine arm to the hoary-haired.'
>   I gave my arm to the king.
> The aged hero seized my hand;
> He heaved a heavy sigh;
> Tears flowed incessant down his cheek.

'Strong art thou, son of the mighty,
Though not so dreadful as Morven's prince. * * *
Let my feast be spread in the hall,
Let every sweet-voiced minstrel sing;
Great is he who is within my wall,
Sons of wave-echoing Croma.' "

Even Ossian himself, the hero-bard, pays tribute
to the superior strength of his father Fingal.

"How beauteous, mighty man, was thy mind,
Why succeeded Ossian without its strength?"

CHAUCER.

What a contrast between the stern and desolate
poetry of Ossian, and that of Chaucer, and even of
Shakspeare and Milton, much more of Dryden, and
Pope, and Gray. Our summer of English poetry, like
the Greek and Latin before it, seems well advanced
toward its fall, and laden with the fruit and foliage
of the season, with bright autumnal tints, but soon
the winter will scatter its myriad clustering and
shading leaves, and leave only a few desolate and
fibrous boughs to sustain the snow and rime, and
creak in the blasts of ages. We cannot escape the impression, that the Muse has stooped a little in her
flight, when we come to the literature of civilized
eras. Now first we hear of various ages and styles of
poetry, but the poetry of runic monuments is for
every age. The bard has lost the dignity and sacredness of his office. He has no more the bardic rage,
and only conceives the deed, which he formerly stood
ready to perform. Hosts of warriors, earnest for
battle, could not mistake nor dispense with the ancient bard. His lays were heard in the pauses of the
fight. There was no danger of his being overlooked
by his contemporaries. But now the hero and the bard
are of different professions. When we come to the

pleasant English verse, it seems as if the storms had all cleared away, and it would never thunder and lighten more. The poet has come within doors, and exchanged the forest and crag for the fireside, the hut of the Gael, and Stonehenge with its circles of stones, for the house of the Englishman. No hero stands at the door prepared to break forth into song or heroic action, but we have instead a homely Englishman, who cultivates the art of poetry. We see the pleasant fireside, and hear the crackling fagots in all the verse. The towering and misty imagination of the bard has descended into the plain, and become a lowlander, and keeps flocks and herds. Poetry is one man's trade, and not all men's religion, and is split into many styles. It is pastoral, and lyric, and narrative, and didactic.

Notwithstanding the broad humanity of Chaucer, and the many social and domestic comforts which we meet with in his verse, we have to narrow our vision somewhat to consider him, as if he occupied less space in the landscape, and did not stretch over hill and valley as Ossian does. Yet, seen from the side of posterity, as the father of English poetry, preceded by a long silence or confusion in history, unenlivened by any strain of pure melody, we easily come to reverence him. Passing over the earlier continental poets, since we are bound to the pleasant archipelago of English poetry, Chaucer's is the first name after that misty weather in which Ossian lived, which can detain us long. Indeed, though he represents so different a culture and society, he may be regarded as in many respects the Homer of the English poets. Perhaps he is the youthfullest of them all. We return to him as to the purest well, the fountain furthest removed from the highway of desultory life. He is so natural and cheerful, compared with

later poets, that we might almost regard him as a
personification of spring. To the faithful reader his
muse has even given an aspect to his times, and
when he is fresh from perusing him, they seem related to the golden age. It is still the poetry of youth
and life, rather than of thought; and though the
moral vein is obvious and constant, it has not yet
banished the sun and daylight from his verse. The
loftiest strains of the muse are, for the most part,
sublimely plaintive, and not a carol as free as nature's. The content which the sun shines to celebrate
from morning to evening is unsung. The muse sol-
aces herself, and is not ravished but consoled. There
is a catastrophe implied, and a tragic element in all
our verse, and less of the lark and morning dews,
than of the nightingale and evening shades. But in
Homer and Chaucer there is more of the innocence
and serenity of youth, than in the more modern and
moral poets. The Iliad is not sabbath but morning
reading, and men cling to this old song, because
they have still moments of unbaptized and uncom-
mitted life, which give them an appetite for more.
It represents no creed nor opinion, and we read it
with a rare sense of freedom and irresponsibility, as
if we trod on native ground, and were autochthones
of the soil.

Chaucer had eminently the habits of a literary
man and a scholar. We do not enough allow for the
prevalence of this class. There were never any times
so stirring, that there were not to be found some
sedentary still. Through all those outwardly active
ages, there were still monks in cloisters writing or
copying folios. He was surrounded by the din of
arms. The battles of Hallidon Hill and Neville's
Cross, and the still more memorable battles of Crecy
and Poictiers, were fought in his youth, but these

did not concern our poet much, Wicliffe much more. He seems to have regarded himself always as one privileged to sit and converse with books. He helped to establish the literary class. His character, as one of the fathers of the English language, would alone make his works important, even those which have little poetical merit. A great philosophical and moral poet gives permanence to the language he uses, by making the best sound convey the best sense. He was as simple as Wordsworth in preferring his homely but vigorous Saxon tongue, when it was neglected by the court, and had not yet attained to the dignity of a literature, and rendered a similar service to his country to that which Dante rendered to Italy. If Greek sufficeth for Greek, and Arabic for Arabian, and Hebrew for Jew, and Latin for Latin, then English shall suffice for him, for any of these will serve to teach truth "right as divers pathes leaden divers folke the right waye to Rome." In the Testament of Love he writes, "Let then clerkes enditen in Latin, for they have the propertie of science, and the knowinge in that facultie, and lette Frenchmen in their Frenche also enditen their queinte termes, for it is kyndely to their mouthes, and let us shewe our fantasies in soche wordes as we lerneden of our dames tonge."

He will know how to appreciate Chaucer best, who has come down to him the natural way, through the meagre pastures of Saxon and ante-Chaucerian poetry; and yet so human and wise he seems after such diet, that he is liable to misjudge him still. In the Saxon poetry extant, in the earliest English, and the contemporary Scottish poetry, there is less to remind the reader of the rudeness and vigor of youth, than of the feebleness of a declining age. It is for the most part translation or imitation merely, with only an

occasional and slight tinge of poetry, and oftentimes
the falsehood and exaggeration of fable, without its
imagination to redeem it. It is astonishing to how
few thoughts so many sincere efforts give utterance.
But as they never sprang out of nature, so they will
never root themselves in nature. There are few
traces of original genius, and we look in vain to find
antiquity restored, humanized, and made blithe
again, by the discovery of some natural sympathy
between it and the present. But when we come to
Chaucer we are relieved of many a load. He is fresh
and modern still, and no dust settles on his true passages. It lightens along the line, and we are reminded
that flowers have bloomed, and birds sung, and
hearts beaten, in England. Before the earnest gaze
of the reader the rust and moss of time gradually
drop off, and the original green life is revealed. He
was a homely and domestic man, and did breathe
quite as modern men do. Only one trait, one little
incident of human biography needs to be truly recorded, that all the world may think the author fit to
wear the laurel crown. In the dearth we have described, and at this distance of time, the bare proc-
esses of living read like poetry, for all of human
good or ill, heroic or vulgar, lies very near to them.
All that is truly great and interesting to men, runs
thus as level a course, and is as unaspiring, as the
plough in the furrow.

There is no wisdom which can take place of humanity, and we find *that* in Chaucer. We can expand
in his breadth and think we could be that man's acquaintance. He was worthy to be a citizen of England,
while Petrarch and Boccaccio lived in Italy, and Tell
and Tamerlane in Switzerland and in Asia, and
Bruce in Scotland, and Wickliffe, and Gower, and
Edward the Third, and John of Gaunt, and the

Black Prince, were his own countrymen; all stout and
stirring names. The fame of Roger Bacon came down
from the preceding century, and the name of Dante
still exerted the influence of a living presence. On
the whole, Chaucer impresses us, as greater than his
reputation, and not a little like Homer and Shakspeare, for he would have held up his head in their
company. Among early English poets he is the land-
lord and host, and has the authority of such. The
affectionate mention, which succeeding early poets
make of him, coupling him with Homer and Virgil,
is to be taken into the account in estimating his character and influence. King James and Dunbar of Scotland speak with more love and reverence of him,
than any modern author of his predecessors of the
last century. The same childlike relation is without
parallel now. We read him without criticism for the
most part, for he pleads not his own cause, but
speaks for his readers, and has that greatness of
trust and reliance which compels popularity. He con-
fides in the reader, and speaks privily with him, keeping nothing back. And in return his reader has great
confidence in him, that he tells no lies, and reads
his story with indulgence, as if it were the circumlo-
cution of a child, but discovers afterwards that he
has spoken with more directness and economy of
words than a sage. He is never heartless,

> "For first the thing is thought within the hart,
> Er any word out from the mouth astart."

And so new was all his theme in those days, that he
had not to invent, but only to tell.

We admire Chaucer for his sturdy English wit. The
easy height he speaks from in his Prologue to the
Canterbury Tales, as if he were equal to any of the
company there assembled, is as good as any particu-

lar excellence in it. But though it is full of good sense and humanity, it is not transcendent poetry. For picturesque description of persons it is, perhaps, without a parallel in English poetry; yet it is essentially humorous, as the loftiest genius never is. Humor, however broad and genial, takes a narrower view than enthusiasm. The whole story of Chanticlere and Dame Partlett, in the Nonne's Preeste's tale, is genuine humanity. I know of nothing better in its kind, no more successful fabling of birds and beasts. If it is said of Shakspeare, that he is now Hamlet, and then Falstaff, it may be said of Chaucer that he sympathizes with brutes as well as men, and assumes their nature that he may speak from it. In this tale he puts on the very feathers and stature of the cock. To his own finer vein he added all the common wit and wisdom of his time, and every where in his works his remarkable knowledge of the world, and nice perception of character, his rare common sense and proverbial wisdom, are apparent. His genius does not soar like Milton's, but is genial and familiar. It shows great tenderness and delicacy, but not the heroic sentiment. It is only a greater portion of humanity with all its weakness. It is not heroic, as Raleigh's, nor pious, as Herbert's, nor philosophical, as Shakspeare's, but it is the child of the English muse, that child which is the father of the man. It is for the most part only an exceeding naturalness, perfect sincerity, with the behavior of a child rather than of a man.

Gentleness and delicacy of character are every where apparent in his verse. The simplest and humblest words come readily to his lips. No one can read the Prioress' tale, understanding the spirit in which it was written, and in which the child sings, *O alma redemptoris mater*, or the account of the de-

parture of Custance with her child upon the sea, in
the Man of Lawe's tale, without feeling the native
innocence and refinement of the author. Nor can we
be mistaken respecting the essential purity of his
character, disregarding the apology of the manners
of the age. His sincere sorrow in his later days for
the grossness of his earlier works, and that he "cannot recall and annull" much that he had written,
"but, alas, they are now continued from man to man,
and I cannot do what I desire," is not to be forgotten.
A simple pathos and feminine gentleness, which
Wordsworth occasionally approaches, but does not
equal, are peculiar to him. We are tempted to say,
that his genius was feminine, not masculine. It was
such a feminineness, however, as is rarest to find in
woman, though not the appreciation of it. Perhaps it
is not to be found at all in woman, but is only the
feminine in man.

Such pure, childlike love of nature is not easily to
be matched. Nor is it strange, that the poetry of so
rude an age should contain such sweet and polished
praise of nature, for her charms are not enhanced
by civilization, as society's are, but by her own original and permanent refinement she at last subdues
and educates man.

Chaucer's remarkably trustful and affectionate
character appears in his familiar, yet innocent and
reverent, manner of speaking of his God. He comes
into his thought without any false reverence, and
with no more parade than the zephyr to his ear. If
nature is our mother, then God is our father. There
is less love and simple practical trust in Shakspeare
and Milton. How rarely in our English tongue do we
find expressed any affection for God. There is no
sentiment so rare as the love of God. Herbert almost
alone expresses it, "Ah, my dear God!" Our poet uses

similar words, and whenever he sees a beautiful person, or other object, prides himself on the "maistry" of his God. He reverently recommends Dido to be his bride,

> "if that God that heaven and yearth made,
> Would have a love for beauty and goodnesse,
> And womanhede, trouth, and semeliness."

He supplies the place to his imagination of the saints of the Catholic calendar, and has none of the attributes of a Scandinavian deity.

But, in justification of our praise, we must refer the hearer to his works themselves; to the Prologue to the Canterbury Tales, the account of Gentilesse, the Flower and the Leaf, the stories of Griselda, Virginia, Ariadne, and Blanche the Dutchesse, and much more of less distinguished merit. There are many poets of more taste and better manners, who knew how to leave out their dulness, but such negative genius cannot detain us long; we shall return to Chaucer still with love. Even the clown has taste, whose dictates, though he disregards them, are higher and purer than those which the artist obeys; and some natures, which are rude and ill developed, have yet a higher standard of perfection, than others which are refined and well balanced. Though the peasant's cot is dark, it has the evening star for taper, while the nobleman's saloon is meanly lighted. If we have to wander through many dull and prosaic passages in Chaucer, we have at least the satisfaction of knowing that it is not an artificial dulness, but too easily matched by many passages in life, and it is, perhaps, more pleasing, after all, to meet with a fine thought in its natural setting. We confess we feel a disposition commonly to concentrate sweets, and accumulate pleasures, but the poet may be presumed always to speak as a traveller, who leads us through a varied scenery, from one eminence to another, and, from time to time, a single casual thought rises naturally and inevitably, with such majesty and escort only as the first stars at evening. And surely fate has enshrined it in these circumstances for some end. Nature strews her nuts and flowers broadcast, and never collects them into heaps. This was the soil it grew in, and this the hour it bloomed in; if sun, wind, and rain, came here to cherish and expand the flower, shall not we come here to pluck it?

A true poem is distinguished, not so much by a felicitous expression, or any thought it suggests, as by the atmosphere which surrounds it. Most have beauty of outline merely, and are striking as the form and bearing of a stranger, but true verses come toward us indistinctly, as the very kernel of all friendliness, and envelope us in their spirit and fragrance. Much of our poetry has the very best manners, but no character. It is only an unusual precision and elasticity of speech, as if its author had taken, not an intoxicating draught, but an electuary. It has the distinct outline of sculpture, and chronicles an early hour. Under the influence of passion all men speak thus distinctly, but wrath is not always divine.

There are two classes of men called poets. The one cultivates life, the other art; one seeks food for nutriment, the other for flavor; one satisfies hunger, the other gratifies the palate. There are two kinds of writing, both great and rare; one that of genius, or the inspired, the other of intellect and taste, in the intervals of inspiration. The former is above criticism, always correct, giving the law to criticism. It vibrates and pulsates with life forever. It is sacred, and to be read with reverence, as the works of nature are studied. There are few instances of a sustained style of this kind; perhaps every man has spoken words, but the speaker is then careless of the record. Such a style removes us out of personal relations with its author, we do not take his words on our lips, but his sense into our hearts. It is the stream of inspiration, which bubbles out, now here, now there, now in this man, now in that. It matters not through what ice-crystals it is seen, now a fountain, now the ocean stream running under ground. It is in Shakspeare, Alpheus, in Burns, Arethuse; but ever the same. The other is self-possessed and wise. It is reverent of genius, and greedy of inspiration. It is conscious in the highest and the least degree. It consists with the most perfect command of the faculties. It dwells in a repose as of the desert, and objects are as distinct in it as oases or palms in the horizon of sand. The train of thought moves with subdued and measured step, like a caravan. But the pen is only an instrument in its hand, and not instinct with life, like a longer arm. It leaves a thin varnish or glaze over all its work. The works of Goethe furnish remarkable instances of the latter.

There is no just and serene criticism as yet. Our taste is too delicate and particular. It says nay to the poet's work, but never yea to his hope. It invites him to adorn his deformities, and not to cast them off by expansion, as the tree its bark. We are a people who live in a bright light, in houses of pearl and porcelain, and drink only light wines, whose teeth are easily set on edge by the least natural sour. If we had been consulted, the back bone of the earth would have been made, not of granite, but of Bristol spar. A modern author would have died in infancy in a ruder age. But the poet is something more than a scald, "a smoother and polisher of language"; he is a Cincinnatus in literature, and occupies no west end of the world, but, like the sun, indifferently selects his rhymes, and with a liberal taste weaves into his verse the planet and the stubble.

In these old books the stucco has long since crumbled away, and we read what was sculptured in the granite. They are rude and massive in their proportions, rather than smooth and delicate in their finish. The workers in stone polish only their chimney ornaments, but their pyramids are roughly done. There is a soberness in a rough aspect, as of unhewn granite, which addresses a depth in us, but a polished surface hits only the ball of the eye. The true finish is the work of time and the use to which a thing is put. The elements are still polishing the pyramids. Art may varnish and gild, but it can do no more. A work of genius is rough-hewn from the first, because it anticipates the lapse of time, and has an ingrained polish, which still appears when fragments are broken off, an essential quality of its substance. Its beauty is at the same time its strength, and it breaks with a lustre. The great poem must have the stamp of greatness as well as its essence. The reader easily goes within the shallowest contemporary poetry, and informs it with all the life and promise of the day, as the pilgrim goes within the temple, and hears the faintest strains of the worshippers; but it will have to speak to posterity, traversing these deserts, through the ruins of its outmost walls, by the grandeur and beauty of its proportions.

Hermes Trismegistus . . .
From the Gulistan of Saadi

HERMES TRISMEGISTUS.

[We subjoin a few extracts from the old English translation (by *Doctor Everard*, London, 1650,) of the Divine Pymander of Hermes Trismegistus. The books ascribed to Hermes are thought to have been written, or at least interpolated, by the new Platonists in the third or fourth century of our era. Dr. Cudworth (Intellectual System, Vol. II. p. 142, Lond. 1820,) thinks them to be for the most part genuine remains of the ancient Egyptian theology, and to have been translated by Apuleius. The book deserves, on account of the purity and depth of its religious philosophy, an honorable place among ethical writings.]

GOOD is voluntary or of its own accord; Evil is involuntary or against its will.

The Gods choose good things as good things.

Nothing in heaven is servanted; nothing upon earth is free. Nothing is unknown in heaven, nothing is known upon earth. The things upon earth communicate not with those in heaven. Things on earth do not advantage those in heaven; but all things in heaven do profit and advantage the things upon earth.

Providence is Divine Order.

What is God and the Father and the Good, but the Being of all things that yet are not, and the existence itself of those things that are?

The sight of good is not like the beams of the sun, which being of a fiery shining brightness maketh the eye blind by his excessive light; rather the contrary, for it enlighteneth and so much increaseth the power of the eye, as any man is able to receive the influence of this intelligible clearness. For it is more swift and sharp to pierce, and harmless withal, and full of immortality, and they that are capable, and can draw any store of this spectacle and sight, do many times fall asleep from the body into this most fair and beauteous vision; which things Celius and Saturn our Progenitors attained unto.

For the knowledge of it is a divine silence, and the rest of all the senses. For neither can he that understands that, understand anything else; nor he that sees that, see anything else, nor hear any other thing, nor move the body. For, shining steadfastly on and round about the whole mind, it enlighteneth all the soul, and loosing it from the bodily senses and motions, it draweth it from the body, and changeth it wholly into the essence of God. For it is possible for the soul, O Son, to be deified while yet it lodgeth in the body of man, if it contemplates the beauty of the Good.

He who can be truly called man is a divine living thing, and is not to be compared to any brute man that lives upon earth, but to them that are above in heaven, that are called Gods. Rather, if we shall be bold to speak the truth, he that is a man indeed, is above them, or at least they are equal in power, one to the other. For none of the things in heaven will come down upon earth, and leave the limits of heaven, but a man ascends up into heaven, and measures it. And he knoweth what things are on high, and what below, and learneth all other things exactly. And that which is the greatest of all, he leaveth not the earth, and yet is above: so great is the greatness of his nature. Wherefore we must be bold to say, that an earthly man is a mortal God, and that the heaven-ly God is an immortal man.

ASCRIPTION.

Who can bless thee, or give thanks for thee or to thee?

When shall I praise thee, O Father; for it is neither possible to comprehend thy hour, nor thy time?

Wherefore shall I praise thee,—as being something of myself, or having anything of mine own, or rather as being another's?

For thou art what I am, thou art what I do, thou art what I say.

Thou art all things, and there is nothing which thou art not.

Thou art thou, all that is made, and all that is not made.

The mind that understandeth;

The Father that maketh;

The Good that worketh;

The Good that doth all things. Of matter the most subtile and slender part is air; of the air, the soul; of the soul, the mind; of the mind, God.

By me the truth sings praise to the truth, the good praiseth the good.

O All! receive a reasonable sacrifice from all things.

Thou art God, thy man cryeth these things unto thee, by the fire, by the air, by the earth, by the water, by the spirit, by thy Creatures.

FROM THE GULISTAN OF SAADI.

Take heed that the orphan weep not; for the Throne of the Almighty is shaken to and fro, when the orphan sets a-crying.

The Dervish in his prayer is saying, O God! have compassion on the wicked, for thou hast given all things to the good in making them good.

Any foe whom you treat courteously will become a friend, excepting lust; which, the more civilly you use it, will grow the more perverse.

Ardishir Babagan asked an Arabian physician, what quantity of food ought to be eaten daily. He replied, Thirteen ounces. The king said, What strength can a man derive from so small a quantity? The physician replied, so much can support you, but in whatever you exceed that, you must support it.

If conserve of roses be frequently eaten, it will cause a surfeit, whereas a crust of bread eaten after a long interval will relish like conserve of roses.

Saadi was troubled when his feet were bare, and he had not wherewithal to buy shoes; but "soon after meeting a man without feet, I was thankful for the bounty of Providence to me, and submitted cheerfully to the want of shoes."

Saadi found in a mosque at Damascus an old Persian of an hundred and fifty years, who was dying, and was saying to himself, "I said, I will enjoy myself for a few moments; alas! that my soul took the path of departure; alas! at the variegated table of life I partook a few mouthfuls, and the fates cried, Enough!"

I heard of a Dervish who was consuming in the flame of want, tacking patch after patch upon his ragged garment, and solacing his mind with verses of poetry. Somebody observed to him, Why do you sit quiet, while a certain gentleman of this city has girt up his loins in the service of the religious independents, and seated himself by the door of their hearts? He would esteem himself obliged by an opportunity of relieving your distress. He said, Be silent, for I swear by Allah, it were equal to the torments of hell to enter into Paradise through the interest of a neighbor.

Sir Walter Raleigh.

PERHAPS no one in English history better represents the heroic character than Sir Walter Raleigh; for Sidney has got to be almost as shadowy as Arthur himself. Raleigh's somewhat antique & Roman virtues appear in his numerous military and naval adventures, in his knightly conduct toward the Queen, in his poems and his employments in the tower, and not least in his death, but more than all in his constant soldier-like bearing and promise. He was the Bayard of peaceful as well as warlike enterprise, & few lives which are the subject of recent & trustworthy history are so agreeable to the imagination. Notwithstanding his temporary unpopularity, he especially possessed those prevalent and popular qualities which command the admiration of men. If an English Plutarch were to be written, Raleigh would be the best Greek or Roman among them all. He was one whose virtues if they were not distinctly great yet gave to virtue a current stamp and value as it were by the very grace and loftiness with which he carried them—one of nature's noblemen, who possessed the requisites to true nobility, without which no heraldry nor blood can avail. Among savages he would still have been the chief. He seems to have had, not a profounder or grander, but, so to speak, more, nature, than other men. The enthusiastic and often extravagant, but always hearty & emphatic tone in which he is spoken of by his contemporaries is not the least remarkable fact about him, and it does not matter much whether the current stories are true or not, since they at least prove his reputation.

It is not his praise to have been a saint and a seer in his generation, but "one of the gallantest worthies that ever England bred". The stories about him testify to a character rather than a virtue. As, for instance, that "he was damnably proud. Old Sir Robert Harley, of Brampton-Brian Castle, (who knew him), would say, 'twas a great question, who was the proudest, Sir Walter or Sir Thomas Overbury, but the difference that was, was judged on Sir Thomas' side;" that "In his youth his companions were boisterous blades, but generally those that had wit." A young contemporary says, "I have heard his enemies confess, that he was one of the weightiest and wisest men that this island ever bred". And another gives this character of him— "Who hath not known or read of this prodigy of wit and fortune, Sir Walter Raleigh, a man unfortunate in nothing else but in the greatness of his wit and advancement, whose eminent worth was such, both in domestic policy, foreign expeditions, and discoveries, in arts and literature, both practic and contemplative, that it might seem at once, to conquer example and imitation".

And what we are told of his personal appearance is accordant with the rest; that "he had in the outward man a good presence, in a handsome and well-compacted person", that "he was a tall, handsome, and bold man," and his "was thought a very good face", though "his countenance was somewhat spoiled by the unusual height of his forehead." "He was such a person (every way), that (as King Charles I. says of the Lord Strafford) a prince would rather be afraid of, than ashamed of—" and had an "awfulness and ascendency in his aspect over other mortals". And we are not disappointed to learn that he indulged in a splendid dress, and "notwithstanding his so great mastership in style, and his conversation with the learnedest and politest persons, yet he spake broad Devonshire to his dying day."

Such a character as this was well suited to the times in which he lived. His age was an unusually stirring one. The discovery of America and the successful progress of the Reformation opened a field for both the intellectual and physical energies of his generation. Its fathers were Calvin, and Knox, and Cranmer, and Pizarro, and Garcilaso; and its immediate forefathers Luther, and Raphael, and Bayard, and Angelo, and Ariosto, and Copernicus, and Machiavel, and Erasmus, and Cabot, and Ximenes, and Columbus. Its device might have been an anchor, a sword, and a quill. The Pizarro laid by his sword at intervals and took to his letters. The Columbus set sail for newer worlds still, by voyages which needed not the patronage of princes. The Bayard alighted from his steed to seek adventures no less arduous than heretofore, upon the ocean, and in the western world; and the Luther who had reformed religion, began now to reform politics and science.

In his youth, however it may have concerned him, Camoens was writing a heroic poem in Portugal, and the arts still had their representative in Paul Veronese of Italy. He may have been one to welcome the works of Tasso and Montaigne to England, and when he looked about him, have found such men as Cervantes & Sidney, men of like pursuits & not altogether dissimilar genius from himself, for his contemporaries, a Drake to rival him on the sea, and a Hudson in western adventure, a Halley, a Galileo, and a Kepler, for his astronomers, a Bacon, a Behmen, and a Burton, for his philosophers, and a Jonson—a Spenser, and a Shakspeare, his poets for refreshment and inspiration.

But that we may know how worthy he himself was to make one of this illustrious company, and appreciate this great activity and versatility of his genius, we will glance hastily at the various aspects of his life.

He was a proper knight, a born cavalier, and in the intervals of war betook himself still to the most vigorous arts of peace, though as if diverted from his proper aim. He makes us doubt if there is not some worthier apology for war than has been discovered, for its modes and manners were an instinct with him, and though in his writings he takes frequent occasion sincerely to condemn its folly, and show the better policy and advantage of peace, yet he speaks with the uncertain authority of a warrior still, to whom those juster wars are not simply the dire necessity implied. In whatever he is engaged we seem to see a plume waving over his head, and a sword dangling at his side. Born in 1552, the last year of the reign of Edward VI, we find that not long after, by such instinct as the young crab seeks the sea shore, he has already marched into France, as one of "a troop of a hundred gentlemen volunteers", who are described as "a gallant company, nobly mounted and accoutred, having on their colors the motto, *Finem det mihi virtus*"—Let valor be my end. And so in fact he marched on through life with this motto in his heart always.

All the peace of those days seems to have been but a truce, or casual interruption of the order of war. War with Spain especially was so much the rule rather than the exception, that the navigators and commanders of these two nations when abroad, acted on the presumption that their countries were at war at home, though they had left them at peace, and their respective colonies in America carried on war at their convenience with no infraction of the treaties between the mother countries. Raleigh especially seems to have regarded the Spaniards as his natural enemies, and he was not backward to develop this part of his nature.

When England was threatened with foreign invasion, the Queen looked to him especially for advice and assistance, and none was better able to give them than he. We cannot but admire the tone in which he speaks of his island, and how it is to be best defended, and the navy its chief strength maintained and improved. He speaks from England as his castle and his, as no other man's, is the voice of the state, for he does not assert the interests of an individual but of a commonwealth, and we see in him revived a Roman patriotism. His actions as they were public and for the public, were fit to be publicly rewarded, and we accordingly read with equanimity of gold chains and monopolies and other emoluments conferred on him from time to time for his various services—his military successes in Ireland "that commonwealth of common woe", as he even then described it,—his enterprise in the harbor of Cadiz,—his capture of Fayal from the Spaniards, and other exploits which perhaps more than anything else got him fame and a name during his life time.

If war was his earnest work, it was his pastime too, for in the peaceful intervals we hear of his participating heartily and bearing off the palm in the birth-day tournaments and tilting matches of the Queen, where the combatants vied with each other mainly who should come on to the ground in the most splendid dress and equipments—those tilts where it is said that his political rival Essex, whose wealth enabled him to lead the costliest train, but who ran very ill, and was thought the poorest knight of all, was wont to change his suit from orange to green, that it might be said that there was one in green who ran worse than one in orange.

ished when Raleigh came to court—his natural companion and other self, as it were, as if nature, in her anxiety to confer one specimen of a true knight and courtier on that age, had cast two in the same mould, lest one should miscarry. These two kindred spirits are said to have been mutually attracted toward each other. And there too was Queen Elizabeth herself, the centre of the court and of the kingdom, to whose service he consecrates himself, not so much as a subject to his sovereign, but as a knight to the service of his mistress. His intercourse with the Queen may well have begun with the incident of the cloak, for such continued to be its character afterwards. It has in the description an air of romance and might fitly have made a part of his friend Sidney's Arcadia. We are inclined to consider him as some knight, and a knight errant too, who had strayed into the precincts of the court, and practised there the arts which he had learned in bower and hall and in the lists.—Not that he knew not how to govern states as well as queens, but he brought to the task the gallantry and graces of chivalry as well as the judgment and experience of a practical modern Englishman. "The Queen", says one, "began to be taken with his elocution, and loved to hear his reasons to her demands, and the truth is she took him for a kind of oracle which nettled them all." He rose rapidly in her favor and became her indispensable counsellor in all matters which concerned the state, for he was minutely acquainted with the affairs of England, and none better understood her commercial interests. But though he made a good use of his influence for the most part when obtained, he could descend to the grossest flattery to obtain it, and we could wish him forever banished from the court, whose favors he so earnestly sought. But that he who was one while "the

Queen of England's poor captive," could sometimes assume a manly and independent tone with her appears from his answer when she once exclaimed, on his asking a favor for a friend, "When, Sir Walter, will you cease to be a beggar?" "When your gracious majesty ceases to be a benefactor."

His court life exhibits him in mean and frivolous relations which make him lose that respect in our eyes which he had acquired elsewhere. The base use he made of his recovered influence, (after having been banished from the court and even suffered imprisonment in consequence of the Queen's displeasure,) to procure the disgrace and finally the execution of his rival Essex, who had been charged with treason, is the foulest stain upon his escutcheon, the one which it is hardest to reconcile with the nobleness and generosity which we are inclined to attribute to such a character. Revenge is most unheroic. Also his acceptance of bribes afterwards for using his influence in behalf of the Earl's adherents is not to be excused by the usage of the times. The times may change, but the laws of integrity and magnanimity are immutable. Nor are the terms on which he was the friend of Cecil, from motives of policy merely, more tolerable to consider. Yet we cannot but think that he frequently travelled a higher, though a parallel course with the mob, and though he had their suffrage, to some extent deserves the praise which Jonson applies to another—

> "That to the vulgar canst thyself apply,
> Treading a better path not contrary."

We gladly make haste to consider him in what the world calls his misfortune, after the death of Elizabeth and the accession of James 1st, when his essentially nobler nature was separated from the base company of the court, and the contaminations which his loyalty could not resist, though by imprisonment and the scaffold.

His enemies had already prejudiced the king against him before his accession to the throne, and when at length the English nobility were presented to his majesty, who, it will be remembered, was a Scotchman, and Raleigh's name was told, "Raleigh", exclaimed the king, "O my soule, mon, I have heard rawly of thee." His efforts to limit the king's power of introducing Scots into England, contributed to increase his jealousy and dislike, and he was shortly after accused by Lord Cobham of participating in a conspiracy to place the Lady Arabella Stuart on the throne, and owing mainly, it is thought, to the King's resentment, was tried and falsely convicted of high treason—though his accuser retracted in writing his whole accusation before the conclusion of the trial.

In connexion with his behavior to Essex, it should be remembered that by his conduct on his own trial he in a great measure removed the ill-will which existed against him on that account. At his trial, which is said to have been most unjustly and insolently conducted by Sir Edward Coke on the part of the Crown, "He answered" says one, "with that temper, wit, learning, courage, and judgment, that save that it went with the hazzard of his life, it was the happiest day that ever he spent. The two first that brought the news [of his condemnation] to the king were Roger Ashton, and a Scotsman, whereof one affirmed that never any man spake so well in times past, nor would do in the world to come: and the other said, that whereas when he saw him first, he was so led with the common hatred, that he would have gone a hundred miles to have seen him hanged, he would, ere he parted, have gone a thousand to have saved his life." Another says he "behaved himself so worthily, so wisely, and so temperately, that in half a day the mind of all the company was changed from the extremest hate to the extremest pity." And another "to the lords humble, but not prostrate; to the jury affable, but not fawning; to the king's counsel patient, but not yielding to the imputations laid upon him, or neglecting to repel them with the spirit which became an injured and honorable man." And finally he followed the sheriff out of court in the expressive words of Sir Thomas Overbury, "with admirable erection, but yet in such sort as became a man condemned."

Raleigh prepared himself for immediate execution, but after his pretended accomplices had gone through the ceremony of a mock execution and been pardoned by the King, it satisfied the policy of his enemies to retain him a prisoner in the tower for 13 years, with the sentence of death still unrevoked. In the meanwhile he solaced himself in his imprisonment with writing a history of the world and cultivating poetry and philosophy as the noblest deeds compatible with his confinement.

It is satisfactory to contrast with his mean personal relations while at court his connexion in the tower with the young prince Henry whose tastes and aspirations were of a stirring kind, as his friend and instructor. He addresses some of his shorter pieces to him, and in some instances they seem to have been written expressly for his use. He preaches to him as he was well able, from experience, a wiser philosophy than he had himself practised, and was particularly anxious to correct in him a love of popularity—which he had discovered, and gave him useful maxims for his conduct when he should take his father's place.

He lost neither health nor spirits by 13 years of captivity, but after having spent this the literary era of his life as in the retirement of his study, and having written the history of the old world, he began to dream of actions which would supply materials to the future historian of the new. It is interesting to consider him, a close prisoner as he was, preparing for voyages and adventures, which would require to roam more broadly than was consistent with the comfort or ambition of his freest contemporaries.

Already in 1595 8 years before his imprisonment, it will be remembered he had undertaken his first voyage to Guiana in person—mainly it is said to recover favor with the Queen—but doubtless it was much more to recover favor with himself and exercise his genius in fields more worthy of him than a corrupt court.

He continued to cherish this his favorite project, though a prisoner, and at length in the 13th year of his imprisonment, through the influence of his friends, and his confident assertions respecting the utility of the expedition to his country, he obtained his release and set sail for Guiana with twelve ships. But unfortunately he neglected to procure a formal pardon from the king, trusting to the opinion of Lord Bacon that this was unnecessary, since the sentence of death against him was virtually annulled, by the lives of others being committed to his hands. Acting on this presumption, and with the best intentions toward his country, and only his usual jealousy of Spain, he undertook to make good his engagements to himself and this world.

It is not easy for us at this day to realize what extravagant expectations Europe had formed respecting the wealth of the new world. We might suppose two whole continents with their adjacent seas & oceans, equal to the present known globe—stretching from pole to pole, and possessing every variety of soil, climate and productions, lying unexplored today—what would be the speculations of Broadway & State street?

The few travellers who had penetrated into the country of Guiana, whither Raleigh was bound, brought back accounts of noble streams flowing through majestic forests and a depth and luxuriance of soil which made England seem a barren waste in comparison. Its mineral wealth was reported to be as inexhaustible as the cupidity of its discoverers was unbounded. The very surface of the ground was said to be resplendent with gold, and men went covered with gold-dust, as Hottentots with grease. Raleigh was informed while at Trinidad by the Spanish governor who was his prisoner, that one John Martinez had at length penetrated into this country and the stories told by him of the wealth and extent of its cities, surpass the narratives of Marco Polo himself. He is said, in particular, to have reached the city of Manoa, to which he first gave the name of El Dorado, or The Gilded, the Indians conducting him blindfolded, "not removing the veil from his eyes till he was ready to enter the city. It was at noon that he passed the gates, and it took him all that day and the next, walking from sunrise to sunset, before he arrived at the Palace of Inga, where he resided for seven months, till he had made himself master of the language of the country". These, and even more fanciful accounts had Raleigh heard and pondered, both before and after his first visit to the country. No one was more familiar with the stories, both true and fabulous, respecting the discovery and resources of the new world, and none had a better right to know what great commanders and navigators had done there or anywhere than he. Such information would naturally flow to him of its own accord. That his ardor and faith were hardly cooled by actual observation may be gathered from the tone of his own description. He was the first English-

ground of hard sand, easy to march on either for horse or foot; the deer crossing in every path; the birds towards the evening singing on every tree with a thousand several tunes; cranes and herons, of white, crimson and carnation, perching on the river's side; the air fresh, with a gentle easterly wind; and every stone that we stopped to take up promising either gold or silver by his complexion."

In another place he says "To conclude, it is a country as yet untouched by the natives of the old world: never sacked, turned, or wrought; the face of the earth hath not been torn, nor the virtue and salt of the soil spent by manurance."

To the fabulous accounts of preceding adventurers Raleigh added many others equally absurd and poetical, as for instance, of a tribe "with eyes in their shoulders, and mouths in their breasts,"—but, it seems to us, with entire good faith, and no such flagrant intent to deceive as he has been accused of. "Weak policy it would be in me", says he, "to betray myself or my country with imaginations; neither am I so far in love with that watching, care, peril, disease, hard fare, and other mischiefs that accompany such voyages, as to woo myself again into any of them, were I not assured that the sun covereth not so much riches in any other part of the earth." It is easy to see that he was tempted not so much by the lustre of the gold, as by the splendor of the enterprise itself. It was the best move that peace allowed. The expeditions to Guiana and the ensuing golden dreams were not wholly unworthy of him, though he accomplished little more in the first voyage than to take formal possession of the country in the name of the Queen, and in the second, of the Spanish town of St. Thomas, as his enemies would say, in the name of himself.

Perceiving that the Spaniards, who had been secretly informed of his designs through their ambassador in England, were prepared to thwart his endeavors, and resist his progress in the country, he procured the capture of this their principal town, which was also burnt against his orders.

But it seems to us that no *particular* exception is to be taken against these high-handed measures, though his enemies have made the greatest handle of them. His behavior on this occasion was part and parcel of his constant character. It would not be easy to say when he ceased to be an honorable soldier and became a freebooter, nor indeed is it of so much importance to inquire of a man what actions he performed at one and what at another period, as what manner of man he was at all periods. It was after all the same Raleigh who had won so much renown by land & sea, at home and abroad. It was his forte to deal vigorously with men, whether as a statesman, a courtier, a navigator, a planter of colonies, an accused person, a prisoner, an explorer of continents, or a military or naval commander, and it was a right hero's maxim of his that "good success admits of no examination", which in a liberal sense is true enough, for good success can only spring from good conduct; and that there was no cant in him on the subject of war, appears from his saying which indeed is very true, that "The necessity of war, which among human actions is most lawless, hath some kind of affinity and near resemblance with the necessity of law." It is to be remembered too that if the Spaniards found him a restless and uncompromising enemy— the Indians experienced in him a humane and gentle defender, and on his second visit to Guiana remembered his name and welcomed him with enthusiasm.

We are told that the Spanish Ambassador, on receiving intelligence of his doings in this country, rushed in to the presence of King James, exclaiming "Piratas—piratas"—pirates—pirates. And the king, to gratify his resentment, without bringing him to trial for this alledged new offence—with characteristic meanness and pusillanimity caused him to be executed upon the old sentence soon after his return to England.

The circumstances of his execution and how he bore himself on that memorable occasion when the sentence of death passed 15 years before was revived against him, after as a historian in his confinement he had visited the old world in his free imagination, and as an unrestrained adventurer the New, with his fleets and in person—are perhaps too well known to be repeated.—The reader will excuse our hasty rehearsal of the final scene.

We can pardon though not without hesitation his supposed attempt at suicide in the prospect of defeat and disgrace. No one can read his letter to his wife written while he was contemplating this act, without being reminded of the Roman Cato, and admiring while he condemns him. "I know", says he "that it is forbidden to destroy ourselves; but I trust it is forbidden in this sort—that we destroy not ourselves despairing of God's mercy."

Though his greatness seems to have forsaken him in his feigning himself sick and the base methods he took to avoid being brought to trial, yet he recovered himself at last, and happily withstood the trials which awaited him.

The night before his execution, besides writing letters of farewell to his wife, containing the most practical advice for the conduct of her life, he appears to have spent the time in writing verses on his condition, and among others this couplet "On the Snuff of a Candle".

> "Cowards fear to die; but courage stout,
> Rather than live in snuff, will be put out."

And perhaps the following verses for an epitaph on himself,

> "Even such is time, that takes on trust
> Our youth, our joys, our all we have,
> And pays us but with age and dust;
> Who in the dark and silent grave,
> When we have wandered all our ways,
> Shuts up the story of our days!
> But from this earth, this grave, this dust,
> The Lord shall raise me up, I trust."

His execution was appointed on Lord Mayor's day, that the pageants and shows might divert the attention of the people, but those pageants have long since been forgotten, while this tragedy is still remembered. He took a pipe of tobacco before he went to the scaffold, and appeared there with a serene countenance so that a stranger could not have told which was the condemned person. After exculpating himself in a speech to the people, and without ostentation having felt the edge of the axe, and disposed himself once as he wished to lie, he made a solemn prayer, and being directed to place himself so that his face should look to the east, his characteristic answer was "It mattered little how the head lay provided the heart was right."

The executioner being over-awed by his behavior was unable at first to perform his office—when Raleigh slowly raising his head exclaimed, "Strike away man, don't be afraid." "He was the most fearless of death," says the Bishop who attended him, "that ever was

Here also he conversed on poetry, philosophy, and literature with Hoskins, his fellow prisoner, whom Ben Jonson mentions as "the person who had polished him." He was a political economist far in advance of his age, and a sagacious and influential speaker in the House of Commons. Science is indebted to him in more ways than one. In the midst of pressing public cares he interested himself to establish some means of universal communication between men of Science, for their mutual benefit, and actually set up what he termed, "an office of address", for this purpose. As a Mathematician he was the friend of Harriot, Dee, and the Earl of Northumberland. As an Antiquarian, he was a member of the first antiquarian society established in England, along with Spelman, Selden, Cotton, Camden, Savile, & Stow. He is said to have been the founder of the Mermaid Club, which met in Fleet Street, to which Shakspeare, Ben Jonson, Fletcher, Beaumont, Carew, Donne, &c., belonged. He has the fame of having first introduced the potato from Virginia, and the cherry from the Canaries into Ireland, where his garden was, and his manor of Sherborne "he beautified with gardens, and orchards, and groves of much variety and delight." And this fact evincing his attention to horticulture is related, that once, on occasion of the Queen's visiting him, he artificially retarded the ripening of some cherries, by stretching a wet canvass over the tree and removed it on a sunny day, so as to present the fruit ripe to the Queen a month later than usual. Not to omit a more doubtful, but not less celebrated benefit, it is said, that on the return of his first colonists from Virginia in 1586, tobacco was first effectually introduced into England, and its use encouraged by his influence and example. —And finally not to be outdone by the quacks, he invented a cordial which became very celebrated and bore his name, and was even administered to the Queen, and to the Prince in his last illness. One Febure writes that "Sir Walter, being a worthy successor of Mithridates, Matheolus, B. Valentine, Paracelsus, and others, has he affirms, selected all that is choicest in the animal, vegetable, and mineral world, and moreover manifested so much art and experience in the preparation of this great and admirable cordial as will of itself render him immortal."

We come at last to consider him as a literary man and a writer, concerning which aspect of his life we are least indebted to the historian for our facts.

As he was heroic with the sword, so was he with the pen. The History of the World, the task which he selected for his prison hours, was heroic in the undertaking and heroic in the achievement. The easy and cheerful heart with which he endured his confinement, turning his prison into a study, a parlor, and a laboratory, and his prison-yard into a garden, so that men did not so much pity as admire him—the steady purpose with which he set about fighting his battles, prosecuting his discoveries, and gathering his laurels, with the pen, if he might no longer do so with regiments & fleets—is itself an exploit. In writing the history of the world he was indeed at liberty; for he who contemplates truth and universal laws is free, whatever walls immure his body;—though to our brave prisoner thus employed mankind may have seemed but his poor fellow prisoners still.

Though this remarkable work interests us more, on the whole, as a part of the history of Raleigh, than as the history of the world, yet it was done like himself, and with no small success. The historian of Greece and Rome is usually unmanned by his subject as a peasant crouches before lords, but Raleigh, though he succumbs to the imposing fame of tradition and antediluvian story, and exhibits unnecessary reverence for a prophet or patriarch, from his habit of innate religious courtesy to the church, has done better than this whenever a hero offered. He stalks down through the aisles of the past, as through the avenues of a camp, with poets and historians for his heralds and guides, and from whatever side the faintest trump reaches his ear that way does he promptly turn, though to the neglect of many a gaudy pavilion.

From a work so little read in these days we will venture to quote as specimens the following criticisms on Alexander and the character of Epaminondas. They will at any rate teach our lips no bad habits. There is a natural emphasis in his style, like a man's tread, and a breathing space between the sentences, which the best of more modern writing does not furnish. His chapters are like English parks or rather like a Western forest, where the larger growth keeps down the underwood, and one may ride on horse back through the openings.

"Certainly the things that this king did, were marvellous, and would hardly have been undertaken by any man else; and though his father had determined to have invaded the lesser Asia, it is like enough that he would have contented himself with some part thereof, and not have discovered the river of Indus, as this man did. The swift course of victory, wherewith he ran over so large a portion of the world, in so short a space, may justly be imputed unto this, that he was never encountered by an equal spirit, concurring with equal power against him. Hereby it came to pass that his actions being limited by no greater opposition, than desart places, and the mere length of tedious journeys could make, were like the

Colossus of Rhodes, and not so much to be admired for the workmanship, though therein also praiseworthy, as for the huge bulk. For certainly the things performed by Xenophon, discover as brave a spirit as Alexander's, and working no less exquisitely, though the effects were less material, as were also the forces and power of command, by which it wrought. But he that would find the exact pattern of a noble commander, must look upon such as Epaminondas, that encountering worthy captains, and those better followed than themselves, have by their singular virtue over-topped their valiant enemies, and still prevailed over those, that would not have yielded one foot to any other. Such as these are, do seldom live to obtain great empires. For it is a work of more labor and longer time, to master the equal force of one hardy and well-ordered state, than to tread down and utterly subdue a multitude of servile nations, compounding the body of a gross unwieldly empire. Wherefore these *Parvo Potentes*, men that with little have done much upon enemies of like ability, are to be regarded as choice examples of worth; but great conquerors, to be rather admired for the substance of their actions, than the exquisite managing: exactness and greatness concurring so seldom, that I can find no instance of both in one, save only that brave Roman, Caesar."

Of Epaminondas he says, "So died Epaminondas, the worthiest man that ever was bred in that nation of Greece, and hardly to be matched in any age or country; for he equalled all others in the several virtues which in each of them were singular. His justice and sincerity, his temperance, wisdom, and high magnanimity, were no way inferior to his military virtues; in every part whereof he so excelled, that he could not but properly be called a wary, a valiant, a politic, a bountiful, and a provident captain. Neither by his very lively understanding and relating of it, especially in those parts in which the mere scholar is most likely to fail. Every reader has observed what a dust the historian commonly raises about the field of battle, to serve as an apology for not making clear the disposition and manoeuvring of the parties, so that the clearest idea one gets is of a very vague counteraction, or standing over against one another of two forces. In this history we, at least, have faith that these things are right. Our author describes an ancient battle with the vivacity and truth of an eye-witness, and perhaps in criticising the disposition of the forces, saying they should have stood thus or so, sometimes enforces his assertions in some such style, as "I remember being in the harbor of Cadiz &c.," so that, as in Herodotus and Thucydides, we associate the historian with the exploits he describes, but in this case not on account of his fame as a writer—but for the conspicuous part he acted on the world's stage—and his name is of equal mark to us with those of his heroes, so in the present instance, not only for his valor as a writer, but the part he acted in his generation, the life of the author seems fit to make the last chapter in the history he is writing. We expect that when his history is brought to a close it will include his own exploits. However, this is hardly a work to be consulted as authority now-a-days, but on the subject of its author's character. The natural breadth and grasp of the man is seen in the preface itself, which is a sermon with human life for its text. In the first books he discusses with childlike earnestness and an ingenuity which they little deserved the absurd and frivolous questions which engaged the theology and philosophy of his day. But even these are recommended by his sincerity and fine imagination, while the subsequent parts, or story itself, have

set in the firmament, to no other end, than to adorn it; but for instruments and organs of his divine Providence, so far as it hath pleased his just will to determine. Origen upon this place of *Genesis, Let there be light in the firmament, &c.*, affirmeth that the stars are not causes (meaning perchance binding causes;) but are as open books, wherein are contained and set down all things whatsoever to come; but not to be read by the eyes of human wisdom: which latter part I believe well, and this saying of Syracides withall; *That there are hid yet greater things than these be, and we have seen but a few of his works.* And though, for the capacity of men, we know somewhat, yet in the true and uttermost virtues of herbs and plants, which our selves sow and set, and which grow under our feet, we are in effect ignorant; much more in the powers and working of celestial bodies. . . . But in this question of fate, the middle course is to be followed, that as with the heathen we do not bind God to his creatures; so on the contrary, we do not rob those beautiful creatures of their powers and offices. . . . And that they wholly direct the reasonless mind, I am resolved; For all those which were created mortal, as birds beasts and the like, are left to their natural appetites; over all which, celestial bodies (as instruments and executioners of God's providence) have absolute dominion. . . . And S. Augustine: *Deus regit inferiora corpora per superiora, God ruleth the bodies below by those above;* . . . . It was therefore truly affirmed, *Sapiens adjuvabit opus astrorum, quemadmodum agricola terrae naturam; A wise man assisteth the work of the stars, as the husbandman helpeth the nature of the soil.* . . . . Lastly, we ought all to know, that God created the stars as he did the rest of the universal; whose influences may be called his re-

and stones, and therefore strong and durable; of
which Ovid;

> *Inde genus durum sumus, experiensque laborum,*
> *Et documenta damus qua simus origine nati:*

> From thence our kind hard-hearted is, enduring
>   pain and care,
> Approving, that our bodies of a stony nature
>   are.

His bloud, which disperseth itself by the branches of
veins through all the body, may be resembled to those
waters, which are carried by brooks and rivers over
all the earth; his breath to the air, his natural heat
to the inclosed warmth which the earth hath in it
self, which, stirred up by the heat of the sun, assisteth nature in the speedier procreation of those
varieties, which the earth bringeth forth; our radical
moisture, oil or balsamum (whereon the natural heat
feedeth and is maintained) is resembled to the fat
and fertility of the earth; the hair of man's body,
which adorns or overshadows it, to the grass, which
covereth the upper face and skin of the earth; our
generative power, to nature, which produceth all
things; our determinations to the light, wandering,
and unstable clouds, carried everywhere with uncertain winds; our eyes to the light of the sun and
moon; and the beauty of our youth, to the flowers of
the spring, which either, in a very short time, or with
the sun's heat, dry up and wither away, or the fierce
puffs of wind blow them from the stalks; the thoughts
of our mind, to the motion of angels; and our pure
understanding (formerly called *mens* and that which
always looketh upwards) to those intellectual natures, which are always present with God; and lastly,
our immortal souls (while they are righteous) are by
God himself beautified with the title of his own image

and similitude." But man is not in all things like nature. "For this tide of man's life, after it once turneth and declineth, ever runneth with a perpetual ebb and falling stream, but never floweth again: our leaf once fallen, springeth no more; neither doth the sun or the summer adorn us again, with the garments of new leaves and flowers."

There is a flowing rhythm in some of these sentences like the rippling of rivers—hardly to be matched in any prose or verse. The following is his poem on the decay of oracles and of pantheism.

"The fire which the Chaldeans worshipped for a god, is crept into every man's chimney, which the lack of fuel starveth, water quencheth, and want of air suffocateth: Jupiter is no more vexed with Juno's jealousies; Death hath persuaded him to chastity, and her to patience; and that time which hath devoured it self, hath also eaten up both the bodies and images of him and his: yea their stately temples of stone and dureful marble. The houses and sumptuous buildings erected to Baal, can no where be found upon the earth, nor any monument of that glorious temple consecrated to Diana. There are none now in Phoenicia that lament the death of Adonis; nor any in Lybia, Creta, Thessalia, or elsewhere, that can ask counsel or help from Jupiter. The great god Pan hath broken his pipes, Apollo's priests are become speechless; and the trade of riddles in Oracles, with the Devil's telling men's fortunes therein, is taken up by counterfeit Egyptians and cozening Astrologers."

In his "Discourse of War in General" commencing with almost a heroic verse, "The ordinary theme and argument of history is war," are many things well thought and many more well said. He thus expands the maxim that corporations have no soul. "But no senate nor civil assembly can be under such natural impulses to honor and justice as single persons. For a majority is no-body when that majority is separated, and a collective body can have no synteresis, or divine ray, which is in the mind of every man, never assenting to evil, but upbraiding and tormenting him when he does it: but the honor and conscience that lies in the majority is too thin and diffusive to be efficacious; for a number can do a great wrong, and call it right, and not one of that majority blush for it." If his philosophy is for the most part poor, yet the conception and expression are rich and generous. His maxims are not true or impartial, but are conceived with a certain magnanimity which was natural to him, as if a selfish policy could easily afford to give place in him to a more universal and true.

As a fact evincing Raleigh's poetic culture and taste, it is said that in a visit to the poet Spenser, on the banks of the Mulla, which is described in "Colin Clout's come home again," he anticipated the judgment of posterity with respect to the Fairy Queen, and by his sympathy and advice encouraged the poet to go on with his work, which, by the advice of other friends, among whom was Sidney, he had laid aside. His own poems, though insignificant in respect to number and length, and not collected into a separate volume, or surely accredited to Raleigh, deserve the distinct attention of the lover of English poetry, and leave such an impression on the mind that this leaf of his laurels, for the time, well nigh overshadows all the rest. In these few rhymes, as in that country he describes, his life naturally culminates, and his secret aspirations appear. They are in some respects more trustworthy testimonials to his character than state papers or tradition; for poetry is a piece of very private history which unostentatiously lets us into the secret of a man's life, and is to the reader, what the eye is to the beholder, the characteristic feature, which cannot be distorted or made to deceive.

The pleasing poem entitled "A Description of the Country's Recreations", also printed among the poems of Sir Henry Wotton, is well known. The following, which bears evident marks of his pen, we will quote for its secure and continent rhythm.

"False Love and True Love."

"As you came from the holy land
    Of Walsingham,
Met you not with my true love
    By the way as you came?
How shall I know your true love,
    That have met many one
As I went to the holy land,
    That have come, that have gone.
She is neither white nor brown,
    But as the heavens fair;
There is none hath so divine a form
    In the earth or the air.
Such a one did I meet, good sir,
    Such an angelic face;
Who like a queen, like a nymph did appear,
    By her gait, by her grace:
She hath left me here all alone,
    All alone as unknown,
Who sometimes did me lead with herself,
    And me loved as her own:
What's the cause that she leaves you alone
    And a new way doth take:
Who loved you once as her own
    And her joy did you make?
I have loved her all my youth,
    But now, old as you see,
Love likes not the falling fruit
    From the withered tree:
Know that love is a careless child
    And forgets promise past,

He is blind, he is deaf, when he list,
    And in faith never fast:
His desire is a dureless content,
    And a trustless joy;
He is won with a world of despair,
    And is lost with a toy:
Of women-kind such indeed is the love,
    Or the word love abused;
Under which many childish desires
    And conceits are excused:
But true love is a durable fire
    In the mind ever burning;
Never sick, never old, never dead,
    From itself never turning."

The following will be new to many of our readers.

"The Shepherd's Praise of his sacred Diana"

"Prais'd be Diana's fair and harmless light;
    Prais'd be the dews wherewith she moists
      the ground;
Prais'd be her beams, the glory of the night;
    Prais'd be her power, by which all
      powers abound!

Prais'd be her nymphs, with whom she decks
    the woods;
    Prais'd be her knights, in whom true
      honor lives;
Prais'd be that force by which she moves the
    floods!
    Let that Diana shine, which all these
      gives!

In heaven, queen she is among the spheres;
    She mistress-like, makes all things to
      be pure;
Eternity in her oft-change she bears;
    She, Beauty is; by her, the fair endure.

Time wears her not; she doth his chariot guide;
    Mortality below her orb is placed;
By her the virtues of the stars down slide;
    In her is Virtue's perfect image cast!

A knowledge pure it is her worth to know:
With Circes let them dwell that think not so!"

Though we discover in his verses the vices of the courtier, and they are not equally sustained, as if his genius were warped by the frivolous society of the Court, he was capable of rising to unusual heights. His genius seems to have been fitted for short flights of unmatched sweetness and vigor, but by no means for the sustained loftiness of the epic poet. One who read his verses would say that he had not grown to be the man he promised. They have occasionally a strength of character and heroic tone rarely expressed or appreciated, and possess an excellence so peculiar, as to be almost unique specimens of their kind in the language. Those which have reference to his death have been oftenest quoted, and are the best. "The Soul's Errand" deserves to be remembered till her mission is accomplished in the world. We quote the following, not so well known—with some omissions, from the commencement of

"His Pilgrimage".

"Give me my scallop-shell of quiet,
    My staff of faith to walk upon;
My scrip of joy, immortal diet;
    My bottle of salvation;
My gown of glory, hope's true gage,
And thus I'll take my pilgrimage.

Blood must be my body's balmer,
    No other balm will here be given,
Whilst my soul like a quiet palmer,
    Travels to the land of heaven,
Over the silver mountains,
Where spring the nectar fountains;

There will I kiss
The bowl of bliss,
And drink mine everlasting fill
Upon every milken hill.
My soul will be adry before,
But after, it will thirst no more.

In that serene and blissful day,
　　More peaceful pilgrims I shall see,
That have cast off their rags of clay,
　　And walk apparell'd fresh like me."

But he wrote his poems, after all, rather with ships and fleets, and regiments of men and horse. At his bidding navies took their place in the channel, and even from prison he fitted out fleets with which to realize his golden dreams, and invited his companions to fresh adventures.

Raleigh might well be studied if only for the excellence of his style, for he is remarkable even in the midst of so many masters. All the distinguished writers of that period possess a greater vigor and naturalness than the more modern, and when we read a quotation from one of them in the midst of a modern author, we seem to have come suddenly upon a greener ground and greater depth and strength of soil. It is as if a green bough were laid across the page, and we are refreshed as by the sight of fresh grass in mid winter or early spring. You have constantly the warrant of life & experience in what you read. The little that is said is supplied by implication of the much that was done. The sentences are verdurous and blooming as evergreen and flowers, because they are rooted in fact and experience, but our false and florid sentences have only the tints of flowers without their sap or roots. Indeed where shall we look for standard English but to the words of a standard man? The word which is best said came very near not being spoken at all, for it is cousin to a deed which would have been better done. It must have taken the place of a deed by some urgent necessity, even by some misfortune, so that the truest writer will be some captive knight after all. And perhaps the fates had such a design, when having stored Raleigh so richly with the substance of life and experience, they made him a fast prisoner, and compelled him to make his words his deeds, and transfer to his expression the emphasis and sincerity of his action.

The necessity of labor, and conversation with many men and things, to the scholar, is rarely well remembered. Steady labor with the hands which engrosses the attention also, is the best method of removing palaver out of one's style both of talking and writing. If he has worked hard from morning till night, though he may have grieved that he could not be watching the train of his thoughts during that time, yet the few hasty lines which at evening record his day's experience will be more musical and true, than his freest but idle fancy could have furnished. He will not idly dance at his work who has wood to cut and cord before night-fall in the short days of winter, but every stroke will be husbanded and ring soberly through the wood; and so will the strokes of that scholar's pen, which at evening record the story of the day, ring soberly on the ear of the reader long after echoes of his axe have died away. The scholar may be sure he writes the tougher truth for the calluses on his palms. They give firmness to the sentence. We are often astonished by the force and precision of style to which hard working men, unpractised in writing, easily attain, when required to make the effort. As if sincerity and plainness, those ornaments of style, were better taught on the farm or in the workshop, than in the schools. The sentences written by such rude hands are nervous and tough, like hardened thongs, the sinews of the deer, or the roots of the pine. The scholar might frequently emulate the propriety and emphasis of the farmer's call to his team, and confess that if that were written it would surpass his labored sentences. Whose are the truly *labored* sentences? From the weak and flimsy periods of the politician and literary man we are glad to turn even to the description of work, the simple record of the month's labor in the farmer's almanack, to restore our tone and spirits. We like that a sentence should read as if its author, had he held a plough instead of a pen, could have drawn a furrow deep and straight to the end. The scholar requires hard labor to give an impetus to his thought; he will learn to grasp the pen firmly so, and wield it gracefully and effectually as an axe or sword. When we consider the weak and nerveless periods of some literary men, who perchance in feet and inches come up to the standard of their race, and are not deficient in girth also, we are amazed at the immense sacrifice of thews and sinews. What! these proportions, these bones, and this their work! Hands which could have felled an ox have hewed this fragile matter which would not have tasked a lady's fingers. Can this be a stalwart man's work, who has a marrow in his back, and a tendon Achilles in his heel? They who set up Stonehenge did somewhat, if they only laid out their strength for once, and stretched themselves.

Yet after all the truly efficient laborer will be found not to crowd his day with work, but saunter to his task surrounded by a wide halo of ease and leisure, and then do but what he likes best. He is anxious only about the kernels of time. Though the hen

Raleigh seems to have been too genial and loyal a soul to resist the temptations of a court; but if to his genius and culture could have been added the temperament of Geo. Fox or Oliver Cromwell, perhaps the world would have had reason longer to remember him. He was however the most generous nature that could be drawn into the precincts of a court, and carried the courtier's life almost to the highest pitch of magnanimity and grace it was capable of. He was liberal and generous, as a prince,—that is, within bounds; heroic, as a knight in armor,—but not as a defenceless man. His was not the heroism of a Luther but of a Bayard, and had more of grace than of honest truth in it. He had more taste than appetite. There may be something petty in a refined taste, —it easily degenerates into effeminacy. It does not consider the broadest use, and is not content with simple good and bad, but is often fastidious, and curious, or nice only.

His faults, as we have hinted before, were those of a courtier and a soldier. In his counsels and aphorisms we see not unfrequently the haste and rashness of the soldier strangely mingled with the wisdom of the philosopher. Though his philosophy was not wide nor profound, it was continually giving way to the generosity of his nature, and he was not hard to be won to the right.

What he touches he adorns by a greater humanity and native nobleness, but he touches not the truest nor deepest. He does not in any sense unfold the new but embellishes the old, and with all his inclination to originality, he never was quite original, or steered his own course. He was of so fair and susceptible a nature rather than broad or deep that he delayed to slake his thirst at the nearest and most turbid wells of truth and beauty, and his homage to the least fair and noble, left no room for homage to the all fair. The misfortune and incongruity of the man appear in the fact that he was at once the author of the "Maxims of State", and "The Soul's Errand."

When we reconsider what we have said in the foregoing pages, we hesitate to apply any of their eulogy to the actual and historical Raleigh, or any of their condemnation to that ideal Raleigh which he suggests, for we must know the man of history as we know our contemporaries, not so much by his deeds, which often belie his real character, as by the expectation he begets in us—and there is a bloom and halo about the character of Raleigh which defies a close and literal scrutiny, and robs us of our critical acumen. With all his heroism, he was not heroic enough; with all his manliness, he was servile and dependent; with all his aspirations, he was ambitious. He was not upright nor constant, yet we would have trusted him; he could flatter and cringe, yet we should have respected him; and he could accept a bribe, yet we should confidently have appealed to his generosity.

Such a life is useful for us to contemplate as suggesting that a man is not to be measured by the virtue of his described actions or the wisdom of his expressed thoughts merely, but by that free character he is, and is felt to be, under all circumstances. Even talent is respectable only when it indicates a depth of character unfathomed. Surely, it is better that our wisdom appear in the constant success of our spirits, than in our business or the maxims which fall from our lips merely. We want not only a revelation but a nature behind to sustain it. Many silent, as well as famous, lives have been the result of no mean thought though it was never adequately expressed nor conceived; and perhaps the most illiterate and unphilosophical mind may yet be accustomed to think to the extent of the noblest action. We all know those in our own circle who do injustice to their entire character in their conversation and in writing, but who, if actually set over against us would not fail to make a wiser impression than many a wise thinker and speaker.

We are not a little profited by any life which teaches us not to despair of the race, and such effect has the steady and cheerful bravery of Raleigh. To march sturdily through life patiently and resolutely looking defiance at one's foes, that is one way, but we cannot help being more attracted by that kind of heroism which relaxes its brows in the presence of danger, and does not need to maintain itself strictly, but by a kind of sympathy with the universe, generously adorns the scene and the occasion, and loves valor so well that itself would be the defeated party only to behold it. When we consider the vast Xerxean army of reformers in these days, we cannot doubt that many a grim soul goes silent, the hero of some small intestine war; and it is somewhat to begin to live on corn bread solely for one who has before lived on bolted wheat;—but of this sort are not the deeds to be sung. These are not the Arthurs that inflame the imaginations of men. All fair action is the product of enthusiasm, and nature herself does nothing in the prose mood. We would fain witness a heroism which is literally illustrious, whose daily life is of the stuff of which our dreams are made—so that the world shall regard less what it does than how it does it, and its actions unsettle the common standards, and have a right to be done, however wrong they may be to the moralist.

Mere gross health and cheerfulness are no slight attraction, and some biographies have this charm mainly. For the most part the best man's spirit makes a fearful sprite to haunt his grave, and it adds not a little therefore to the credit of Little John, the celebrated follower of Robin Hood, reflecting favorably on the character of his life, that his grave was "long celebrous for the yielding of excellent whetstones".

A great cheerfulness indeed have all great wits and heroes possessed, almost a prophane levity to such as understood them not, but their religion had the broader basis of health and permanence. For the hero too has his religion, though it is the very opposite to that of the ascetic. It demands not a narrower cell but a wider world. He is perhaps the very best man of the world; the poet active, the saint enterprising; not the most godlike, but the most manlike. There have been souls of a heroic stamp, for whom this world seemed expressly made; as if creation had at last succeeded, for it seems to be thrown away on the saint; and their presence enhances the beauty and ampleness of nature herself, and where they walk, as Virgil says of the abodes of the blessed,

"*Largior hic campos aether et lumine vestit*
Purpureo: Solemque suum, sua sidera norunt."

Here a more copious air invests the fields, and clothes
With purple light: And they know their own sun
and their own stars.

Thomas Carlyle and His Works.

THOMAS CARLYLE is a Scotchman, born about fifty years ago, "at Ecclefechan, Annandale," according to one authority. "His parents 'good farmer people,' his father an elder in the Secession church there, and a man of strong native sense, whose words were said to 'nail a subject to the wall.'" We also hear of his "excellent mother," still alive, and of "her fine old covenanting accents, concerting with his transcendental tones." He seems to have gone to school at Annan, on the shore of the Solway Frith, and there, as he himself writes, "heard of famed professors, of high matters classical, mathematical, a whole Wonderland of Knowledge," from Edward Irving, then a young man "fresh from Edinburgh, with college prizes, &c."—"come to see our schoolmaster, who had also been his." From this place, they say, you can look over into Wordsworth's country. Here first he may have become acquainted with Nature, with woods, such as are there, and rivers and brooks, some of whose names we have heard, and the last lapses of Atlantic billows. He got some of his education, too, more or less liberal, out of the University of Edinburgh, where, according to the same authority, he had to "support himself," partly by "private tuition, translations for the booksellers, &c.," and afterward, as we are glad to hear, "taught an academy in Dysart, at the same time that Irving was teaching in Kirkaldy," the usual middle passage of a literary life. He was destined for the church, but not by the powers that rule man's life; made his literary début in Fraser's Magazine, long ago; read here and there in English and French, with more or less profit, we may suppose, such of us at least as are not particularly informed, and at length found some words which spoke to his condition in the German language, and set himself earnestly to unravel that mystery—with what success many readers know.

After his marriage he "resided partly at Comely Bank, Edinburgh; and for a year or two at Craigenputtock, a wild and solitary farm-house in the upper part of Dumfriesshire," at which last place, amid barren heather hills, he was visited by our countryman Emerson. With Emerson he still corresponds. He was early intimate with Edward Irving, and continued to be his friend until the latter's death. Concerning this "freest, brotherliest, bravest human soul," and Carlyle's relation to him, those whom it concerns will do well to consult a notice of his death in Fraser's Magazine for 1835, reprinted in the Miscellanies. He also corresponded with Goethe. Latterly, we hear, the poet Sterling was his only intimate acquaintance in England.

He has spent the last quarter of his life in London, writing books; has the fame, as all readers know, of having made England acquainted with Germany, in late years, and done much else that is novel and remarkable in literature. He especially is the literary man of those parts. You may imagine him living in altogether a retired and simple way, with small family, in a quiet part of London, called Chelsea, a little out of the din of commerce, in "Cheyne Row," there, not far from the "Chelsea Hospital." "A little past this, and an old ivy-clad church, with its buried generations lying around it," writes one traveller, "you come to an antique street running at right angles with the Thames, and, a few steps from the river, you find Carlyle's name on the door."

"A Scotch lass ushers you into the second story front chamber, which is the spacious workshop of the world maker." Here he sits a long time together, with many books and papers about him; many new books, we have been told, on the upper shelves, un- cut, with the "author's respects" in them; in late months, with many manuscripts in an old English hand, and innumerable pamphlets, from the public libraries, relating to the Cromwellian period; now, perhaps, looking out into the street on brick and pavement, for a change, and now upon some rod of grass ground in the rear; or, perchance, he steps over to the British Museum, and makes that his studio for the time. This is the fore part of the day; that is the way with literary men commonly; and then in the afternoon, we presume, he takes a short run of a mile or so through the suburbs out into the country; we think he would run that way, though so short a trip might not take him to very sylvan or rustic places. In the meanwhile, people are calling to *see* him, from various quarters, very few worthy of being *seen* by him, "distinguished travellers from America," not a few, to all and sundry of whom he gives freely of his yet unwritten rich and flashing soliloquy, in exchange for whatever they may have to offer; speak- ing his English, as they say, with a "broad Scotch accent," talking, to their astonishment and to ours, very much as he writes, a sort of Carlylese, his dis- course "coming to its climaxes, ever and anon, in long, deep, chest-shaking bursts of laughter."

He goes to Scotland sometimes to visit his native heath-clad hills, having some interest still in the earth there; such names as Craigenputtock and Ec- clefechan, which we have already quoted, stand for habitable places there to him; or he rides to the seacoast of England in his vacations, upon his horse Yankee, bought by the sale of his books here, as we have been told.

How, after all, he gets his living; what proportion of his daily bread he earns by day-labor or job-work with his pen, what he inherits, what steals—questions whose answers are so significant, and not to be omitted in his biography—we, alas! are unable to answer here. It may be worth the while to state that he is not a Reformer, in our sense of the term, eats, drinks, and sleeps, thinks and believes, professes and practices, not according to the New England standard, nor to the Old English wholly. Nevertheless, we are told that he is a sort of lion in certain quarters there, "an amicable centre for men of the most opposite opinions," and "listened to as an oracle," "smoking his perpetual pipe."

A rather tall, gaunt figure, with intent face, dark hair and complexion, and the air of a student; not altogether well in body, from sitting too long in his workhouse, he, born in the border country and descended from moss-troopers, it may be. We have seen several pictures of him here; one, a full length portrait, with hat and overall, if it did not tell us much, told the fewest lies; another, we remember, was well said to have "too combed a look;" one other also we have seen in which we discern some features of the man we are thinking of; but the only ones worth remembering, after all, are those which he has unconsciously drawn of himself.

When we remember how these volumes came over to us, with their encouragement and provocation from month to month, and what commotion they created in many private breasts, we wonder that the country did not ring, from shore to shore, from the Atlantic to the Pacific, with its greeting; and the Boones and Crocketts of the West make haste to hail him, whose wide humanity embraces them too. Of all that the packets have brought over to us, has there been any richer cargo than this? What else has been English news for so long a season? What else, of late years, has been England to us—to us who read books, we mean? Unless we remembered it as the scene where the age of Wordsworth was spending itself, and a few younger muses were trying their wings, and from time to time, as the residence of Landor; Carlyle alone, since the death of Coleridge, has kept the promise of England. It is the best apology for all the bustle and the sin of commerce, that it has made us acquainted with the thoughts of this man. Commerce would not concern us much if it were not for such results as this. New England owes him a debt which she will be slow to recognize. His earlier essays reached us at a time when Coleridge's were the only recent words which had made any notable impression so far, and they found a field unoccupied by him, before yet any words of moment had been uttered in our midst. He had this advantage, too, in a teacher, that he stood near to his pupils; and he has no doubt afforded reasonable encouragement and sympathy to many an independent but solitary thinker. Through him, as usher, we have been latterly, in a great measure, made acquainted with what philosophy and criticism the nineteenth century had to offer—admitted, so to speak, to the privileges of the century; and what he may yet have to say, is still expected here with more interest than any thing else from that quarter.

It is remarkable, but on the whole, perhaps, not to be lamented, that the world is so unkind to a new book. Any distinguished traveller who comes to our shores, is likely to get more dinners and speeches of welcome than he can well dispose of, but the best books, if noticed at all, meet with coldness and suspicion, or, what is worse, gratuitous, off-hand criticism. It is plain that the reviewers, both here and abroad, do not know how to dispose of this man. They approach him too easily, as if he were one of the men of letters about town, who grace Mr. Some-body's administration, merely; but he already belongs to literature, and depends neither on the favor of reviewers, nor the honesty of booksellers, nor the pleasure of readers for his success. He has more to impart than to receive from his generation. He is another such a strong and finished workman in his craft as Samuel Johnson was, and like him, makes the literary class respectable. As few are yet out of their apprenticeship, or even if they learn to be able writers, are at the same time able and valuable thinkers. The aged and critical eye, especially, is in-capacitated to appreciate the works of this author. To such their meaning is impalpable and evanescent, and they seem to abound only in obstinate manner-isms, Germanisms, and whimsical ravings of all kinds, with now and then an unaccountably true and sensible remark. On the strength of this last, Carlyle is admitted to have what is called genius. We hardly know an old man to whom these volumes are not hopelessly sealed. The language, they say, is foolish-ness and a stumbling-block to them; but to many a clear-headed boy, they are plainest English, and des-patched with such hasty relish as his bread and milk. The fathers wonder how it is that the children take to this diet so readily, and digest it with so little difficulty. They shake their heads with mistrust at their free and easy delight, and remark that "Mr. Carlyle is a very learned man;" for they, too, not to be out of fashion, have got grammar and dictionary, if the truth were known, and with the best faith cudgelled their brains to get a little way into the jungle, and they could not but confess, as often as they found the clue, that it was as intricate as Blackstone to follow, if you read it honestly. But merely reading, even with the best intentions, is not enough, you must almost have written these books yourself. Only he who has had the good fortune to read them in the nick of time, in the most perceptive and recipient season of life, can give any adequate account of them.

Many have tasted of this well with an odd suspicion, as if it were some fountain Arethuse which had flowed under the sea from Germany, as if the materials of his books had lain in some garret there, in danger of being appropriated for waste paper. Over what German ocean, from what Hercynian forest, he has been imported, piece-meal, into England, or whether he has now all arrived, we are not informed. This article is not invoiced in Hamburg, nor in London. Perhaps it was contraband. However, we suspect that this sort of goods cannot be imported in this way. No matter how skillful the stevedore, all things being got into sailing trim, wait for a Sunday, and aft wind, and then weigh anchor, and run up the main-sheet—straightway what of transcendent and permanent value is there resists the aft wind, and will doggedly stay behind that Sunday—it does not travel Sundays; while biscuit and pork make headway, and sailors cry heave-yo! it must part company, if it open a seam. It is not quite safe to send out a venture in this kind, unless yourself go supercargo. Where a man goes, there he is; but the slightest virtue is immovable—it is real estate, not personal; who would keep it, must consent to be bought and sold with it.

However, we need not dwell on this charge of a German extraction, it being generally admitted, by this time, that Carlyle is English, and an inhabitant of London. He has the English for his mother tongue, though with a Scotch accent, or never so many accents, and thoughts also, which are the legitimate growth of native soil, to utter therewith. His style is eminently colloquial—and no wonder it is strange to meet with in a book. It is not literary or classical; it has not the music of poetry, nor the pomp of philosophy, but the rhythms and cadences of conversation endlessly repeated. It resounds with emphatic, natural, lively, stirring tones, muttering, rattling, exploding, like shells and shot, and with like execution. So far as it is a merit in composition, that the written answer to the spoken word, and the spoken word to a fresh and pertinent thought in the mind, as well as to the half thoughts, the tumultuary misgivings and expectancies, this author is, perhaps, not to be matched in literature. In the streets men laugh and cry, but in books, never; they "whine, put finger i' the eye, and sob" only. One would think that all books of late, had adopted the falling inflexion. "A mother, if she wishes to sing her child to sleep," say the musical men, "will always adopt the falling inflexion." Would they but choose the rising inflexion, and wake the child up for once.

He is no mystic either, more than Newton or Arkwright, or Davy—and tolerates none. Not one obscure line, or half line, did he ever write. His meaning lies plain as the daylight, and he who runs may read; indeed, only he who runs *can* read, and keep up with the meaning. It has the distinctness of picture to his mind, and he tells us only what he sees printed in largest English type upon the face of things. He utters substantial English thoughts in plainest English dialects; for it must be confessed, he speaks more than one of these. All the shires of England, and all the shires of Europe, are laid under contribution to his genius; for to be English does not mean to be exclusive and narrow, and adapt one's self to the apprehension of his nearest neighbor only. And yet no writer is more thoroughly Saxon. In the translation of those fragments of Saxon poetry, we have met with the same rhythm that occurs so often in his poem on the French Revolution. And if you would know where many of those obnoxious Carlyle-isms and Germanisms came from, read the best of Milton's prose, read those speeches of Cromwell which he has brought to light, or go and listen once more to your mother's tongue. So much for his German extraction.

Indeed, for fluency and skill in the use of the English tongue, he is a master unrivaled. His felicity and power of expression surpass even any of his special merits as a historian and critic. Therein his experience has not failed him, but furnished him with such a store of winged, aye, and legged words, as only a London life, perchance, could give account of; we had not understood the wealth of the language before. Nature is ransacked, and all the resorts and purlieus of humanity are taxed, to furnish the fittest symbol for his thought. He does not go to the dictionary, the word-book, but to the word-manufactory itself, and has made endless work for the lexicographers—yes, he has that same English for his mother-tongue, that you have, but with him it is no dumb, muttering, mumbling faculty, concealing the thoughts, but a keen, unwearied, resistless weapon. He has such command of it as neither you nor I have; and it would be well for any who have a lost horse to advertise, or a town-meeting warrant, or a sermon, or a letter to write, to study this universal letter-writer, for he knows more than the grammar or the dictionary.

The style is worth attending to, as one of the most important features of the man which we at this distance can discern. It is for once quite equal to the matter. It can carry all its load, and never breaks down nor staggers. His books are solid and work-manlike, as all that England does; and they are graceful and readable also. They tell of huge labor done, well done, and all the rubbish swept away, like the bright cutlery which glitters in shop-windows, while the coke and ashes, the turnings, filings, dust, and borings, lie far away at Birmingham, unheard of. He is a masterly clerk, scribe, reporter, and writer. He can reduce to writing most things—gestures, winks, nods, significant looks, patois, brogue, accent, pantomime, and how much that had passed for silence before, does he represent by written words. The countryman who puzzled the city lawyer, requir-ing him to write, among other things, his call to his horses, would hardly have puzzled him; he would have found a word for it, all right and classical, that would have started his team for him. Consider the ceaseless tide of speech forever flowing in countless cellars, garrets, *parlors;* that of the French, says Carlyle, "only ebbs toward the short hours of night," and what a drop in the bucket is the printed word. Feeling, thought, speech, writing, and we might add, poetry, inspiration—for so the circle is completed; how they gradually dwindle at length, passing through successive colanders, into your history and classics, from the roar of the ocean, the murmur of the forest, to the squeak of a mouse; so much only parsed and spelt out, and punctuated, at last. The few who can talk like a book, they only get reported commonly. But this writer reports a new "Lieferung."

One wonders how so much, after all, was expressed in the old way, so much here depends upon the emphasis, tone, pronunciation, style, and spirit of the reading. No writer uses so profusely all the aids to intelligibility which the printer's art affords. You wonder how others had contrived to write so many pages without emphatic or italicised words, they are so expressive, so natural, so indispensable here, as if none had ever used the demonstrative pronouns demonstratively before. In another's sentences the thought, though it may be immortal, is, as it were, embalmed, and does not *strike* you, but here it is so freshly living, even the body of it, not having passed through the ordeal of death, that it stirs in the very extremities, and the smallest particles and pronouns are all alive with it. It is not simple dictionary *it*, yours or mine, but IT. The words did not come at the command of grammar, but of a tyrannous, inexorable meaning; not like standing soldiers, by vote of parliament, but any able-bodied countryman pressed into the service, for "sire, it is not a revolt, it is a revolution."

We have never heard him speak, but we should say that Carlyle was a rare talker. He has broken the ice, and streams freely forth like a spring torrent. He does not trace back the stream of his thought, silently adventurous, up to its fountain-head, but is borne away with it, as it rushes through his brain like a torrent to overwhelm and fertilize. He holds a talk with you. His audience is such a tumultuous mob of thirty thousand, as assembled at the University of Paris, before printing was invented. Philosophy, on the other hand, does not talk, but write, or, when it comes personally before an audience, lecture or read; and therefore it must be read to-morrow, or a thousand years hence. But the talker must naturally be attended to at once; he does not talk on without an audience; the winds do not long bear the sound of his voice. Think of Carlyle reading his French Revolution to any audience. One might say it was never written, but spoken; and thereafter reported and printed, that those not within sound of his voice might know something about it. Some men read to you something which they have written, in a dead *language*, of course, but it may be in a living *letter*, in a Syriac, or Roman, or Runic character. Men must *speak* English who can *write* Sanscrit; and they must speak a modern language who write, perchance, an ancient and universal one. We do not live in those days when the learned used a learned language. There is no writing of Latin with Carlyle, but as Chaucer, with all reverence to Homer, and Virgil, and Messieurs the Normans, sung his poetry in the homely Saxon tongue,—and Locke has at least the merit of having done philosophy into English—so Carlyle has done a different philosophy still further into English, and thrown open the doors of literature and criticism to the populace.

Such a style—so diversified and variegated! It is like the face of a country; it is like a New England landscape, with farm-houses and villages, and cultivated spots, and belts of forests and blueberry-swamps round about it, with the fragrance of shad-blossoms and violets on certain winds. And as for the reading of it, it is novel enough to the reader who has used only the diligence, and old-line mail-coach. It is like travelling, sometimes on foot, sometimes in a gig tandem; sometimes in a full coach, over highways, mended and unmended, for which you will prosecute the town; on level roads, through French departments, by Simplon roads over the Alps, and now and then he hauls up for a relay, and yokes in an unbroken colt of a Pegasus for a leader, driving off by cart-paths, and across lots, by corduroy roads and gridiron bridges; and where the bridges are gone, not even a string-piece left, and the reader has to set his breast and swim. You have got an expert driver this time, who has driven ten thousand miles, and was never known to upset; can drive six in hand on the edge of a precipice, and touch the leaders anywhere with his snapper.

With wonderful art he grinds into paint for his picture all his moods and experiences, so that all his forces may be brought to the encounter. Apparently writing without a particular design or responsibility, setting down his soliloquies from time to time, taking advantage of all his humors, when at length the hour comes to declare himself, he puts down in plain English, without quotation marks, what he, Thomas Carlyle, is ready to defend in the face of the world, and fathers the rest, often quite as defensible, only more modest, or plain spoken, or insinuating, upon "Sauerteig," or some other gentleman long employed on the subject. Rolling his subject how many ways in his mind, he meets it now face to face, wrestling with it at arm's length, and striving to get it down, or throws it over his head; and if that will not do, or whether it will do or not, tries the back-stitch and side-hug with it, and downs it again—scalps it, draws and quarters it, hangs it in chains, and leaves it to the winds and dogs. With his brows knit, his mind made up, his will resolved and resistless, he advances, crashing his way through the host of weak, half-formed, *dilettante* opinions, honest and dishonest ways of thinking, with their standards raised, sentimentalities and conjectures, and tramples them all into dust. See how he prevails; you don't even hear the groans of the wounded and dying. Certainly it is not so well worth the while to look through any man's eyes at history, for the time, as through his; and his way of looking at things is fastest getting adopted by his generation.

It is not in man to determine what his style shall be. He might as well determine what his thoughts shall be. We would not have had him write always as in the chapter on Burns, and the Life of Schiller, and elsewhere. No; his thoughts were ever irregular and impetuous. Perhaps as he grows older and writes more he acquires a truer expression; it is in some respects manlier, freer, struggling up to a level with its fountain-head. We think it is the richest prose style we know of.

Who cares what a man's style is, so it is intelligible—as intelligible as his thought. Literally and really, the style is no more than the *stylus*, the pen he writes with—and it is not worth scraping and polishing, and gilding, unless it will write his thoughts the better for it. It is something for use, and not to look at. The question for us is not whether Pope had a fine style, wrote with a peacock's feather, but whether he uttered useful thoughts. Translate a book a dozen times from one language to another, and what becomes of its style? Most books would be worn out and disappear in this ordeal. The pen which wrote it is soon destroyed, but the poem survives. We believe that Carlyle has, after all, more readers, and is better known to-day for this very originality of style, and that posterity will have reason to thank him for emancipating the language, in some measure, from the fetters which a merely conservative, aimless, and pedantic literary class had imposed upon it, and setting an example of greater freedom and naturalness. No man's thoughts are new, but the style of their expression is the never failing novelty which cheers and refreshes men. If we were to answer the question, whether the mass of men, as we know them, talk as the standard authors and reviewers write, or rather as this man writes, we should say that he alone begins to write their language at all, and that the former is, for the most part, the mere effigies of a language, not the best method of concealing one's thoughts even, but frequently a method of doing without thoughts at all.

In his graphic description of Richter's style, Carlyle describes his own pretty nearly; and no doubt he first got his own tongue loosened at that fountain, and was inspired by it to equal freedom and originality. "The language," as he says of Richter, "groans with indescribable metaphors and allusions to all things, human and divine, flowing onward, not like a river, but like an inundation; circling in complex eddies, chafing and gurgling, now this way, now that;" but in Carlyle, "the proper current" never "sinks out of sight amid the boundless uproar." Again: "His very language is Titanian—deep, strong, tumultuous, shining with a thousand hues, fused from a thousand elements, and winding in labyrinthic mazes."

In short, if it is desirable that a man be eloquent, that he talk much, and address himself to his own age mainly, then this is not a bad style of doing it. But if it is desired rather that he pioneer into unexplored regions of thought, and speak to silent centuries to come, then, indeed, we could wish that he had cultivated the style of Goethe more, that of Richter less; not that Goethe's is the kind of utterance most to be prized by mankind, but it will serve

for a model of the best that can be successfully cultivated.

But for style, and fine writing, and Augustan ages
—that is but a poor style, and vulgar writing, and a
degenerate age, which allows us to remember these
things. This man has something to communicate.
Carlyle's are not, in the common sense, works of art
in their origin and aim; and yet, perhaps, no living
English writer evinces an equal literary talent. They
are such works of art only as the plough, and corn-
mill, and steam-engine—not as pictures and statues.
Others speak with greater emphasis to scholars, as
such, but none so earnestly and effectually to all who
can read. Others give their advice, he gives his
sympathy also. It is no small praise that he does not
take upon himself the airs, has none of the whims,
none of the pride, the nice vulgarities, the starched,
impoverished isolation, and cold glitter of the spoiled
children of genius. He does not need to husband his
pearl, but excels by a greater humanity and sincerity.

He is singularly serious and untrivial. We are
every where impressed by the rugged, unwearied,
and rich sincerity of the man. We are sure that he
never sacrificed one jot of his honest thought to art
or whim, but to utter himself in the most direct and
effectual way, that is the endeavor. These are merits
which will wear well. When time has worn deeper
into the substance of these books, this grain will
appear. No such sermons have come to us here out
of England, in late years, as those of this preacher;
sermons to kings, and sermons to peasants, and
sermons to all intermediate classes. It is in vain that
John Bull, or any of his cousins, turns a deaf ear, and
pretends not to hear them, nature will not soon be
weary of repeating them. There are words less ob-

viously true, more for the ages to hear, perhaps, but none so impossible for this age not to hear. What a cutting cimiter was that "Past and Present," going through heaps of silken stuffs, and glibly through the necks of men, too, without their knowing it, leaving no trace. He has the earnestness of a prophet. In an age of pedantry and dilettantism, he has no grain of these in his composition. There is no where else, surely, in recent readable English, or other books, such direct and effectual teaching, reproving, encouraging, stimulating, earnestly, vehemently, almost like Mahomet, like Luther; not looking behind him to see how his *Opera Omnia* will look, but forward to other work to be done. His writings are a gospel to the young of this generation; they will hear his manly, brotherly speech with responsive joy, and press forward to older or newer gospels.

We should omit a main attraction in these books, if we said nothing of their humor. Of this indispensable pledge of sanity, without some leaven of which the abstruse thinker may justly be suspected of mysticism, fanaticism, or insanity, there is a superabundance in Carlyle. Especially the transcendental philosophy needs the leaven of humor to render it light and digestible. In his later and longer works it is an unfailing accompaniment, reverberating through pages and chapters, long sustained without effort. The very punctuation, the italics, the quotation marks, the blank spaces and dashes, and the capitals, each and all are pressed into its service.

Every man, of course, has his fane, from which even the most innocent conscious humor is excluded; but in proportion as the writer's position is high above his fellows, the range of his humor is extended. To the thinker, all the institutions of men, as all imperfection, viewed from the point of equanimity, are legitimate subjects of humor. Whatever is not necessary, no matter how sad or personal, or universal a grievance, is, indeed, a jest more or less sublime.

Carlyle's humor is vigorous and Titanic, and has more sense in it than the sober philosophy of many another. It is not to be disposed of by laughter and smiles merely; it gets to be too serious for that—only they may laugh who are not hit by it. For those who love a merry jest, this is a strange kind of fun—rather too practical joking, if they understand it. The pleasant humor which the public loves, is but the innocent pranks of the ball-room, harmless flow of animal spirits, the light plushy pressure of dandy pumps, in comparison. But when an elephant takes to treading on your corns, why then you are lucky if you sit high, or wear cowhide. His humor is always subordinate to a serious purpose, though often the real charm for the reader, is not so much in the essential progress and final upshot of the chapter, as in this indirect side-light illustration of every hue. He sketches first with strong, practical English pencil, the essential features in outline, black on white, more faithfully than Dryasdust would have done, telling us wisely whom and what to mark, to save time, and then with brush of camel's hair, or sometimes with more expeditious swab, he lays on the bright and fast colors of his humor everywhere. One piece of solid work, be it known, we have determined to do, about which let there be no jesting, but all things else under the heavens, to the right and left of that, are for the time fair game. To us this humor is not wearisome, as almost every other is. Rabelais, for instance, is intolerable; one chapter is better than a volume—it may be sport to him, but it is death to us. A mere humorist, indeed, is a most unhappy man; and his readers are most unhappy also.

Humor is not so distinct a quality as for the purposes of criticism, it is commonly regarded, but allied to every, even the divinest faculty. The familiar and cheerful conversation about every hearth-side, if it be analyzed, will be found to be sweetened by this principle. There is not only a never-failing, pleasant, and earnest humor kept up there, embracing the domestic affairs, the dinner, and the scolding, but there is also a constant run upon the neighbors, and upon church and state, and to cherish and maintain this, in a great measure, the fire is kept burning, and the dinner provided. There will be neighbors, parties to a very genuine, even romantic friendship, whose whole audible salutation and intercourse, abstaining from the usual cordial expressions, grasping of hands, or affectionate farewells, consists in the mutual play and interchange of a genial and healthy humor, which excepts nothing, not even themselves, in its lawless range. The child plays continually, if you will let it, and all its life is a sort of practical humor of a very pure kind, often of so fine and ethereal a nature, that its parents, its uncles and cousins, can in no wise participate in it, but must stand aloof in silent admiration, and reverence even. The more quiet the more profound it is. Even nature is observed to have her playful moods or aspects, of which man seems sometimes to be the sport.

But, after all, we could sometimes dispense with the humor, though unquestionably incorporated in the blood, if it were replaced by this author's gravity. We should not apply to himself, without qualification, his remarks on the humor of Richter. With more repose in his inmost being, his humor would become more thoroughly genial and placid. Humor is apt to imply but a half satisfaction at best. In his pleasantest and most genial hour, man smiles but as the globe smiles, and the works of nature. The fruits *dry* ripe, and much as we relish some of them in their green and pulpy state, we lay up for our winter store, not out of these, but the rustling autumnal harvests. Though we never weary of this vivacious wit, while we are perusing its work, yet when we remember it from afar, we sometimes feel balked and disappointed, missing the security, the simplicity, and frankness, even the occasional magnanimity of acknowledged dullness and bungling. This never-failing success and brilliant talent become a reproach. To the most practical reader the humor is certainly too obvious and constant a quality. When we are to have dealings with a man, we prize the good faith and valor of soberness and gravity. There is always a more impressive statement than consists with these victorious comparisons. Besides, humor does not wear well. It is commonly enough said, that a joke will not bear repeating. The deepest humor will not keep. Humors do not circulate but stagnate, or circulate partially. In the oldest literature, in the Hebrew, the Hindoo, the Persian, the Chinese, it is rarely humor, even the most divine, which still survives, but the most sober and private, painful or joyous thoughts, maxims of duty, to which the life of all men may be referred. After time has sifted the literature of a people, there is left only their SCRIPTURE, for that is WRITING, *par excellence*. This is as true of the poets, as of the philosophers and moralists by profession; for what subsides in any of these is the moral only, to re-appear as dry land at some remote epoch.

We confess that Carlyle's humor is rich, deep, and variegated, in direct communication with the back bone and risible muscles of the globe—and there is nothing like it; but much as we relish this jovial, this rapid and delugeous way of conveying one's views and impressions, when we would not converse but meditate, we pray for a man's diamond edition of his thought, without the colored illuminations in the margin—the fishes and dragons, and unicorns, the red or the blue ink, but its initial letter in distinct skeleton type, and the whole so clipped and condensed down to the very essence of it, that time will have little to do. We know not but we shall immigrate soon, and would fain take with us all the treasures of the east, and all kinds of *dry*, portable soups, in small tin canisters, which contain whole herds of English beeves, boiled down, will be acceptable.

The difference between this flashing, fitful writing and pure philosophy, is the difference between flame and light. The flame, indeed, yields light, but when we are so near as to observe the flame, we are apt to be incommoded by the heat and smoke. But the sun, that old Platonist, is set so far off in the heavens, that only a genial summer-heat and ineffable day-light can reach us. But many a time, we confess, in wintery weather, we have been glad to forsake the sun-light, and warm us by these Promethean flames.

Carlyle must undoubtedly plead guilty to the charge of mannerism. He not only has his vein, but his peculiar manner of working it. He has a style which can be imitated, and sometimes is an imitator of himself. Every man, though born and bred in the metropolis of the world, will still have some provincialism adhering to him; but in proportion as his aim is simple and earnest, he approaches at once the most ancient and the most modern men. There is no mannerism in the Scriptures. The style of proverbs, and indeed of all *maxims*, whether measured by sentences or by chapters, if they may be said to have any style, is one, and as the expression of one voice, merely an account of the matter by the latest witness. It is one advantage enjoyed by men of science, that they use only formulas which are universal. The common language and the common sense of mankind, it is most uncommon to meet with in the individual. Yet liberty of thought and speech is only liberty to think the universal thought, and speak the universal language of men, instead of being enslaved to a particular mode. Of this universal speech there is very little. It is equable and sure; from a depth within man which is beyond education and prejudice.

Certainly, no critic has anywhere said what is more to the purpose, than this which Carlyle's own writings furnish, which we quote, as well for its intrinsic merit as for its pertinence here. "It is true," says he, thinking of Richter, "the beaten paths of literature lead the safeliest to the goal; and the talent pleases us most, which submits to shine with new gracefulness through old forms. Nor is the noblest and most peculiar mind too noble or peculiar for working by prescribed laws; Sophocles, Shakspeare, Cervantes, and in Richter's own age, Goethe, how little did they innovate on the given forms of composition, how much in the spirit they breathed into them! All this is true; and Richter must lose of our esteem in proportion." And again, in the chapter on Goethe, "We read Goethe for years before we come to see wherein the distinguishing peculiarity of his understanding, of his disposition, even of his way of writing, consists! It seems quite a simple style, [that of his?] remarkable chiefly for its calmness, its perspicuity, in short, its commonness; and yet it is the most uncommon of all styles." And this, too, translated for us by the same pen from Schiller, which we will apply not merely to the outward form of his works, but to their inner form and substance. He is speaking of the artist. "Let some beneficent divinity snatch him, when a suckling, from the breast of his mother, and nurse him with the milk of a better time, that he may ripen to his full stature beneath a distant Grecian sky. And having grown to manhood, let him return, a foreign shape, into his century; not, however, to delight it by his presence, but, dreadful, like the son of Agamemnon, to purify it. The matter of his works he will take from the present, but their form he will derive from a nobler time; nay, from beyond all time, from the absolute unchanging unity of his own nature."

But enough of this. Our complaint is already out of all proportion to our discontent.

Carlyle's works, it is true, have not the stereotyped success which we call classic. They are a rich but inexpensive entertainment, at which we are not concerned lest the host has strained or impoverished himself to feed his guests. It is not the most lasting word, nor the loftiest wisdom, but rather the word which comes last. For his genius it was reserved to give expression to the thoughts which were throbbing in a million breasts. He has plucked the ripest fruit in the public garden; but this fruit already least concerned the tree that bore it, which was rather perfecting the bud at the foot of the leaf stalk. His works are not to be studied, but read with a swift satisfaction. Their flavor and gust is like what poets tell of the froth of wine, which can only be tasted once and hastily. On a review we can never find the pages we had read. The first impression is the truest and the deepest, and there is no reprint, no *double entendre*, so to speak, for the alert reader. Yet they are in some degree true natural products in this respect. All things are but once, and never repeated. The first faint blushes of the morning, gilding the mountain tops, the pale phosphor and saffron-colored clouds do verily transport us to the morning of creation; but what avails it to travel eastward, or look again there an hour hence? We should be as far in the day ourselves, mounting toward our meridian. These works were designed for such complete success that they serve but for a single occasion. It is the luxury of art, when its own instrument is manufactured for each particular and present use. The knife which slices the bread of Jove ceases to be a knife when this service is rendered.

But he is wilfully and pertinaciously unjust, even scurrilous, impolite, ungentlemanly; calls us "Imbeciles," "Dilettantes," "Philistines," implying sometimes what would not sound well expressed. If he would adopt the newspaper style, and take back these hard names—but where is the reader who does not derive some benefit from these epithets, applying them to himself? Think not that with each repetition of them there is a fresh overflowing of bile; oh no! Perhaps none at all after the first time, only a faithfulness, the right name being found, to apply it—"They are the same ones we meant before"—and ofttimes with a genuine sympathy and encouragement expressed. Indeed, there appears in all his writings a hearty and manly sympathy with all misfortune and wretchedness, and not a weak and sniveling one. They who suspect a Mephistophiles, or sneering, satirical devil, under all, have not learned the secret of true humor, which sympathizes with the gods themselves, in view of their grotesque, half-finished creatures.

He is, in fact, the best tempered, and not the least impartial of reviewers. He goes out of his way to do justice to profligates and quacks. There is somewhat even Christian, in the rarest and most peculiar sense, in his universal brotherliness, his simple, child-like endurance, and earnest, honest endeavor, with sympathy for the like. And this fact is not insignificant, that he is almost the only writer of biography, of the lives of men, in modern times. So kind and generous a tribute to the genius of Burns cannot be expected again, and is not needed. We honor him for his noble reverence for Luther, and his patient, almost reverent study of Goethe's genius, anxious that no shadow of his author's meaning escape him for want of trustful attention. There is nowhere else, surely, such determined and generous love of whatever is manly in history. His just appreciation of any, even inferior talent, especially of all sincerity, under whatever guise, and all true men of endeavor, must have impressed every reader. Witness the chapters on Werner, Heyne, even Cagliostro, and others. He is not likely to underrate his man. We are surprised to meet with such a discriminator of kingly qualities in these republican and democratic days, such genuine loyalty all thrown away upon the world.

Carlyle, to adopt his own classification, is himself the hero, as literary man. There is no more notable working-man in England, in Manchester or Birmingham, or the mines round about. We know not how many hours a-day he toils, nor for what wages, exactly, we only know the results for us. We hear through the London fog and smoke the steady systole, diastole, and vibratory hum, from "Somebody's Works" there; the "Print Works," say some; the "Chemicals," say others; where something, at any rate, is manufactured which we remember to have seen in the market. This is the place, then. Literature has come to mean, to the ears of laboring men, something idle, something cunning and pretty merely, be-

cause the nine hundred and ninety-nine really write
for fame or for amusement. But as the laborer works,
and soberly by the sweat of his brow earns bread for
his body, so this man *works* anxiously and *sadly*, to
get bread of life, and dispense it. We cannot do better
than quote his own estimate of labor from Sartor
Resartus.

"Two men I honor, and no third. First; the toil-
worn craftsman that with earth-made implement la-
boriously conquers the earth, and makes her man's.
Venerable to me is the hard hand; crooked, coarse,
wherein, notwithstanding, lies a cunning virtue, in-
defeasibly royal, as of the sceptre of this planet.
Venerable, too, is the rugged face, all weather-tanned,
besoiled, with its rude intelligence; for it is the face
of a man living manlike. Oh, but the more venerable
for thy rudeness, and even because we must pity as
well as love thee. Hardly-entreated brother! For us
was thy back so bent, for us were thy straight limbs
and fingers so deformed; thou wert our conscript, on
whom the lot fell, and fighting our battles wert so
marred. For in thee, too, lay a god-created form, but
it was not to be unfolded; encrusted must it stand
with the thick adhesions and defacements of labor;
and thy body, like thy soul, was not to know freedom.
Yet toil on, toil on; *thou* art in thy duty, be out of it
who may; thou toilest for the altogether indispensable, for daily bread."

"A second man I honor, and still more highly; him
who is seen toiling for the spiritually indispensable;
not daily bread, but the bread of life. Is not he, too,
in his duty, endeavoring toward inward harmony, revealing this, by act or by word, through all his outward endeavors, be they high or low? Highest of all,
when his outward and his inward endeavor are one;
when we can name him Artist; not earthly crafts-

man only, but inspired thinker, that with heaven-made implement conquers heaven for us. If the poor and humble toil that we have food, must not the high and glorious toil for him in return, that he have light, have guidance, freedom, immortality? These two in all their degrees, I honor; all else is chaff and dust, which let the wind blow whither it listeth."

"Unspeakably touching is it, however, when I find both dignities united; and he that must toil outwardly for the lowest of man's wants, is also toiling inwardly for the highest. Sublimer in this world know I nothing than a peasant saint, could such now anywhere be met with. Such a one will take thee back to Nazareth itself; thou wilt see the splendor of heaven spring forth from the humblest depths of earth, like a light shining in great darkness."

Notwithstanding the very genuine, admirable, and loyal tributes to Burns, Schiller, Goethe, and others, Carlyle is not a critic of poetry. In the book of heroes, Shakspeare, the hero, as poet, comes off rather slimly. His sympathy, as we said, is with the men of endeavor; not using the life got, but still bravely getting their life. "In fact," as he says of Cromwell, "every where we have to notice the decisive, practical *eye* of this man; how he drives toward the practical and practicable; has a genuine insight into what *is* fact." You must have very stout legs to get noticed at all by him. He is thoroughly English in his love of practical men, and dislike for cant, and ardent enthusiastic heads that are not supported by any legs. He would kindly knock them down that they may regain some vigor by touching their mother earth. We have often wondered how he ever found out Burns, and must still refer a good share of his delight in him to neighborhood and early association.

The Lycidas and Comus appearing in Blackwood's Magazine, would probably go unread by him, nor lead him to expect a Paradise Lost. The condition of England question is a practical one. The condition of England demands a hero, not a poet. Other things demand a poet; the poet answers other demands. Carlyle in London, with this question pressing on him so urgently, sees no occasion for minstrels and rhapsodists there. Kings may have their bards when there are any kings. Homer would *certainly* go a begging there. He lives in Chelsea, not on the plains of Hindostan, nor on the prairies of the West, where settlers are scarce, and a man must at least go *whistling* to himself.

What he says of poetry is rapidly uttered, and suggestive of a thought, rather than the deliberate development of any. He answers your question, What is poetry? by writing a special poem, as that Norse one, for instance, in the Book of Heroes, altogether wild and original;—answers your question, What is light? by kindling a blaze which dazzles you, and pales sun and moon, and not as a peasant might, by opening a shutter. And, certainly, you would say that this question never could be answered but by the grandest of poems; yet he has not dull breath and stupidity enough, perhaps, to give the most deliberate and universal answer, such as the fates wring from illiterate and unthinking men. He answers like Thor, with a stroke of his hammer, whose dint makes a valley in the earth's surface.

Carlyle is not a *seer*, but a brave looker-on and *reviewer;* not the most free and catholic observer of men and events, for they are likely to find him preoccupied, but unexpectedly free and catholic when they fall within the focus of his lens. He does not live in the present hour, and read men and books as they occur for his theme, but having chosen this, he directs his studies to this end.

But if he supplies us with arguments and illustrations against himself, we will remember that we may perhaps be convicted of error from the same source—stalking on these lofty reviewer's stilts so far from the green pasturage around. If we look again at his page, we are apt to retract somewhat that we have said. Often a genuine poetic feeling dawns through it, like the texture of the earth seen through the dead grass and leaves in the spring. There is indeed more poetry in this author than criticism on poetry. He often reminds us of the ancient Scald, inspired by the grimmer features of life, dwelling longer on Dante than on Shakspeare. We have not recently met with a more solid and unquestionable piece of poetic work than that episode of "The Ancient Monk," in Past and Present, at once idyllic, narrative, heroic; a beautiful restoration of a past age. There is nothing like it elsewhere that we know of. The History of the French Revolution is a poem, at length got translated into prose; an Iliad, indeed, as he himself has it—"The destructive wrath of Sansculottism: this is what we speak, having unhappily no voice for singing."

One improvement we could suggest in this last, as indeed in most epics, that he should let in the sun oftener upon his picture. It does not often enough appear, but it is all revolution, the old way of human life turned simply bottom upward, so that when at length we are inadvertently reminded of the "Brest Shipping," a St. Domingo colony, and that anybody thinks of owning plantations, and simply turning up the soil there, and that now at length, after some years of this revolution, there is a falling off in the importation of sugar, we feel a queer surprise. Had they not sweetened their water with Revolution then? It would be well if there were several chapters headed "Work for the Month"—Revolution-work inclusive, of course—"Altitude of the Sun," "State of the Crops and Markets," "Meteorological Observations," "Attractive Industry," "Day Labor," &c., just to remind the reader that the French peasantry did something beside go without breeches, burn châteaus, get ready knotted cords, and embrace and throttle one another by turns. These things are sometimes hinted at, but they deserve a notice more in proportion to their importance. We want not only a background to the picture, but a ground under the feet also. We remark, too, occasionally, an unphilosophical habit, common enough elsewhere, in Alison's History of Modern Europe, for instance, of saying, undoubtedly with effect, that if a straw had not fallen this way or that, why then—but, of course, it is as easy in philosophy to make kingdoms rise and fall as straws. The old adage is as true for our purpose, which says that a miss is as good as a mile. Who shall say how near the man came to being killed who was not killed? If an apple had not fallen then we had never heard of Newton and the law of gravitation; as if they could not have contrived to let fall a pear as well.

The poet is blithe and cheery ever, and as well as nature. Carlyle has not the simple Homeric health of Wordsworth, nor the deliberate philosophic turn of Coleridge, nor the scholastic taste of Landor, but, though sick and under restraint, the constitutional vigor of one of his old Norse heroes, struggling in a lurid light, with Jötuns still, striving to throw the old woman, and "she was Time"—striving to lift the big cat—and that was "The Great World-Serpent, which, tail in mouth, girds and keeps up the whole created world." The smith, though so brawny and tough, I should not call the healthiest man. There is too much shop-work, too great extremes of heat and cold, and incessant ten-pound-ten and thrashing of the anvil, in his life. But the haymaker's is a true sunny perspiration, produced by the extreme of summer heat only, and conversant with the blast of the zephyr, not of the forge-bellows. We know very well the nature of this man's sadness, but we do not know the nature of his gladness. There sits Bull in the court all the year round, with his hoarse bark and discontented growl—not a cross dog, only a canine habit, verging to madness some think—now separated from the shuddering travellers only by the paling, now heard afar in the horizon, even melodious there; baying the moon o' nights, *baying the sun by day*, with his mastiff mouth. He never goes after the cows, nor stretches in the sun, nor plays with the children. Pray give him a longer rope, ye gods, or let him go at large, and never taste raw meat more.

The poet will maintain serenity in spite of all disappointments. He is expected to preserve an unconcerned and healthy outlook over the world while he lives. *Philosophia practica est eruditionis meta*, philosophy practiced is the goal of learning; and for that other, *Oratoris est celare artem*, we might read, *Herois est celare pugnam*, the hero will conceal his struggles. Poetry is the only life got, the only work done, the only pure product and free labor of man, performed only when he has put all the world under his feet, and conquered the last of his foes.

Carlyle speaks of Nature with a certain unconscious pathos for the most part. She is to him a receded but ever memorable splendor, casting still a reflected light over all his scenery. As we read his books here in New England, where there are potatoes enough, and every man can get his living peacefully and sportively as the birds and bees, and need think no more of that, it seems to us as if by the world he often meant London, at the head of the tide upon the Thames, the sorest place on the face of the earth, the very citadel of conservatism. Possibly a South African village might have furnished a more hopeful, and more exacting audience, or in the silence of the wilderness and the desert, he might have addressed himself more entirely to his true audience posterity.

In his writings, we should say that he, as conspicuously as any, though with little enough expressed or even conscious sympathy, represents the Reformer class, and all the better for not being the acknowledged leader of any. In him the universal plaint is most settled, unappeasable and serious. Until a thousand named and nameless grievances are righted, there will be no repose for him in the lap of nature, or the seclusion of science and literature. By foreseeing it he hastens the crisis in the affairs of England, and is as good as many years added to her history.

As we said, we have no adequate word from him concerning poets—Homer, Shakspeare; nor more, we might add, of Saints—Jesus; nor philosophers—Socrates, Plato; nor mystics—Swedenborg. He has no articulate sympathy at least with such as these as yet. Odin, Mahomet, Cromwell, will have justice at his hands, and we would leave him to write the eulogies of all the giants of the will, but the kings of men, whose kingdoms are wholly in the hearts of their subjects, strictly transcendent and moral greatness, what is highest and worthiest in character, he is not inclined to dwell upon or point to. To do himself justice, and set some of his readers right, he should give us some transcendent hero at length, to rule his demigods and Titans; develop, perhaps, his reserved and dumb reverence for Christ, not speaking to a London or Church of England audience merely. Let *not* "sacred silence meditate that sacred matter" forever, but let us have sacred speech and sacred scripture thereon. True reverence is not necessarily dumb, but ofttimes prattling and hilarious as children in the spring.

Every man will include in his list of worthies those whom he himself best represents. Carlyle, and our countryman Emerson, whose place and influence must ere long obtain a more distinct recognition, are, to a certain extent, the complement of each other. The age could not do with one of them, it cannot do with both. To make a broad and rude distinction, to suit our present purpose, the former, as critic, deals with the men of action—Mahomet, Luther, Cromwell; the latter with the thinkers—Plato, Shakspeare, Goethe, for though both have written upon Goethe, they do not meet in him. The one has more sympathy with the heroes, or practical reformers, the other with the observers, or philosophers. Put these worthies together, and you will have a pretty fair representation of mankind; yet with one or more memorable exceptions. To say nothing of Christ, who yet awaits a just appreciation from literature, the peacefully practical hero, whom Columbus may represent, is obviously slighted; but above and after all, the Man of the Age, come to be called working-man, it is obvious that none yet speaks to his condition, for the speaker is not yet in his condition. There is poetry and prophecy to cheer him, and advice of the head and heart to the hands; but no very memorable coöperation, it must be confessed, since the Christian era, or rather since Prometheus tried it. It is even a note-worthy fact, that a man addresses effectually in another only himself still, and what he himself does and is, alone can he prompt the other to do and to become. Like speaks to like only; labor to labor, philosophy to philosophy, criticism to criticism, poetry to poetry, &c. Literature speaks how much still to the past, how little to the future, how much to the east, how little to the west—

> In the East fames are won,
> In the West deeds are done.

One more merit in Carlyle, let the subject be what it may, is the freedom of prospect he allows, the entire absence of cant and dogma. He removes many cart-loads of rubbish, and leaves open a broad highway. His writings are all unfenced on the side of the future and the possible. He does not place himself across the passage out of his books, so that none may go freely out, but rather by the entrance, inviting all to come in and go through. No gins, no net-work, no pickets here, to restrain the free thinking reader. In many books called philosophical, we find ourselves running hither and thither, under and through, and sometimes quite unconsciously straddling some imaginary fence-work, which in our clairvoyance we had not noticed, but fortunately, not with such fatal consequences as happen to those birds which fly against a white-washed wall, mistaking it for fluid air. As we proceed the wreck of this dogmatic tissue collects about the organs of our perception, like cobwebs about the muzzles of hunting dogs in dewy mornings. If we look up with such eyes as these authors furnish, we see no heavens, but a low pent-roof of straw or tiles, as if we stood under a shed, with no sky-light through which to glimpse the blue.

Carlyle, though he does but inadvertently direct our eyes to the open heavens, nevertheless, lets us wander broadly underneath, and shows them to us reflected in innumerable pools and lakes. We have from him, occasionally, some hints of a possible science of astronomy even, and revelation of heavenly arcana, but nothing definite hitherto.

These volumes contain not the highest, but a very practicable wisdom, which startles and provokes, rather than informs us. Carlyle does not oblige us to think; we have thought enough for him already, but he compels us to act. We accompany him rapidly through an endless gallery of pictures, and glorious reminiscences of experiences unimproved. "Have you not had Moses and the prophets? Neither will ye be persuaded if one should rise from the dead." There is no calm philosophy of life here, such as you might put at the end of the Almanac, to hang over the farmer's hearth, how men shall live in these winter, in these summer days. No philosophy, properly speaking, of love, or friendship, or religion, or politics, or education, or nature, or spirit; perhaps a nearer approach to a philosophy of kingship, and of the place of the literary man, than of any thing else. A rare preacher, with prayer, and psalm, and sermon, and benediction, but no contemplation of man's life from serene oriental ground, nor yet from the stirring occidental. No thanksgiving sermon for the holydays, or the Easter vacations, when all men submit to float on the full currents of life. When we see with what spirits, though with little heroism enough, wood-choppers, drovers, and apprentices, take and spend life, playing all day long, sunning themselves, shading themselves, eating, drinking, sleeping, we think that the philosophy of their life written would be such a level natural history as the Gardener's Calendar, and the works of the early botanists, inconceivably slow to come to practical conclusions; its premises away off before the first morning light, ere the heather was introduced into the British isles, and no inferences to be drawn during this noon of the day, not till after the remote evening shadows have begun to fall around.

There is no philosophy here for philosophers, only as every man is said to have his philosophy. No system but such as is the man himself; and, indeed, he stands compactly enough. No progress beyond the first assertion and challenge, as it were, with trumpet blast. One thing is certain, that we had best be doing something in good earnest, henceforth forever; that's an indispensable philosophy. The before impossible precept, *"know thyself,"* he translates into the partially possible one, *"know what thou canst work at."* Sartor Resartus is, perhaps, the sunniest and most philosophical, as it is the most autobiographical of his works, in which he drew most largely on the experience of his youth. But we miss everywhere a calm depth, like a lake, even stagnant, and must submit to rapidity and whirl, as on skates, with all kinds of skillful and antic motions, sculling, sliding, cutting punch-bowls and rings, forward and backward. The talent is very nearly equal to the genius. Sometimes it would be preferable to wade slowly through a Serbonian bog, and feel the juices of the meadow. We should say that he had not speculated far, but faithfully, living up to it. He lays all the stress still on the most elementary and initiatory maxims, introductory to philosophy. It is the experience of the religionist. He pauses at such a quotation as, "It is only with renunciation that life, properly speaking, can be said to begin;" or, "Doubt of any sort cannot be removed except by action;" or, "Do the duty which lies nearest thee." The chapters entitled, "The Everlasting No," and "The Everlasting Yea," contain what you might call the religious experience of his hero. In the latter,

he assigns to him these words, brief, but as significant as any we remember in this author:—"One BIBLE
I know, of whose plenary inspiration doubt is not so
much as possible; nay, with my own eyes I saw the
God's-hand writing it: thereof all other Bibles are but
leaves." This belongs to "The Everlasting Yea;" yet
he lingers unaccountably in "The Everlasting No,"
under the negative pole. "Truth!" he still cries with
Teufelsdröckh, "though the heavens crush me for
following her: no falsehood! though a whole celestial
Lubberland were the price of apostacy." Again, "Living without God in the world, of God's light I was
not utterly bereft; if my as yet sealed eyes, with their
unspeakable longing, could nowhere see Him, nevertheless, in my heart He was present, and His heaven-
written law still stood legible and sacred there." Again,
"Ever from that time, [*the era of his Protest*,] the
temper of my misery was changed: not fear or whin-
ing sorrow was it, but indignation and grim, fire-eyed
defiance." And in the "Centre of Indifference," as editor, he observes, that "it was no longer a quite hope-
less unrest," and then proceeds, not in his best style,
"For the fire-baptized soul, long so scathed and thun-
der-riven, here feels its own freedom, which feeling
is its Baphometic Baptism: the citadel of its whole
kingdom it has thus gained by assault, and will keep
inexpugnable; outward from which the remaining
dominions, not, indeed, without hard battling, will
doubtless by degrees be conquered and pacificated."

Beside some philosophers of larger vision, Carlyle
stands like an honest, half-despairing boy, grasping
at some details only of their world systems. Philosophy, certainly, is some account of truths, the fragments and very insignificant parts of which man will
practice in this work-shop; truths infinite and in harmony with infinity; in respect to which the very ob-

experience, but in some nook or corner of his works, you will find that this, too, was sometimes dreamed of in his philosophy.

To sum up our most serious objections, in a few words, we should say that Carlyle indicates a depth, —and we mean not impliedly, but distinctly,—which he neglects to fathom. We want to know more about that which he wants to know as well. If any luminous star, or undissolvable nebula, is visible from his station, which is not visible from ours, the interests of science require that the fact be communicated to us. The universe expects every man to do his duty in his parallel of latitude. We want to hear more of his inmost life; his hymn and prayer, more; his elegy and eulogy, less; that he should speak more from his character, and less from his talent; communicate centrally with his readers, and not by a side; that he should say what he believes, without suspecting that men disbelieve it, out of his never-misunderstood nature. Homer and Shakspeare speak directly and confidently to us. The confidence implied in the unsuspicious tone of the world's worthies, is a great and encouraging fact. Dig up some of the earth you stand on, and show that. If he gave us religiously the meagre results of his experience, his style would be less picturesque and diversified, but more attractive and impressive. His genius can cover all the land with gorgeous palaces, but the reader does not abide in them, but pitches his tent rather in the desert and on the mountain peak.

When we look about for something to quote, as the fairest specimen of the man, we confess that we labor under an unusual difficulty; for his philosophy is so little of the proverbial or sentential kind, and opens so gradually, rising insensibly from the reviewer's level, and developing its thought completely and in detail, that we look in vain for the brilliant passages, for point and antithesis, and must end by quoting his works entire. What in a writer of less breadth would have been the proposition which would have bounded his discourse, his column of victory, his Pillar of Hercules, and *ne plus ultra*, is in Carlyle frequently the same thought unfolded; no Pillar of Hercules, but a considerable prospect, north and south, along the Atlantic coast. There are other pillars of Hercules, like beacons and light-houses, still further in the horizon, toward Atlantis, set up by a few ancient and modern travellers; but, so far as this traveller goes, he clears and colonizes, and all the surplus population of London is bound thither at once. What we would quote is, in fact, his vivacity, and not any particular wisdom or sense, which last is ever synonymous with sentence, [*sententia*,] as in his cotemporaries, Coleridge, Landor and Wordsworth.

We have not attempted to discriminate between his works, but have rather regarded them all as one work, as is the man himself. We have not examined so much as remembered them. To do otherwise, would have required a more indifferent, and perhaps even less just review, than the present. The several chapters were thankfully received, as they came out, and now we find it impossible to say which was best; perhaps each was best in its turn. They do not require to be remembered by chapters—that is a merit—but are rather remembered as a well-known strain, reviving from time to time, when it had nearly died away, and always inspiring us to worthier and more persistent endeavors.

In his last work, "The Letters and Speeches of Oliver Cromwell," Carlyle has added a chapter to the history of England; has actually written a chapter of her history, and, in comparison with this, there seems to be no other,—this, and the thirty thousand or three hundred thousand pamphlets in the British Museum, and that is all. This book is a practical comment on Universal History. What if there were a British Museum in Athens and Babylon, and nameless cities! It throws light on the history of the Iliad and the labors of Pisistratus. History is, then, an account of memorable events that have sometime transpired, and not an incredible and confused fable, quarters for scholars merely, or a gymnasium for poets and orators. We may say that he has dug up a hero, who was buried alive in his battle-field, hauled him out of his cairn, on which every passer had cast a pamphlet. We had heard of their digging up Arthurs before to be sure they were there; and, to be sure they were there, their bones, seven feet of them; but they had to bury them again. Others have helped to make known Shakspeare, Milton, Herbert, to give a name to such treasures as we all possessed; but, in this instance, not only a lost character has been restored to our imaginations, but palpably a living body, as it were, to our senses, to wear and sustain the former. His Cromwell's restoration, if England will read it faithfully, and addressed to New England too. Every reader will make his own application.

To speak deliberately, we think that in this instance, vague rumor and a vague history have for the first time been subjected to a rigid scrutiny, and the wheat, with at least novel fidelity, sifted from the chaff; so that there remain for result,—First, Letters and Speeches of Oliver Cromwell, now for the first time read or readable, and well nigh as complete as the fates will permit; secondly, Deeds, making an imperfect and fragmentary life, which may, with probability, be fathered upon him; thirdly, this wreck of an ancient picture, the present editor has, to the best of his ability, restored, sedulously scraping away the daubings of successive bunglers, and endeavoring to catch the spirit of the artist himself. Not the worst, nor a barely possible, but for once the most favorable construction has been put upon this evidence of the life of a man, and the result is a picture of the ideal Cromwell, the perfection of the painter's art. Possibly this was the actual man. At any rate, this only can contain the actual hero. We confess that when we read these Letters and Speeches, unquestionably Cromwell's, with open and confident mind, we get glimpses occasionally of a grandeur and heroism, which even this editor has not proclaimed. His "Speeches" make us forget modern orators, and might go right into the next edition of the Old Testament, without alteration. Cromwell *was* another sort of man than *we* had taken him to be. These Letters and Speeches have supplied the lost key to his character. Verily another soldier than Bonaparte; rejoicing in the triumph of a psalm; to whom psalms were for Magna Charta and Heralds' Book, and whose victories were "crowning mercies." For stern, antique, and practical religion, a man unparalleled, since the Jewish dispensation, in the line of kings. An old Hebrew warrior, indeed, and last right-hand man of the Lord of Hosts, that has blown his ram's horn about Jericho. Yet, with a remarkable common sense and unexpected liberality, there was joined in him, too, such a divine madness, though with large and sublime features, as that of those dibblers of beans on St. George's Hill, whom Carlyle tells of. He still listened to ancient and decaying oracles. If his actions were not always what Christianity or the truest philosophy teaches, still they never fail to impress us as noble, and however violent, will always be pardoned to the great purpose and sincerity of the man. His unquestionable hardness, not to say willfulness, not prevailing by absolute truth and greatness of character, but honestly striving to bend things to his will, is yet grateful to consider in this or any age. As John Maidstone said, "He was a strong man in the dark perils of war; in the high places of the field, hope shone in him like a pillar of fire, when it had gone out in the others." And as Milton sang, whose least testimony cannot be spared—

> "Our chief of men,
> Guided by faith and matchless fortitude."

None ever spake to Cromwell before, sending a word of cheer across the centuries—not the "hear!" "hear!" of modern parliaments, but the congratulation and sympathy of a brother soul. The Letters and Speeches owe not a little to the "Intercalations" and "Annotations" of the "latest of the Commentators." The reader will not soon forget how like a happy merchant in the crowd, listening to his favorite speaker, he is all on the alert, and sympathetic, nudging his neighbors from time to time, and throwing in his responsive or interrogatory word. All is good, both that which he didn't hear, and that which he did. He not only makes him speak audibly, but he makes all parties listen to him, all England sitting round, and give in their comments, "groans," or "blushes," or "assent;" indulging sometimes in triumphant malicious applications to the present day, when there is a palpable hit; supplying the look and attitude of the speaker, and the tone of his voice, and even rescuing his unutterable, wrecked and submerged thought,—for this orator begins speaking anywhere within sight of the beginning, and leaves off when the conclusion is visible. Our merchant listens, restless, meanwhile, encouraging his fellow-auditors,

when the speech grows dim and involved, and pleas-
antly congratulating them, when it runs smoothly; or,
in touching soliloquy, he exclaims, "Poor Oliver, noble
Oliver"—"Courage, my brave one!"

And all along, between the Letters and Speeches, as
readers well remember, he has ready such a fresh top-
of-the-morning salutation as conjures up the spirits
of those days, and men go marching over English
sward, not wired skeletons, but with firm, elastic
muscles, and clang of armor on their thighs, if they
wore swords, or the twang of psalms and canticles on
their lips. His blunt, "Who are you?" put to the shadowy ghosts of history, they vanish into deeper obscurity than ever. Vivid phantasmagorian pictures of what
is transpiring in England in the meanwhile, there are,
not a few, better than if you had been there to see.

All of Carlyle's works might well enough be embraced under the title of one of them, a good specimen brick, "On Heroes, Hero-worship, and the Heroic
in History." Of this department, he is the Chief Professor in the World's University, and even leaves
Plutarch behind. Such intimate and living, such loyal
and generous sympathy with the heroes of history,
not one in one age only, but forty in forty ages, such
an unparalleled reviewing and greeting of all past
worth, with exceptions, to be sure,—but exceptions
were the rule, before,—it was, indeed, to make this
the age of review writing, as if now one period of the
human story were completing itself, and getting its
accounts settled. This soldier has told the stories with
new emphasis, and will be a memorable hander-down
of fame to posterity. And with what wise discrimina-
tion he has selected his men, with reference both to
his own genius and to theirs: Mahomet, – Dante, –
Cromwell, – Voltaire, – Johnson, – Burns, – Goethe, –

Richter, − Schiller, − Mirabeau; could any of these have been spared? These we wanted to hear about. We have not as commonly the cold and refined judgment of the scholar and critic merely, but something more human and affecting. These eulogies have the glow and warmth of friendship. There is sympathy not with mere fames, and formless, incredible things, but with kindred men,−not transiently, but life-long he has walked with them.

The attitude of some, in relation to Carlyle's love of heroes, and men of the sword, reminds us of the procedure at the anti-slavery meetings, when some member, being warmed, begins to speak with more latitude than usual of the Bible or the Church, for a few prudent and devout ones to spring a prayer upon him, as the saying is; that is, propose suddenly to unite in prayer, and so solemnize the minds of the audience, or dismiss them at once; which may oftener be to interrupt a true prayer by most gratuitous profanity. But the spring of this trap, we are glad to learn, has grown somewhat rusty, and is not so sure of late.

No doubt, some of Carlyle's worthies, should they ever return to earth, would find themselves unpleasantly put upon their good behavior, to sustain their characters; but if he can return a man's life more perfect to our hands, than it was left at his death, following out the design of its author, we shall have no great cause to complain. We do not want a Daguerreotype likeness. All biography is the life of Adam,−a much-experienced man,−and time withdraws something partial from the story of every individual, that the historian may supply something general. If these virtues were not in this man, perhaps they are in his biographer,−no fatal mistake. Really, in any other sense, we never do, nor desire to, come at the historical man,—unless we rob his grave, that is the nearest approach. Why did he die, then? *He* is with his bones, surely.

No doubt, Carlyle has a propensity to *exaggerate* the heroic in history, that is, he creates you an ideal hero rather than another thing, he has most of that material. This we allow in all its senses, and in one narrower sense it is not so convenient. Yet what were history if he did not exaggerate it? How comes it that history never has to wait for facts, but for a man to write it? The ages may go on forgetting the facts never so long, he can remember two for every one forgotten. The musty records of history, like the catacombs, contain the perishable remains, but only in the breast of genius are embalmed the souls of heroes. There is very little of what is called criticism here; it is love and reverence, rather, which deal with qualities not relatively, but absolutely great; for whatever is admirable in a man is something infinite, to which we cannot set bounds. These sentiments allow the mortal to die, the immortal and divine to survive. There is something antique, even in his style of treating his subject, reminding us that Heroes and Demigods, Fates and Furies, still exist, the common man is nothing to him, but after death the hero is apotheosized and has a place in heaven, as in the religion of the Greeks.

Exaggeration! was ever any virtue attributed to a man without exaggeration? was ever any vice, without infinite exaggeration? Do we not exaggerate ourselves to ourselves, or do we recognize ourselves for the actual men we are? Are we not all great men? Yet what are we actually to speak of? We live by exaggeration, what else is it to anticipate more than we enjoy? The lightning is an exaggeration of the light. Exaggerated history is poetry, and truth referred to a new standard. To a small man every greater is an exaggeration. He who cannot exaggerate is not qualified to utter truth. No truth we think was ever expressed but with this sort of emphasis, so that for the time there seemed to be no other. Moreover, you must speak loud to those who are hard of hearing, and so you acquire a habit of shouting to those who are not. By an immense exaggeration we appreciate our Greek poetry and philosophy, and Egyptian ruins; our Shakspeares and Miltons, our Liberty and Christianity. We give importance to this hour over all other hours. We do not live by justice, but by grace. As the sort of justice which concerns us in our daily intercourse is not that administered by the judge, so the historical justice which we prize is not arrived at by nicely balancing the evidence. In order to appreciate any, even the humblest man, you must first, by some good fortune, have acquired a sentiment of admiration, even of reverence, for him, and there never were such exaggerators as these. Simple admiration for a hero renders a juster verdict than the wisest criticism, which necessarily degrades what is high to its own level. There is no danger in short of saying too much in praise of one man, provided you can say more in praise of a better man. If by exaggeration a man can create for us a hero, where there was nothing but dry bones before, we will thank him, and let Dryasdust administer historical justice. This is where a true history properly begins, when some genius arises, who can turn the dry and musty records into poetry. As we say, looking to the future, that what is best is truest, so, in one sense, we may say looking into the past, for the only past that we are to look at, must also be future to us. The great danger is not of excessive partiality or sympathy with one, but of a shallow justice to many, in which, after all, none gets

him, but until you get accustomed to the panorama, you may easily mistake one of his court for the king." It stands there a piece of mute brass, that seems nevertheless to know in what vicinity it is: and there perchance it will stand, when the nation that placed it there has passed away, still in sympathy with the mountains, forever discriminating in the desert.

So, we may say, stands this man, pointing as long as he lives, in obedience to some spiritual magnetism, to the summits in the historical horizon, for the guidance of his fellows.

Truly, our greatest blessings are very cheap. To have our sunlight without paying for it, without any duty levied,—to have our poet there in England, to furnish us entertainment, and what is better, provocation, from year to year, all our lives long, to make the world seem richer for us, the age more respectable, and life better worth the living,—all without expense of acknowledgment even, but silently accepted out of the east, like morning light as a matter of course.

Love.

WHAT the essential difference between man and woman is that they should be thus attracted to one another, no one has satisfactorily answered. Perhaps we must acknowledge the justness of the distinction which assigns to man the sphere of wisdom, and to woman that of love, though neither belongs exclusively to either. Man is continually saying to woman, Why will you not be more wise? Woman is continually saying to man, Why will you not be more loving? It is not in their wills to be wise or to be loving; but, unless each is both wise and loving, there can be neither wisdom nor love.

All transcendent goodness is one, though appreciated in different ways, or by different senses. In beauty we see it, in music we hear it, in fragrance we scent it, in the palatable the pure palate tastes it, and in rare health the whole body feels it. The variety is in the surface or manifestation; but the radical identity we fail to express. The lover sees in the glance of his beloved the same beauty that in the sunset paints the western skies. It is the same daimon, here lurking under a human eyelid, and there under the closing eyelids of the day. Here, in small compass, is the ancient and natural beauty of evening and morning. What loving astronomer has ever fathomed the ethereal depths of the eye?

The maiden conceals a fairer flower and sweeter fruit than any calyx in the field; and, if she goes with averted face, confiding in her purity and high resolves, she will make the heavens retrospective, and all nature humbly confess its queen.

Under the influence of this sentiment, man is a string of an Æolian harp, which vibrates with the zephyrs of the eternal morning.

There is at first thought something trivial in the commonness of love. So many Indian youths and maidens along these banks have in ages past yielded to the influence of this great civilizer. Nevertheless, this generation is not disgusted nor discouraged, for love is no individual's experience; and though we are imperfect mediums, it does not partake of our imperfection; though we are finite, it is infinite and eternal; and the same divine influence broods over these banks, whatever race may inhabit them, and perchance still would, even if the human race did not dwell here.

Perhaps an instinct survives through the intensest actual love, which prevents entire abandonment and devotion, and makes the most ardent lover a little reserved. It is the anticipation of change. For the most ardent lover is not the less practically wise, and seeks a love which will last forever.

Considering how few poetical friendships there are, it is remarkable that so many are married. It would seem as if men yielded too easy an obedience to nature without consulting their genius. One may be drunk with love without being any nearer to finding his mate. There is more of good nature than of good sense at the bottom of most marriages. But the good nature must have the counsel of the good spirit or Intelligence. If common sense had been consulted, how many marriages would never have taken place; if uncommon or divine sense, how few marriages such as we witness would ever have taken place!

Our love may be ascending or descending. What is its character, if it may be said of it,—

"We must *respect* the souls above,
But only *those below* we *love*."

Love is a severe critic. Hate can pardon more than love. They who aspire to love worthily, subject themselves to an ordeal more rigid than any other.

Is your friend such a one that an increase of worth on your part will surely make her more your friend? Is she retained,—is she attracted,—by more nobleness in you,—by more of that virtue which is peculiarly yours; or is she indifferent and blind to that? Is she to be flattered and won by your meeting her on any other than the ascending path? Then duty requires that you separate from her.

Love must be as much a light as a flame.

Where there is not discernment, the behavior even of the purest soul may in effect amount to coarseness.

A man of fine perceptions is more truly feminine than a merely sentimental woman. The heart is blind, but Love is not blind. None of the gods is so discriminating.

In Love & Friendship the imagination is as much exercised as the heart, and if either is outraged, the other will be estranged. It is commonly the imagination which is wounded first, rather than the heart, it is so much the more sensitive.

Comparatively, we can excuse any offence against the heart, but not against the imagination. The imagination knows—nothing escapes its glance from out its eyry—and it controls the breast. My heart may still yearn toward the valley, but my imagination will not permit me to jump off the precipice that debars me from it, for it is wounded, its wings are clipt, and it cannot fly, even descendingly. Our "blundering hearts"! some poet says. The imagination never forgets, it is a re-membering. It is not foundationless, but most reasonable, and it alone uses all the knowledge of the intellect.

Love is the profoundest of secrets. Divulged, even to the beloved, it is no longer Love. As if it were merely I that loved you. When love ceases, then it is divulged.

In our intercourse with one we love, we wish to have answered those questions at the end of which we do not raise our voice; against which we put no interrogation-mark,—answered with the same unfailing, universal aim toward every point of the compass.

I require that thou knowest everything without being told anything. I parted from my beloved because there was one thing which I had to tell her. She *questioned* me. She should have known all by sympathy. That I had to tell it her was the difference between us,—the misunderstanding.

A lover never hears anything that is *told*, for that is commonly either false or stale; but he hears things taking place, as the sentinels heard Trenck mining in the ground, and thought it was moles.

The relation may be profaned in many ways. The parties may not regard it with equal sacredness. What if the lover should learn that his beloved dealt in incantations and philters! What if he should hear that she consulted a clairvoyant! The spell would be instantly broken.

If to chaffer and higgle are bad in trade, they are much worse in Love. It demands directness as of an arrow.

There is danger that we lose sight of what our friend is absolutely, while considering what she is to us alone.

The lover wants no partiality. He says, Be so kind as to be just.

> Canst thou love with thy mind,
>   And reason with thy heart?
> Canst thou be kind,
>   And from thy darling part?
>
> Canst thou range earth, sea, and air,
>   And so meet me everywhere?
> Through all events I will pursue thee,
>   Through all persons I will woo thee.

I need thy hate as much as thy love. Thou wilt not repel me entirely when thou repellest what is evil in me.

> Indeed, indeed, I cannot tell,
> Though I ponder on it well,
> Which were easier to state,
> All my love or all my hate.
> Surely, surely, thou wilt trust me
> When I say thou dost disgust me.
> O I hate thee with a hate
> That would fain annihilate;
> Yet, sometimes, against my will,
> My dear Friend, I love thee still.
> It were treason to our love,
> And a sin to God above,
> One iota to abate
> Of a pure, impartial hate.

It is not enough that we are truthful; we must cherish and carry out high purposes to be truthful about.

It must be rare, indeed, that we meet with one to whom we are prepared to be quite ideally related, as she to us. We should have no reserve; we should give the whole of ourselves to that society; we should have no duty aside from that. One who could bear to be so wonderfully and beautifully exaggerated every day. I would take my friend out of her low self and set her higher, infinitely higher, and *there* know her. But, commonly, men are as much afraid of love as of hate.

They have lower engagements. They have near ends to serve. They have not imagination enough to be thus employed about a human being, but must be coopering a barrel, forsooth.

What a difference, whether, in all your walks, you meet only strangers, or in one house is one who knows you, and whom you know. To have a brother or a sister! To have a gold mine on your farm! To find diamonds in the gravel heaps before your door! How rare these things are! To share the day with you,—to people the earth. Whether to have a god or a goddess for companion in your walks, or to walk alone with hinds and villains and carles. Would not a friend enhance the beauty of the landscape as much as a deer or hare? Everything would acknowledge and serve such a relation; the corn in the field, and the cranberries in the meadow. The flowers would bloom, and the birds sing, with a new impulse. There would be more fair days in the year.

The object of love expands and grows before us to eternity, until it includes all that is lovely, and we become all that can love.

Chastity & Sensuality.

THE subject of Sex is a remarkable one, since, though its phenomena concern us so much both directly and indirectly, and, sooner or later it occupies the thoughts of all, yet, all mankind, as it were, agree to be silent about it, at least the sexes commonly one to another. One of the most interesting of all human facts is veiled more completely than any mystery. It is treated with such secrecy and awe, as surely do not go to any religion. I believe that it is unusual even for the most intimate friends to communicate the pleasures and anxieties connected with this fact,— much as the external affairs of love, its comings & goings, are bruited. The Shakers do not exaggerate it so much by their manner of speaking of it, as all mankind by their manner of keeping silence about it. Not that men should speak on this or any subject without having any thing worthy to say; but it is plain that the education of man has hardly commenced, there is so little genuine intercommunication.

In a pure society, the subject of copulation would not be so often avoided from shame and not from reverence, winked out of sight, and hinted at only, but treated naturally and simply,—perhaps simply avoided, like the kindred mysteries. If it cannot be spoken of for shame, how can it be acted of? But doubtless there is far more purity as well as more impurity, than is apparent.

Men commonly couple with their idea of marriage a slight degree at least of sensuality; but every lover, the world over, believes in its inconceivable purity.

If it is the result of a pure love, there can be nothing sensual in marriage. Chastity is something positive, not negative. It is the virtue of the married

especially. All lusts or base pleasures must give place
to loftier delights. They who meet as superior beings
cannot perform the deeds of inferior ones. The deeds
of love are less questionable than any action of an
individual can be, for, it being founded on the rarest
mutual respect, the parties incessantly stimulate each
other to a loftier and purer life, and the act in which
they are associated must be pure and noble indeed,
for innocence and purity can have no equal. In this
relation we deal with one whom we respect more religiously even than we respect our better selves, and
we shall necessarily conduct as in the presence of
God. What presence can be more awful to the lover
than that of his beloved?

If you seek the warmth even of affection from a
similar motive to that from which cats and dogs and
slothful persons hug the fire, because your tempera-
ture is low through sloth, you are on the downward
road, and it is but to plunge yet deeper into sloth.
Better the cold affection of the sun reflected from
fields of ice and snow, or his warmth in some still
wintry dell. The warmth of celestial love does not relax, but nerves and braces its enjoyer. Warm your
body by healthful exercise, not by cowering over a
stove. Warm your spirit by performing independently
noble deeds, not by ignobly seeking the sympathy of
your fellows who are no better than yourself. A man's
social and spiritual discipline must answer to his corporeal. He must lean on a friend who has a hard
breast, as he would lie on a hard bed. He must drink
cold water for his only beverage. So he must not hear
sweetened and colored words, but pure and refreshing truths. He must daily bathe in truth cold as spring
water, not warmed by the sympathy of friends.

Can love be in aught allied to dissipation? Let us
love by refusing not accepting one another. Love and

lust are far asunder. The one is good, the other bad. When the affectionate sympathize by their higher natures, there is love; but there is danger that they will sympathize by their lower natures, and then there is lust. It is not necessary that this be deliberate, hardly even conscious, but in the close contact of affection there is danger that we may stain and pollute one another, for we cannot embrace but with an entire embrace.

We must love our friend so much that she shall be associated with our purest and holiest thoughts alone. When there is impurity, we have "descended to meet," though we knew it not.

The *luxury* of affection,—there's the danger. There must be some nerve and heroism in our love, as of a winter morning. In the religion of all nations a purity is hinted at, which, I fear, men never attain to. We may love and not elevate one another. The love that takes us as it finds us, degrades us. What watch we must keep over the fairest and purest of our affections, lest there be some taint about them. May we so love as never to have occasion to repent of our love.

There is to be attributed to sensuality the loss to language of how many pregnant symbols.

Flowers, which, by their infinite hues and fragrance celebrate the marriage of the plants are intended for a symbol of the open and unsuspected beauty of all true marriage, when man's flowering season arrives.

Virginity too is a budding flower, and by an impure marriage the virgin is deflowered. Whoever loves flowers, loves virgins and chastity. Love and lust are as far asunder as a flower garden is from a brothel.

J. Biberg, in the "Amoenitates Botanicae", edited by Linnaeus, observes, (I translate from the Latin) "the organs of generation which in the animal king-

dom are for the most part concealed by nature as if
they were to be ashamed of, in the vegetable kingdom
are exposed to the eyes of all; and when the nuptials
of plants are celebrated, it is wonderful what delight
they afford to the beholder, refreshing the senses with
the most agreeable color and the sweetest odor, and at
the same time bees and other insects, not to mention
the humming bird, extract honey from their nectaries,
and gather wax from their effete pollen." Linnaeus
himself calls the calyx the *thalamus*, or bridal chamber, and the corolla the *aulaeum* or tapestry of it, and
proceeds to explain thus every part of the flower.

Who knows but evil spirits might corrupt the flowers themselves, rob them of their fragrance and their
fair hues, and turn their marriage into a secret shame
& defilement? Already they are of various qualities,
and there is one whose nuptials fill the lowlands in
June with the odor of carrion.

The intercourse of the sexes, I have dreamed, is in-
credibly beautiful, too fair to be remembered. I have
had thoughts about it, but they are among the most
fleeting and irrecoverable in my experience. It is
strange that men will talk of miracles, revelation,
inspiration, and the like, as things past, while love
remains.

A true marriage will differ in no wise from illumination. In all perception of the truth there is a divine
ecstasy, an inexpressible delirium of joy, as when a
youth embraces his betrothed virgin. The ultimate
delights of a true marriage are one with this.

No wonder that out of such a union, not as end,
but as accompaniment, comes the undying race of
man. The womb is a most fertile soil.

Some have asked if the stock of men could not be
improved,—if they could not be bred as cattle. Let
Love be purified and all the rest will follow. A pure

Index

Editorial Appendix

Notes on Illustrations

Harvard University in 1833   following page 298

On August 20, 1833, Thoreau and Charles Stearns Wheeler settled into Hollis Hall 20 as roommates. Harvard Hall housed the College library and chapel. President Quincy officiated from the third floor of University Hall, above commons and recitation rooms, while Thoreau attended classes in Massachusetts Hall, flanking Harvard Yard. This lithograph (reduced detail) is from Benjamin Peirce, *A History of Harvard University* (Cambridge, Mass., 1833).— Harvard University Archives.

"The Love of stories, . . ." a manuscript page
          from a college theme

The first page of Thoreau's theme on the love of stories, "real or fabulous, in young and old," endorsed "Thoreau 1836," the year apparently in a later handwriting. Professor Channing's records date the assignment September 30. The numbers above the title are non-authorial, as is the revision near the bottom of the page, and on line 20 (page 45) of the printed text.—Pierpont Morgan Library.

"Chastity & Sensuality," a manuscript page
          from the fair copy

The first page from an essay Thoreau sent to his friend H. G. O. Blake as a wedding gift in September 1852. Unpublished in Thoreau's lifetime, the essay first appeared in Emerson's edition of Thoreau's *Letters to Various Persons* (Boston, 1865). Text appears on page 274 in the present edition.—Humanities Research Center, The University of Texas at Austin.

Thoreau's college diploma

> On August 30, 1837, Harvard University awarded the bachelor of arts degree to "Davidem Henricum Thoreau." The story that he refused to accept a diploma is apocryphal, although apparently he declined the master of arts degree conferred three years later to those graduates still living and willing to render unto Harvard five dollars. Referring to the dubious honor of academic credentials, Thoreau wrote Emerson on November 14, 1847: "They have been foolish enough to put at the end of all this earnest the old joke of a diploma. Let every sheep keep but his own skin, I say."–*The Writings of Henry D. Thoreau* Archives.

"Thomas Carlyle and His Works," a page
     from the periodical version

> First page from the 1847 *Graham's Magazine* publication of "Thomas Carlyle and His Works," featured as the lead article. Text appears on pages 219-221 of the present edition.–Photograph, by Roger Smith, courtesy of Walter Harding.

Holworthy. Stoughton. Holden Chapel. Hollis. Harvard Hall. University. Massachusetts. Dane College.

Pendleton's Lithog. Boston

Harvard University in 1833

"Chastity and Sensuality," a manuscript page
from the fair copy

"The Love of stories, . . ." a manuscript page
from a college theme

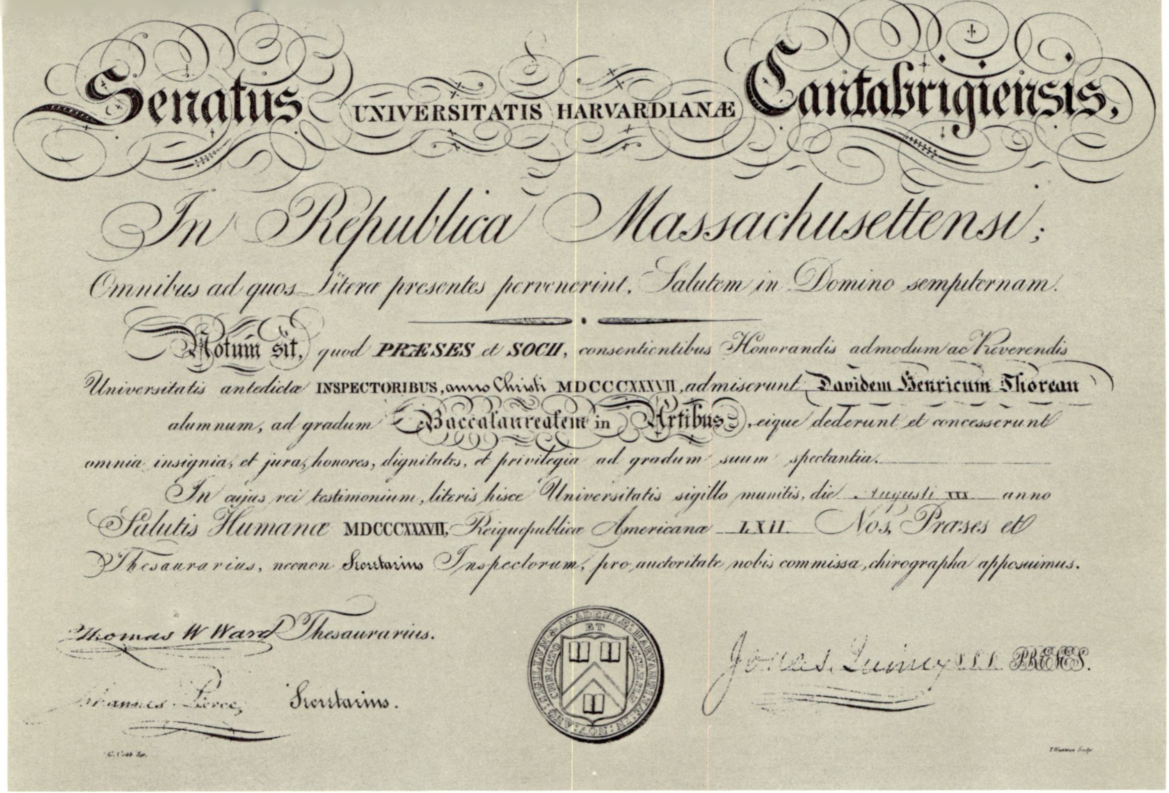
Senatus UNIVERSITATIS HARVARDIANÆ Cantabrigiensis,

In Republica Massachusettensi;

Omnibus ad quos literæ presentes pervenerint, Salutem in Domino sempiternam.

Notum sit, quod PRÆSES et SOCII, consentientibus Honorandis admodum ac Reverendis Universitatis antedictæ INSPECTORIBUS, anno Christi MDCCCXXXVII, admiserunt Davidem Henricum Thoreau alumnum, ad gradum Baccalaureatem in Artibus, eique dederunt et concesserunt omnia insignia, et jura, honores, dignitates, et privilegia ad gradum suum spectantia.

In cujus rei testimonium, literis hisce Universitatis sigillo munitis, die Augusti XXX anno Salutis Humanæ MDCCCXXXVII, Reique publicæ Americanæ LXII Nos, Præses et Thesaurarius, necnon Secretarius Inspectorum, pro auctoritate nobis commissa, chirographa apposuimus.

Thomas W Ward Thesaurarius.

Secretarius.

PRÆSES.

Thoreau's college diploma

THOMAS CARLYLE AND HIS WORKS.

BY HENRY D. THOREAU.

THOMAS CARLYLE is a Scotchman, born about fifty years ago, "at Ecclefechan, Annandale," according to one authority. "His parents 'good farmer people,' his father an elder in the Secession church there, and a man of strong native sense, whose words were said to 'nail a subject to the wall.'" We also hear of his "excellent mother," still alive, and of "her fine old covenanting accents, concerting with his transcendental tones." He seems to have gone to school at Annan, on the shore of the Solway Frith, and there, as he himself writes, "heard, of famed professors, of high matters classical, mathematical, a whole Wonderland of Knowledge," from Edward Irving, then a young man "fresh from Edinburgh, with college prizes, &c."—"come to see our schoolmaster, who had also been his." From this place, they say, you can look over into Wordsworth's country. Here first he may have become acquainted with Nature, with woods, such as are there, and rivers and brooks, some of whose names we have heard, and the last lapses of Atlantic billows. He got some of his education, too, more or less liberal, out of the University of Edinburgh, where, according to the same authority, he had to "support himself," partly by "private tuition, translations for the booksellers, &c.," and afterward, as we are glad to hear, "taught an academy in Dysart, at the same time that Irving was teaching in Kirkaldy," the usual middle passage of a literary life. He was destined for the church, but not by the powers that rule man's life; made his literary début in Fraser's Magazine, long ago; read here and there in English and French, with more or less profit, we may suppose, such of us at least as are not particularly informed, and at length found some words which spoke to his condition in the German language, and set himself earnestly to unravel that mystery—with what success many readers know.

After his marriage he "resided partly at Comely Bank, Edinburgh; and for a year or two at Craigen-

puttock, a wild and solitary farm-house in the upper part of Dumfriesshire," at which last place, amid barren heather hills, he was visited by our countryman Emerson. With Emerson he still corresponds. He was early intimate with Edward Irving, and continued to be his friend until the latter's death. Concerning this "freest, brotherliest, bravest human soul," and Carlyle's relation to him, those whom it concerns will do well to consult a notice of his death in Fraser's Magazine for 1835, reprinted in the Miscellanies. He also corresponded with Goethe. Latterly, we hear, the poet Stirling was his only intimate acquaintance in England.

He has spent the last quarter of his life in London, writing books; has the fame, as all readers know, of having made England acquainted with Germany, in late years, and done much else that is novel and remarkable in literature. He especially is the literary man of those parts. You may imagine him living in altogether a retired and simple way, with small family, in a quiet part of London, called Chelsea, a little out of the din of commerce, in "Cheyne Row," there, not far from the "Chelsea Hospital." "A little past this, and an old ivy-clad church, with its buried generations lying around it," writes one traveler, "you come to an antique street running at right angles with the Thames, and, a few steps from the river, you find Carlyle's name on the door."

"A Scotch lass ushers you into the second story front chamber, which is the spacious workship of the world maker." Here he sits a long time together, with many books and papers about him; many new books, we have been told, on the upper shelves, uncut, with the "author's respects" in them; in late months, with many manuscripts in an old English hand, and innumerable pamphlets, from the public libraries, relating to the Cromwellian period; now, perhaps, looking out into the street on brick and pavement, for a change, and now upon some rod of grass ground in the rear; or, perchance,

Acknowledgments

FOR permission to refer to, copy, and publish manuscript material, as particularized in the Checklist of Manuscripts, the editors are indebted to the Huntington Library, San Marino, California; the Abernethy Library of American Literature, Middlebury College; the Pierpont Morgan Library; the Harvard College Library; the Harvard University Archives; the Humanities Research Center, the University of Texas at Austin; the Concord Free Public Library; Manuscript Division, Library of Congress; the Clifton Waller Barrett Library, University of Virginia Library; the Morris Library, Special Collections, Southern Illinois University, Carbondale; Henry W. and Albert A. Berg Collection, the New York Public Library, Astor, Lenox and Tilden Foundations; the Robert H. Taylor Collection, Princeton, New Jersey; the Brown University Library; Mr. Albert E. Lownes; and Mr. Kenneth W. Cameron and the *Emerson Society Quarterly*. Mr. Cameron also graciously allowed manuscript material previously edited and published by him in *The Transcendentalists and Minerva* to be re-edited in this volume of THE WRITINGS OF HENRY D. THOREAU.

Contributions of expertise, time, and good will, for which the editors offer their warmest gratitude, were made by Mary Isabel Fry, Lola L. Szladits, Carolyn Jakeman, Marcia Moss, Herbert Cahoon, John R. McKenna, Robert Buckeye, Stuart C. Sherman, David A. Jonah, Floyd S. Merritt, Kimball C. Elkins, Charlotte Johnson, Elizabeth Ryall, Audrey Scott, Gay Wilson Allen, Walter Harding, J. Lyndon Shanley, William Gibson, Raymond D. Gozzi, O M Brack, Thomas Blanding, Hershel Parker, Douglass S. Parker, William L. Howarth, Joel Myerson, M. Ali Jazayeri, and Kenneth M. Sanderson; also by the reference staff at the New England Depository Library, the Boston Athenæum Library, and the libraries of the University of Massachusetts at Amherst, the University of Texas at Austin, and Harvard University.

Graduate students at the University of Iowa who assisted in the preparation of a "Sir Walter Raleigh" transcript include Marsha Madsen, Gordon Kelly, Keith Swigger, Ruth Kantzer, Tom Morain, Kay Mussell, Charles Dee, Linda Schuppener, and David Day. Elizabeth Worthington rendered expert stenographic help during the last year of work on the volume as a whole.

The scholars who confirmed the final texts against manuscripts, a task indispensable to the completion of this project, are named in "Editorial Contributions."

Material assistance was generously provided by the University of Massachusetts, the Huntington Library, the Newberry Library, the Graduate College of the University of Iowa, and the National Endowment for the Humanities through the Modern Language Association and the Center for Editions of American Authors.

Editorial Contributions

MUCH of the preliminary work on the Early Essays was done by Edwin Moser, who located and described all but one of the manuscript copy-texts, prepared typed transcripts, oversaw an initial validation of these against the originals, and proposed various emendations. Joseph J. Moldenhauer reread the transcripts against photocopy, found and studied Thoreau's source materials, drew up the final emendations, notes on textual problems, and other apparatus, and supervised a second reading of the typescript against manuscript copy-texts. Alexander C. Kern developed working materials for "Sir Walter Raleigh," among them a typed duplicate of the manuscript from photocopy and microfilm. Aided by Mr. Kern's documents and Thomas Blanding's study of changes in the original, Mr. Moldenhauer oversaw the validation of his text against the original, established emendations, and prepared the apparatus. He was responsible for the remaining Miscellanies texts and apparatus, though some working materials had been assembled by Mr. Moser. The Introduction was written by Mr. Moldenhauer, who also, as Textual Editor, supervised production of the volume and made such decisions as that function required.

The final validation of texts and apparatus against original manuscript copy-texts was performed by Mr. Moldenhauer for the pieces at Middlebury College, the Pierpont Morgan Library, Brown University, and the University of Texas; by Bruce Bebb for those at the Huntington Library; by Joel Myerson for those at Harvard University and the Concord Free Public Library; by Gillian G. M. Kyles for the piece at the University of Virginia; by John C. Broderick for that in the

Library of Congress; by William L. Howarth for that at Princeton University; and by Manuel Schonhorn for the authorially annotated printed copy-texts at Southern Illinois University.

J. J. M.

Introduction

1 . WORKS INCLUDED

ALL Thoreau's extant writings in English up
to and including the Harvard years (1833-1837) that
could reasonably be regarded as independent compositions are here collected under the heading "Early
Essays." Dominating this group of apprentice works
are the 23 identifiable themes and 6 forensic exercises
Thoreau wrote in Edward Tyrrel Channing's rhetoric
course as a sophomore, junior, and senior. "Early
Essays" also contains the only known school essay
from the period before 1833 and several compositions
contemporary with Thoreau's college years but not,
it seems, directly related to his rhetoric course work:
a Harvard commencement exercise and class book
autobiographical sketch; four book reviews or sum-
maries, which Thoreau may have written for an un-
dergraduate literary society; three fragmentary essays
on topics not listed among E. T. Channing's assignments; an analysis of Milton's companion poems; and
a personal essay, akin to the later *Journal*, which Thoreau entitled "Musings. April 20th 1835." Excluded
from "Early Essays" are Thoreau's direct notes from
his reading. The summary-reviews, while consisting
largely of paraphrase and quotation, are organized as
coherent compositions, with transitional matter of
Thoreau's own devising and, at times, independent
flights of thought provoked by the book on his desk.

The dozen separate writings collected as "Miscellanies" were almost all composed before the publication of *A Week on the Concord and Merrimack Rivers*
in 1849.[1] Their number includes, besides some am-

---

[1] "Miscellanies" bears no relationship to Volume X of the
Riverside Edition, *Miscellanies* (1893), and Volume IV of the

bitious works of literary history and criticism, a newspaper obituary, a series of edited extracts from eastern scripture, and a pair of essays on the subject of
love. By definition, "Miscellanies" is a mixed assemblage whose chief claim to coherence is that these
pieces issued from, and reflect back upon, the mind
of the author. They are shorter works that fit none of
the categories into which THE WRITINGS OF HENRY D.
THOREAU is divided: the *Journal, Fruits and Seeds,
Reform Papers* (essays on politics and morality),
Translations (Thoreau's *own* translations from ancient and modern languages),[2] *Correspondence, Ex-
cursions* (the brief pieces on nature and on walking-
tours, including the pieces first collected under this
title in 1863), and *Poems*, plus the four book-length
works published during Thoreau's lifetime and immediately after his death (*A Week, Walden, The
Maine Woods, Cape Cod*). Certain anomalous writings
not presently scheduled for inclusion elsewhere in
THE WRITINGS have been rejected from "Miscellanies"
as well, notably the large and numerous commonplace
books of extracts from Thoreau's reading in literature,
natural history, history, and anthropology.

Publication or intended publication during Thoreau's lifetime is not a criterion for the inclusion of
works in this volume. Among the Miscellanies only
the *Dial* pieces, the obituary for Anna Jones, and
"Thomas Carlyle" received contemporary publication,

Manuscript Edition or the Walden Edition, *Cape Cod and
Miscellanies* (1906). Only "Thomas Carlyle," among the
"Miscellanies" in the present volume, appeared in those earlier
collections.

[2] "The Preaching of Buddha," a piece from *The Dial* belonging to the same family of scriptural extracts as several
Miscellanies in this volume, will appear in *Translations*. The
"Buddha" article was almost entirely translated by Thoreau
from French texts in the 1843 *Revue indépendante*.

and none of the Early Essays appeared in print before the twentieth century.

The writings gathered here are arranged in chronological sequence. Pieces not dated in Thoreau's own hand are placed by reference to all available internal, physical, and historical evidence, with this data cited in the apparatus. "Musings" has a date as part of its title; but the title of each of the other compositions in the Early Essays section is preceded by the date of composition in conventional and regularized form. The assignment of a date to each Early Essay within the text can be justified on both textual and practical grounds: the order of composition of these apprentice writings is important to the study of Thoreau's intellectual development; their chronology has long been an area of confusion and misunderstanding; and many of the essays contain a whole or partial date in Thoreau's endorsement. The editor's role in the formulation of each dateline is acknowledged in the apparatus.

2. THEORY OF COPY-TEXT AND PRINCIPLES OF EMENDATION

Like all other volumes in THE WRITINGS OF HENRY D. THOREAU, and like all volumes in the other large projects proceeding under the auspices of the Center for Editions of American Authors, *Early Essays and Miscellanies* is an unmodernized, purified, eclectic or critical text. The editorial theory and procedures by which this volume has been prepared conform essentially to those employed in the Centenary Edition of Hawthorne and the Northwestern-Newberry Edition of Melville.[3] The interested reader should consult the

---

[3] See Fredson Bowers, "The Centenary Texts: Editorial Principles," appended to the second and subsequent Haw-

Center's working manual for all projects under its sponsorship, the *Statement of Editorial Principles and Procedures* (1972). He should also examine several essays and monographs that explain the theory of copy-text more fully, subtly, and systematically than the present introduction does: W. W. Greg, "The Rationale of Copy-Text," *Studies in Bibliography*, 3 (1950), 19-36; Fredson Bowers, "Current Theories of Copy-Text, with an Illustration from Dryden," *Modern Philology*, 48 (1950), 12-20; Bowers, "Some Principles for Scholarly Editions of Nineteenth-Century American Authors," *Studies in Bibliography*, 17 (1964), 223-228; and James Thorpe, *Principles of Textual Criticism* (San Marino, Calif.: Huntington Library, 1972). What follows in these pages is a capsule discussion concentrating on those aspects of the theory most pertinent to the editing of *Early Essays and Miscellanies*.

An eclectic or critical text is not an exact transcription of a manuscript nor an exact reprint of any particular printed form of the text. It is, rather, that one of the documentary forms of the finished text over which the author exercised the greatest degree of control (e.g., a fair-copy manuscript, or a set of corrected proofs for the first printing if the fair copy is lost, or a first printed form if both fair copy and corrected proofs have disappeared), as emended by the editor to reproduce as nearly as possible the author's intentions. Such emendation of the "copy-text" derives for the most part from other relevant forms of the text. The category of relevant or authoritative materials includes the author's working manuscripts and those

---

thorne volumes, and pp. xxix-xlii of the first, *The Scarlet Letter* (Columbus: Ohio State University Press, 1962); also, the discussion of editorial procedures in each of the Melville volumes.

printed forms of the text over which he demonstrably, or probably, exercised authority. It is crucial that the editor have access to all known relevant documents, for he selects his copy-text from among these, and uses the others ("pre-copy-texts"—usually working manuscripts—and "post-copy-texts"—usually revised reprints) to guide him in emendation.

Since some of his emendations will not derive from an authoritative document, but rather from independent editorial judgment, the editor must be familiar with the author's style both in working draft and fair copy, with his composition habits at the time he wrote the work, with external data bearing on the composition and—if applicable—first authoritative publication of the text, and, in the case of printed copy-texts, with the style norms of the editors, publishers, and printers to whom authoritative printings and reprintings were entrusted.

A primary assumption in modern textual theory is that the form closest in time to the author's composition is the most reliable in its "accidentals"—the details of punctuation, capitalization, word-division, spelling, and paragraphing. The accidentals of later printed forms, even those produced during the author's lifetime, are less authoritative. This is so because in most cases, Thoreau's "Thomas Carlyle and His Works" not excepted, a later printing is set from an earlier published form, even when the reprinting may contain authorial revisions. As the text is reset, further house stylings may be imposed upon the accidentals, and new compositor's errors are introduced. In the choice of copy-text, therefore, the author's fair or final manuscript enjoys the highest priority, followed by three other forms in this usual sequence: authorially corrected proofsheets for the initial printing (no instances in *Early Essays and Miscellanies*), authorially annotated post-publication copy of the first printing (two instances), and unmarked first printed copy (nine instances).

Though the copy-text has maximum general authority among relevant forms of the text with respect to accidentals, its substantives—the words themselves —are not binding where they differ from the substantives of a later *relevant* printing. The later substantives are adopted if it can be argued from internal or external evidence that they issued from the author's hand. Otherwise, they are rejected as sophistications, errors, or indifferent modifications by a copy-editor or compositor, and are presented as variant readings in the apparatus, with discussion, if necessary, in textual notes.

These two steps, the choice of copy-text from among the relevant forms, and the emendation of copy-text from other relevant forms or from the editor's independent judgment, are the heart of the editorial process. Accordingly, the editor is under strict obligation to identify his copy-text for the reader, to explain on what grounds he chose and validated it, and to document every change he makes from it. This documentation is of especial importance, for it enables the reader to follow the editorial labor back to the original form of the copy-text, and to judge for himself the validity of any particular emendation.

Copy-texts for the fifty-three pieces included in *Early Essays and Miscellanies* have been separately determined. By good fortune the texts of all but four Early Essays can be drawn directly from fair manuscript. The exceptions are "Titles of Books," for which a photoprint of the manuscript must serve, "T. Pomponius Atticus," taken entire from the first printing in Franklin Benjamin Sanborn's *The Life of Henry David Thoreau* (Boston and New York: Houghton

Mifflin Company, 1917), and "L'Allegro & Il Penseroso" and "Gaining or Exercising Public Influence," where the surviving manuscripts are less complete than when Sanborn copied them, so that readings for several gaps must be supplied from the 1917 *Life*. As indicated in textual notes for these last two pieces, Sanborn's versions of the missing parts are obviously imprecise. But where the manuscript is mutilated beyond recovery, Sanborn's readings are presented for want of any others. Here, and in "T. Pomponius Atticus," it is improbable that Sanborn invented long passages out of whole cloth; more likely he performed the same kinds of styling and diction "improvements" on the texts of now lost and mutilated manuscripts as on those for which full manuscripts are extant. The reader is invited to compare Sanborn's 1917 versions of college essays with the versions from manuscript copy-text in the present volume—noting, of course, the record of editorial emendations in the end matter.

Fair copies of two Miscellanies—"Sir Walter Raleigh" and "Chastity & Sensuality"—and a fair-copy leaf from another—the essay on "Love"—are extant and serve as copy-texts in this edition. The *Dial* essays and edited extracts present special problems of copy-text choice. Fair copies of these pieces are lost, but Thoreau pencilled corrections and other changes onto the printed pages of four *Dial* pieces in his personal copies of the magazine. It would seem appropriate to use these annotated printings of "Aulus Persius Flaccus," "The Laws of Menu," "Dark Ages," and "Homer. Ossian. Chaucer." as copy-texts in the present edition. For the first two titles this is done: Thoreau's changes, all of which correct *Dial* errors, are treated as copy-text readings, and the superseded *Dial* readings are listed as rejected precopy-text variants. But Thoreau's annotations on "Dark Ages" and "Homer . . ." go far beyond mere correction

as "impositions" of a sort. This edition presents as text the original reading wherever it is clear that Thoreau's alteration followed a notation by his teacher—unless, of course, the original reading is an error that the editor would have emended had Thoreau himself not corrected it. Those changes Thoreau appears to have entered before submitting a theme to Channing are respected as free revisions and are adopted as text.

To distinguish between independent and imposed changes requires a familiarity with Channing's methods of reading student papers. The most important document for this purpose is a manuscript entitled "Themes given out by Prof Channing to the Class of Harvard University. From Sept 1834 to Sept 1837." Written by William Allen, Thoreau's classmate and close friend, it lists in order Channing's theme assignments and contains in addition a guide to "Prof Channing's Corrections":[4]

P is to shew the proper place for a paragraph.

D is for an imperfect sentence, statement or translation.

O, for obscurity.

C, for want of connection with other parts, or with the subject.

T, for a passage doubtful in point of taste.

R, for repetition.

S, for a change in the form of a sentence.

———— placed under two or more words or phrases
indicates some imperfection in the connection.

[4] Harvard University Archives, HUC 8834.386. The document is partially transcribed and facsimiled by Kenneth W. Cameron in "Thoreau, Edward Tyrrel Channing and College Themes," *Emerson Society Quarterly*, 42 (IV Quarter, 1966), 15-34; reprinted in *Thoreau's Harvard Years* (Hartford: Transcendental Books, 1966), Part II, pp. 1-19.

A, B, C, &c placed under a word when used too frequently or under several words of similar sound coming too near each other.

1, 2, 3, &c to show that the words or sentences require a different arrangement corresponding to the numbers.

"[   ]" Passage thus enclosed, to be erased.

"W" placed against passages that abound in needless words, truisms or trite remarks.

"sp", shews that bad spelling is in the line.

"p" shews that punctuation is wrong.

"————" under a word shews that it is not English, or is used ungramatically, or that it is vague or unappropriate.

Other marks are for the professor's own use.

Allen also records Channing's injunction to "Make the corrections in ink as far as possible, and leave the pencil marks untouched." Thoreau honored this directive, making ink changes in response to the invariably pencilled correction symbols Channing entered on his themes.

The editor must assume, then, that all changes in the manuscript *not* accompanied by Channing's notations were made on Thoreau's own initiative, probably before a theme was handed in. Very little has come to light respecting the conditions under which Channing's students corrected their exercises. If a specific theme was passed back by Channing, "improved" by the student at his leisure and then resubmitted to the teacher before it was finally returned, this editorial assumption is sound. If, on the other hand, the student made revisions in Channing's presence, in a tutorial session or exercise, it is possible that *some* changes not signalled by pencil notes are imposed revisions. In that event, the distinction between the two kinds of alterations would often be dubious.[5] The list of alterations for each Early Essay records all Thoreau's revisions in the manuscript and every mark Channing entered on lines of themes where authorial changes have been (or may have been) made.

Allen's consecutive list of Channing's assignments complements another list, in the professor's own handwriting, entitled "Lists of Subjects for Students' Themes in Harvard College, 1823-1851."[6] It contains abbreviated titles or topics of the assignments, plus assignment numbers and the dates on which themes were due. Those of Thoreau's themes which are dated by at least month and day in the endorsement agree exactly with Channing's recorded deadlines for 1835-1837. When the editor of the present volume supplies a date for a theme, he draws it from the Channing document, called "Channing's Lists" in the apparatus. It must be understood that theme dates (whether in

[5] Channing's semiannual reports to the Harvard Overseers for the years in question do not describe in sufficient detail the procedures for student revision of written work. He declared in the first report for 1834-1835, Thoreau's sophomore year, that themes and translations "were examined by the Professor & returned to the student for correction; & were afterwards gone over again, with the student, at a stated Exercise." In the final report for that year Channing wrote that each student "presents a Theme every fortnight, for inspection & correction, & attends an Exercise, at which his Theme is re-examined." Channing informed the Overseers at the end of Thoreau's junior year that he spent six hours correcting each set of themes, and that "A critical exercise with a whole class, upon the corrected compositions, takes nearly two hours." During Thoreau's senior year, Channing reported that the seniors' themes "were examined & returned for correction." (*Reports to the Overseers*, Harvard University Archives; edited by Kenneth W. Cameron in "Chronology of Thoreau's Harvard Years," *Thoreau's Harvard Years* [Hartford: Transcendental Books, 1966], Part I, pp. 5, 6, 8, 9.)

[6] Harvard University Archives, HUC 8823.286; transcribed by Cameron in "Thoreau, Edward Tyrrel Channing and College Themes."

Thoreau's handwriting on the manuscripts or inter-polated by the editor) do not represent the exact times of composition, but rather the last possible day on which Thoreau could have written a theme before submitting it. (The remote possibility that Thoreau could back-date a late exercise should also be borne in mind.) Forensics assigned by Channing in the junior and senior years seem to have been due within a given month. Thoreau dated four of the six forensics in the present edition without reference to day; these have been arbitrarily placed after any spe-cifically dated or datable exercises for the same month. The two forensics Thoreau dated by day as well as month are placed in their exact chronological posi-tion. The assignment numbers entered on Thoreau's forensics agree with those in Channing's Lists.

The titles of the fragmentary themes "Popular Feel-ing" and "Travellers & Inhabitants" are derived from Channing's Lists, and their subtitles are taken from the William Allen document, called "Channing's Themes" in the apparatus. Channing's Themes also provides the title of "T. Pomponius Atticus as an Example."

All the themes and forensics Thoreau submitted to his rhetoric teacher were written on folio sheets folded in half to produce booklets of four sides. After writing his assignment on one or more booklets, Thoreau held the composition face up and folded it in half ver-tically, so that the last or back page formed the outer faces of the new, tall folder. "Folded in theme fashion" in the apparatus designates this manner of handling. If the last page was not covered with writing, Tho-reau endorsed it on the right side—the upper face of the tall folder—with his name and often a full or par-tial date, plus, for the forensics, the assignment num-ber. Occasionally the endorsement appears elsewhere than on the last page. On the themes, Channing added in pencil, for his own filing or record-keeping purposes, Thoreau's initial, the theme assignment number, and a short form of the year (e.g., "35"). No grades are recorded on either themes or forensics.[7]

Most of the college manuscripts came into the possession of F. B. Sanborn, who published them, liberally edited, in *The Life of Henry David Thoreau* (1917). The originals bear notations in Sanborn's hand, chiefly Roman numbers agreeing with the essay headings in his biography, and capital letters *C* to indicate that he had copied them. Sanborn also drew heavy pencil lines before Channing's faint year-dates, apparently in order to call them subsequently to his own attention.

In the present edition, printer's copy for every piece based on manuscript copy-text was prepared on the typewriter from a photocopy of the original. Typescript was then read several times against the photocopy and at least once—usually twice—against the original. Printer's copy of works based on printed forms was prepared on photocopies of the copy-texts after Hinman machine collation demonstrated that different specimens of each copy-text were textually identical. (Prints of a copy of *The Dial* other than Thoreau's own were marked for printer's copy of "Aulus Persius Flaccus" and "The Laws of Menu.") The printed copy-text and post-copy-text of "Thomas Carlyle" were collated three times by hand to insure the identification of all differences between the 1847 and 1866 printings.

In keeping with the guidelines established by the Center for Editions of American Authors for all editions published under its auspices, this volume has

[7] See Edwin Moser, "Thoreau's Theme Grades," *Thoreau Society Bulletin*, 91 (Spring, 1965), 1-2.

been examined in printer's copy by an independent textual expert, and has been proofread at least five times by three different individuals, including the editor, in galley and page proof.

3. TYPES OF EMENDATION

A.   Since the present edition is not intended as a type-facsimile of the copy-texts, such details of printed copy-text design as display type, running heads, repetition of title and author in a second installment ("Thomas Carlyle") and notices of continuation and termination are silently omitted. The original pagination, printer's signatures, and smudges are of course disregarded; broken but legible characters are treated as though they were whole. No textual significance should be assigned to the running heads in this edition. Although chosen for their appropriateness to the texts, and sometimes duplicating Thoreau's own titles, they are elements of design, not of text. Set-off lines of verse, whether from printed or manuscript copy-text, appear here in reduced type. Italic display type (at a flush-left margin) has been chosen for the datelines of all Thoreau's early essays save one: "Musings" contains the date in its title, and no separate dateline is needed. When datelines are drawn from Thoreau's autograph endorsements of his essays, the original forms are recorded in the apparatus.

Many of the Early Essays—themes, forensics, and the commencement piece on "The Commercial Spirit" —begin not with true *titles* but rather with *topics* assigned by Thoreau's teacher. These topics occur in the form of single or multiple short paragraphs in the manuscripts; in this typesetting the topic material is inset but no additional indentation is given the first topic paragraph. Subsequent paragraphs in a single topic begin, however, with further indentation. The texts of themes, forensics, and the commencement piece begin flush left with the first word or two in capitals and small capitals, except where the beginning of an essay has been mutilated or lost. Thoreau's theme on T. Pomponius Atticus—from printed copytext—is headed with a topic so like a true title that it has been handled differently (see below).

The remaining essays Thoreau wrote before his graduation from Harvard, and all the Miscellanies, begin—or in the case of fragmentary manuscripts, may be assumed to have begun—with actual titles. They are headed, that it to say, by titular material set in display type in printed copy-texts, or by titles evidently of Thoreau's own election, if not invention, in manuscript copy-texts (including the book-title headings of Thoreau's college-period reviews). Titles chosen by the editor as appropriate to fragmentary texts, such as "Sir Henry Vane," fall into the same category. Together with the "Atticus" heading, all these titles have been set flush left in the present edition. As a rule, the beginning of Thoreau's text is given a deep paragraph indentation unless the beginning is lost, or a subtitle or preliminary matter intervenes between title and text. Subtitles (all from *Dial* copy-text, and there centered) are likewise set flush left.

Three *Dial* compilations of wisdom literature, "Sayings of Confucius," "Chinese Four Books," and the selection from Hermes and Saadi, are headed "Ethnical Scriptures" in their magazine publication. Apparently chosen by Emerson, this caption was also used for *Dial* extracts other than those assembled by Thoreau. The editor views it as a *Dial* department heading rather than a true textual element, and deletes it from the text of the present edition. Since the Hermes and Saadi selection bears no other general title than "Ethnical Scriptures" in the *Dial* publication (there, subtitles head the divisions of text), the present editor supplies the title "Hermes Trismegistus . . . From the Gulistan of Saadi." Thoreau's preliminary notes to "The Laws of Menu," "Chinese Four Books," and the Hermes extracts have been inset much like the topics of themes and forensics, for the same design reasons.

No effort was made to reproduce the format of a list of titles on page forty-four, which is neither centered nor aligned on a margin in Thoreau's manuscript: an indented left margin is employed in this edition. For rules in Thoreau's manuscript and printed pieces the editor and designer substitute wide spacing. Deletion of individual rules within essays is noted in the apparatus for each affected text; terminal rules are silently disregarded. Superscript suffixes in dates and other ordinals, e.g., "13th," which occur rather often in the manuscript copy-texts, are regularly lowered to the line, and dots beneath the superscripts, where these occur, are ignored as insignificant. (The superscribed "th" suffix is often so perfunctory as to resemble a ditto or quotation mark; "d" and "nd," as in "3d" and "2nd," are normally legible.)[8]

No changes in the above categories are recorded as emendations; all others are.

[8] There are fourteen instances of lowered superscripts in the text, besides duplications in the apparatus wherever any of these ordinals are cited: 14.24, 18.7, 18.7, 43.21, 43.28, 53.27, 57.16, 64.33, 66.1, 66.20, 113.21, 113.27, 185.34, and 188.14. Superscript suffixes have been lowered in the emendation entries for datelines of works from manuscript copy-text at 26.13, 36.17, 37.29, 42.1, 50.1, 79.1, 83.22, 86.15, 93.7, 99.6, 101.12, 105.1, and 108.16; and in a quotation in the copy-text note for "The Book of the Seasons." In the endorsement to "Life and Works of Sir W. Scott" a superscript flourish after "Cam" (Cambridge) has been ignored.

B. Quoted lines of poetry, erratically and confusingly treated in the manuscript copy-texts, are uniformly indented. Paragraph indentations are also regularized, although in some manuscript instances the only paragraph signal is the conclusion of the preceding line well before the right-hand margin or the presence of a large vertical space before the new paragraph. Wide spacing in contractions (twice only, in "Thomas Carlyle") is reduced.

C. Periods are supplied after abbreviations when they are lacking in the copy-texts. In a few instances, abbreviations of proper nouns are expanded for clarity of reference: e.g., "K. Ch." is emended to "King Charles," but "Geo. Fox" is left undisturbed.

D. Authorial substantive changes in post-copy-text forms are adopted as explained in the previous section of this introduction.

E. Positive spelling errors, whether authorial, nonauthorial, or of undetermined origin, are corrected. The editor has checked unusual spellings against four dictionaries of which Thoreau owned copies, retaining the copy-text spellings if they are listed in at least one of them. The lexicons consulted are Nathan Bailey's *An Universal Etymological English Dictionary*, seventeenth edition (London: T. Osborne *et al.*, 1759); Samuel Johnson and John Walker, *Johnson's English Dictionary* (Boston: Charles Ewer and T. H. Carter, 1828); John Walker, *A Critical Pronouncing Dictionary . . . of the English Language* (New York: Collins and Hannay, 1823); and Noah Webster, *An American Dictionary of the English Language* (New York: N. and J. White, 1838).[9]

---

[9] Thoreau's manuscript library list does not specify which editions of Webster or Bailey he owned; the editions named

Where copy-text is a printed form, the editor has attempted to isolate any elements of house-spelling. The single-l treatment of Thoreau's habitual "traveller," "travelled," and "travelling" in the *Graham's Magazine* "Carlyle" text is seen as an editorial imposition and the several instances are emended. Similarly the form "Shakespeare" in Sanborn's text of a section of "L'Allegro & Il Penseroso" where the manuscript is mutilated is emended to "Shakspeare," Thoreau's normal spelling during the college period. The evidence for these emendations is provided in textual notes.

No effort has been made to modernize archaic spellings in Thoreau's quotations from early English works (e.g., in "Sir Walter Raleigh" and "Homer. Ossian. Chaucer.").

The editor has tried to determine whether certain unusual spellings of names were tolerated within the appropriate discipline—classical studies, for example— even where Thoreau follows a source in a name-spelling that modern readers may find peculiar. Emendation is performed only on those forms that by this standard appear to be positive errors in the copy-text.

F.   In the manuscript pieces Thoreau sometimes forgot to enter apostrophes in possessives: they are supplied by the present editor. Misplaced apostrophes are properly located. The terminal dash, a common feature of Thoreau's working drafts, occasionally appears in his clean copies and is emended to a period. The other accidentals of the copy-texts, both manuscript and print, are emended only when they threaten

---

were thought by the editor to approximate or duplicate those on Thoreau's shelves. The Bailey and Johnson lexicons seem to have been acquired by Thoreau before 1840, and perhaps before he went to Harvard. See Walter Harding, *Thoreau's Library* (Charlottesville: University of Virginia Press, 1957).

to obscure the meaning.[10] To regularize copy-text accidentals to the statistically dominant forms in Thoreau's manuscripts—a difficult task both practically and theoretically, since the manuscripts often disclose no clear preference—would be to misrepresent Thoreau's normal, that is, inconsistent, practices. Regularization of any sort, even to the dominant forms of a copy-text or to an inconsistent author's most frequent forms, constitutes a form of modernization that the present edition avoids. The irregularity of accidentals reflects, then, both Thoreau's style and the nineteenth-century printshop policies that permitted such diversity.

We may fairly assume that many accidentals (including punctuation, word-division, and tolerated spellings) in the printed copy-texts are nonauthorial, but because of Thoreau's own inconsistency we can only rarely be sure which ones are impositions by a copyist, editor, or compositor.

G. Demonstrable copyist's or compositor's misreadings of substantives in the printed copy-texts are corrected. These errors include incredible or implausible wordings and plausible ones that can be shown to be nonauthorial corruptions of more appropriate readings in manuscript pre-copy-text. In "Love,"

---

[10] In the formal penmanship of the Early Essays Thoreau's capital and lowercase letters S and C are often indistinguishable, and when in doubt the editor has perforce chosen that reading, lowercase or uppercase, which best agrees with the sense. One or more such choices have been made in each of the following pieces: "Musings," "Style May . . . Offend against Simplicity," "The Book of the Seasons," "Literary Digressions," "Life and Works of Sir W. Scott," "Cultivation of the Imagination," "The Greek Classic Poets," "The Meaning of 'Fate,'" "Whether the Government Ought to Educate," "Travellers & Inhabitants," "History . . . of the Roman Republic," and "Barbarities of Civilized States."

for example, Thoreau's working draft term "surely" comes out as "rarely" in *Letters to Various Persons*, the copy-text. Pre-copy-text manuscripts have also been read against fair manuscript copy-texts as a check upon copying errors by Thoreau himself; a few were found and emended.

H.   Wherever possible the editor has located and examined the sources for Thoreau's direct quotations and paraphrases in *Early Essays and Miscellanies*, in the editions Thoreau used. As a check against typographer's errors in printed copy-texts and inadvertent copying errors in Thoreau's fair manuscripts, these sources have been read against the texts. The few emendations which resulted are discussed in textual notes.

I.   The Early Essays are given uniform date-lines as explained in the first section of this introduction, and titles, where lacking, are supplied.[11]

Early Essays and Miscellanies embodies the clear-text principle: no footnotes or square brackets except Thoreau's own interrupt the text. Only one editorial symbol is employed in the text. It is the pair of angle brackets containing ellipses dots ($\langle . . . \rangle$) for matter made unrecoverable by mutilation of the manuscript. Reconstructions from partially mutilated portions, readings drawn from pre-copy-text or post-copy-text, and readings taken from transcripts made before the mutilation occurred are entered into the text without

---

11 In the table of contents and textual apparatus—but not in the texts themselves—essays with long topic headings or titles are identified by short titles. These are key phrases drawn from the full headings appearing on the copy-texts or supplied from Channing's Lists or Channing's Themes. No editorial interpolations or symbols except for occasionally necessary ellipses dots, and the adjustment of initial letters to conventional uppercase or lowercase forms, occur in the short titles.

symbolic accompaniment; explanations appear in the apparatus.

4. FORMS OF DOCUMENTATION

All editorial apparatus for each essay, except for the detailed identification of manuscripts pertinent to the text and the list of line-end hyphenations, is grouped individually by essay immediately following this introduction. Since the kinds of copy-text employed in the present edition are various—holograph manuscript, autograph with nonauthorial matter and imposed authorial revisions, printed copy, and print with autograph corrections—the kinds of documentary apparatus needed for full and accurate reporting of textual information must also vary somewhat.

Uniform for all pieces in the volume, however, are the first two types of end matter, textual notes and (where emendation has occurred) a list of emendations. The initial textual note is sometimes the only one. It specifies the copy-text for this edition (if manuscript, "MS" plus an abbreviated repository name; if a printed form, full bibliographical citation), categorizes the piece (e.g., theme, forensic, essay, summary-review), dates it, gives the endorsement, and discusses any problems of authenticity or attribution. (Authenticity is at issue in "The Seasons" and in Sanborn's readings for a lost essay and mutilated parts of others; attribution is at issue for the unsigned *Dial* extracts from eastern writings, particularly "Sayings of Confucius," "Chinese Four Books," and "Hermes Trismegistus . . . From the Gulistan of Saadi.") Additional textual notes are explanations of specific decisions to emend or not to emend where the decision was complex or problematical. Textual notes of the latter sort begin with a page and line reference and the key word or phrase.[12]

The list of emendations is a tabular presentation of all changes made from copy-text other than those remarked earlier as silent design changes or typographical conveniences. The source or sources of the emendations are identified briefly in a headnote to the list. At the left margin the emendation is located by page and line (if this reference is marked with an asterisk the emendation is discussed in a textual note); the middle column gives the emended reading and the right-hand column the original, copy-text reading:

22.5-6	concurred	concured

Where editorial description rather than simple presentation is required in an emendations list entry, as, for example, where the editor supplies matter or changes the format, the descriptive words are italicized to distinguish them from textual matter per se:

* 9.23	January 31, 1835	*lacking*
16.2	vast	*last two letters illegible*
26.12	Resigns	*not indented*

In those instances where descriptive, editorial words follow the author's words in a column entry, the italicized description is further set off by parentheses:

* 21.5	September, 1835	Sept. 1835 (*at end*)
18.22	swollen	swolen (*corrected by Channing*)

---

[12] Line references are by literal tally. That is, blank lines are disregarded, but every line of type, whether normal, reduced, or display type, is included in the count. On pages of solid normal type the line-guide may conveniently be used.

Those few entries where the descriptive element precedes the textual element are straightforward, and parentheses are not needed:

87.2   there   *possibly* then

Two conventional symbols are commonly used in the emendations lists. A wavy dash ($\sim$) in the right-hand column stands for the word occupying this position in the Princeton Edition reading to the left. An inferior caret ($_\wedge$) in either column signifies the absence of a punctuation mark:

104.3-4   support. $\sim$ —

(the copy-text reading is "support–")

101.13   Chap.   Chap $_\wedge$
105.6   theirs. $\sim$ $_\wedge$

A third symbol occasionally employed here is the virgule, always representing a line-end division. Thus, in the following example, the word "spinning" was divided at the end of the line after the first syllable, without a hyphen, in the copy-text:

59.12   spinning   spin $_\wedge$ / ning

Angle brackets surrounding ellipses have the same meaning in the apparatus as in the text:

87.31   ⟨ . . . ⟩   *remainder of MS*
                                             missing

For essays taken from manuscript copy-text, the next element of apparatus is a list of alterations, reporting all changes Thoreau made on the copy-text. They are presented by means of simple descriptive phrases following a page and line reference, a key word or phrase, and a square bracket. Once again, all authorial words are printed in the original Roman and all editorial words in italics:

102.22 hill] *altered by erasure from* hills
78.19 blemishes] *altered from* belmishes
78.20-21 pleasing] *preceded by cancelled* striking passage a

The changes described in the last two examples were made in the basic writing medium, which for all texts from manuscript in this volume is ink. When Thoreau made an alteration in pencil the fact is noted in the entry:

178.14 he] *added in pencil above cancelled* his were

In this last example, the cancellation line as well as the entered word should be understood to be in pencil. No mention is made of the presence of carets, which almost always accompany a simple interlinear addition (one not involving a cancellation) in the same writing medium as the added matter.

Many entries in alterations lists for the college themes cite changes Thoreau made—apparently always in ink—in response to pencilled criticisms by E. T. Channing. In keeping with the policy about imposed revisions which has already been described, such alterations are not incorporated into the text unless they are corrections of positive errors, which the editor would emend had Thoreau not corrected them at Channing's direction. Every evidence of Channing's role in a given alteration is noted in the entry:

95.14 indifference] *sixth letter added interlinearly following Channing's marginal "sp"*
95.20 origin] *cancelled and* beginning *added interlinearly following Channing's underlining*

The editor has carefully studied all lines marked by Channing, but in some instances he is not sure whether Thoreau made or did not make alterations. Such lines are noted in the alterations list:

96.16-17 fight . . . calm] *marked "p" in margin by Channing; no alteration apparent*

The descriptive phrase *"followed by,"* as in

96.24 our] *followed by cancelled* our

refers to the appearance of the text. It should not be confused with the descriptive formula *"following Channing's"* (see examples above), which refers to Thoreau's response, when correcting a theme, to Channing's pencil symbols and revisions. *"Followed by"* and *"following Channing's"* are never used in the same entry.

Paralleling the list of alterations for essays from manuscript copy-text is a presentation of Thoreau's corrections and revisions in those four essays from *The Dial* where Thoreau's copy of the magazine bears his autograph annotations. For "Aulus Persius Flaccus" and "The Laws of Menu," this presentation takes the form of a list of rejected (print) pre-copy-text readings superseded by autograph corrections, since the *Dial* printing *as corrected* is copy-text. For "Dark Ages" and "Homer . . . ," where the unannotated *Dial* printing serves as copy-text, all of Thoreau's holograph changes not adopted (and listed) as emendations are particularized in a list of "Thoreau's Corrections and Revisions." In either case the organization is columnar; the central column contains copy-text readings (followed in the present edition), and the right-hand column records the superseded *Dial* readings (in lists for "Persius" and "Menu") or the rejected autograph alterations (in lists for "Dark Ages" and "Homer . . ."). The following examples are drawn from the "Homer . . ." list:

| 154.11 | is rhymed or measured | is either rhymed or in some way musically measured |
| 154.14 | Yet | *marked with paragraph sign* |

A headnote to each list of corrections and revisions explains its organization.

A table of textual variations is provided for "DIED . . . Miss Anna Jones," "Thomas Carlyle," "Love," and "Chastity & Sensuality." The table presents substantive differences between copy-text and relevant or possibly relevant post-copy-text, plus, in a very few instances, variant substantives from pre-copy-text manuscript which Thoreau or a compositor might inadvertently have changed to equally plausible copy-text forms, or which an editor or compositor might deliberately have altered in the absence of authorial control. In these collations the source of variant readings and the particular specimen used are identified in a headnote. The organization of the textual variations table is columnar, and again, where the listing of a variant requires descriptive editorial phrases, the non-textual matter is set in italics:

| 231.28 | throws | throw (Y) |
| 235.32-236.4 | Every . . . sublime. | *deleted* (Y) |

Aside from editorial ellipses in the column citing the reading in the present edition, internal punctuation of the phrases in either column follows the collated texts, but adjacent punctuation is ignored. Thus, where a variant text abbreviates a sentence in the copy-text

division at the end of the line in the present edition. Every instance of line-end hyphenation of a hyphenated or possibly hyphenated compound in the copy-text required an editorial decision as to the form the construction should take in this text. Such judgments were based on other appearances of the term in Thoreau's manuscripts of the same period, on source readings where the ambiguous phenomenon occurred in a quotation, and, where possible, on other appearances of the term in the copy-text itself. The form recorded in the hyphenation list (for example, "dragon-fly" or "bluestockings") is the form to which the editor resolved each line-end hyphenation in the copy-texts. By coincidence, some few compounds—such as "arm-chair" at 42.29-30—are hyphenated at the end of the line in *both* the copy-text and the present edition: these are listed in the forms to which the editor has resolved them notwithstanding the new typesetting. The word-division list for THE WRITINGS OF HENRY D. THOREAU records those compounds hyphenated at the end of the line in this edition that appeared as hyphenated compounds in the copy-text. Terms divided at the end of the line in THE WRITINGS but not listed here were continuous in the copy-text. (Again, since the present typesetting occasionally duplicated copy-text line-end hyphenations, certain entries in and omissions from this list reflect editorial decisions: "preoccupied" at 246.33-34, for instance, is line-end hyphenated in both the copy-text and this edition, but since the editor resolves it as a continuous word it is excluded from the second list; "block-head" at 57.23-24, line-end hyphenated in both texts, is included in the second list because the editor resolves it as a hyphenated form.) The information provided in this list will enable a reader to reconstruct copy-text forms that would otherwise be disguised, and will permit accurate transcription of the text for quotation and reprinting.

Finally, the checklist of manuscripts describes, for each piece in *Early Essays and Miscellanies*, the extant Thoreau manuscripts associated with it. The description of manuscript *copy-texts* includes paper color, ink color, number of pages, pagination by Thoreau (if present), folding pattern, and any identifying notations by Channing or Sanborn. Pagination and other additions by collectors and librarians are not reported. For every manuscript cited in the checklist, whether copy-text, pre-copy-text, or subsequent autograph use of the text, the name of the holding library or archive and the manuscript's call number or shelf designation are reported.

Early Essays

Textual Notes and Tables

The Seasons

Copy-text: MS, Concord Free Public Library. The conjectural dating is by Walter Harding in *The Days of Henry Thoreau* (New York: Knopf, 1966), p. 26, and agrees with that offered by Kenneth W. Cameron in "Young Henry Thoreau in the Annals of the Concord Academy (1829-1833)," *Emerson Society Quarterly*, 9 (IV Quarter, 1957), 4. The composition date 1827 suggested by F. B. Sanborn in *The Life of Henry David Thoreau* (Boston and New York: Houghton Mifflin Company, 1917), p. 51, would anticipate Thoreau's studies in the Concord Academy by at least a year—he seems to have been first enrolled in late 1828—and thus does not comport with the provenance of the manuscript, reported below. The signature "Henry D. Thoreau" appears at the end. Thoreau is referred to as "Henry Thoreau" in minutes of the Concord Academic Debating Society, contemporary with his Concord Academy years (see Cameron, *op. cit.*), but in formal Academy records he is identified as "David Henry Thoreau" (see Hubert H. Hoeltje, "Thoreau and the Concord Academy," *New England Quarterly*, 21 [1948], 105), and apart from "The Seasons" there is no firm evidence of his having reversed the order of his baptismal names or initials until after he graduated from Harvard. In the endorsements of his college-period compositions, the heading of his class book autobiography, and other surviving dated or datable signatures of the Harvard years, he used the forms "D. H. Thoreau," "David Henry Thoreau," "Thoreau, David H.," and simply "Thoreau." The immature handwriting of "The Seasons" cannot fairly be compared with Thoreau's later autograph. Against the question of authenticity raised by the signature, one should weigh the manuscript's provenance: it was transmitted on May 14, 1892, by Horatio F. Allen, the son of Thoreau's Academy preceptor Phineas Allen, to Alfred W. Hosmer of Concord.

Emendations

* 3.1	1828-1829?	*lacking*
3.5	It is	It it
3.9	beginning	begining
3.14	song.	~ ∧
3.18	beautiful	beutiful
3.22	leaves	leavs
3.22	which	whith
3.23	retiring	retireing
3.25	Winter.	~ ∧
3.25-26	covered	coverd

ANXIETIES AND DELIGHTS OF A DISCOVERER

Copy-text: MS, Huntington. Theme, endorsed "D. H. Thoreau". Date is drawn from E. T. Channing's Lists.

Emendations

* 4.1	December 6, 1834	*lacking*
4.24	satisfaction.	~ ∧
4.30	Genoese	Genoesse
5.2	irresistible	irresistable

Alterations

4.7   disappointments]   *sixth letter added interlinearly*
4.17   will]   *altered by erasure and overwriting from* shall
4.22   have sunk]   have *preceded by erased* w
4.31   disappointment]   *sixth letter added interlinearly*
5.19   did]   *followed by erased* he
5.20   to]   *followed by cancelled* to
5.20   heighten]   *second letter added interlinearly*

MEN WHOSE PURSUIT IS MONEY

Copy-text: MS, University of Virginia. Theme, endorsed "D. H. Thoreau"; dated from Channing's Lists.

Emendations

* 5.22	December 20, 1834	*lacking*
7.4-5	"But . . . cheat;	*on same line as preceding word*
7.9	one's	ones
7.11	and	and and (*corrected by Channing*)

Alterations

  6.8   striving] *fourth letter added interlinearly*
  6.20 own,] *comma possibly inserted after first writing*
  6.22 Aristocrats] *changed by erasure from* Aristocrates
  6.22 liberty] *fifth letter added interlinearly*
  6.23 rights] *altered from* are *by erasure and overwriting*
  6.32 enjoyment] *preceded by cancelled* mere
  6.33 merely,] *added interlinearly*
  6.35 he, who] *comma inserted over erased comma;* who *followed by erased comma*
  6.36 upon] *cancelled and* to *added interlinearly following Channing's partially erased pencil revision*
  7.10 interest] *altered by erasure from* interests,
  7.15 undertaken] *followed by erased semicolon*
  7.16 with . . . zeal;] *added interlinearly*
  7.16 one] *written over erased* it were
  7.22 himself,] *comma possibly inserted after first writing*
  7.24 whose] *preceded by cancelled* whose

OF KEEPING A PRIVATE JOURNAL

Copy-text: MS, Huntington. Theme, endorsed "*D. H. Thoreau*"; dated from Channing's Lists and from a notation, "Jany 17. 1835" after the endorsement in an unidentified hand. A rule after the topic heading is deleted in this edition.

Emendations

* 8.1	January 17, 1835	*lacking*
8.29	in	in in (*corrected by Channing*)

Alterations

  8.15-16 to us . . . use-] *marked "?" in margin by Channing; no alterations apparent*
  8.17 practice] *altered from* practise *following Channing's marginal "sp"*
  8.20 importance.] *followed by erased* in keepin
  8.31 may] *altered by erasure and overwriting from* might

8.32   have]   *last two letters written over erased* d
9.10   our]   *altered by erasure and overwriting from*
their
9.14   for one]   *added interlinearly*
9.15   borrow]   *followed by cancelled* of another
9.21   take]   *followed by erased* f

"WE ARE APT TO BECOME WHAT OTHERS . . . THINK US
TO BE"

Copy-text: MS, Huntington. Theme, endorsed "D. H. Thoreau"; dated from Channing's Lists.

Emendations

* 9.23	January 31, 1835	*lacking*
9.26	others'	other's
9.27	opinion."	$\sim_\wedge$ "
10.6	been	ben
10.6	brought	*followed by dash or misplaced crossing of* t
10.7	I	Il (*superfluous stroke*)
10.14	of	*lacking*
10.17	haven't	havn't
10.17	concluded.	$\sim$,
10.20	waves;	$\sim$,
11.1	customs	customes

Alterations

10.16   act]   *last letter written over unrecoverable*
erased letters
10.21   but,]   *comma erased and/or comma after* hand
added following Channing's marginal "p"
10.23-24   drifted . . . secure]   *marked with marginal*
line by Channing; no alterations apparent
10.26   down]   *added interlinearly*
10.28   which party]   *first letter of* which *written over*
erased p
10.29   their actions]   *underlined with an "a" beneath*
and "x C" in margin by Channing; no alteration apparent
10.30   mere]   *changed by cancellation from* merely
10.31   they]   *altered from* their

11.2-3   entire . . . character]   *underlined with "a"
beneath and "x C" in margin by Channing, with the
bracketed comment "Do [sign] not retain their character?"
at end; no alteration apparent*

FORMS, CEREMONIES, AND RESTRAINTS OF POLITE SOCIETY

Copy-text: MS, Brown University. Theme, endorsed "D. H.
Thoreau,". Dated from Channing's Lists.

Emendations

* 11.4	February 14, 1835	*lacking*
11.26	neighbour's	neighbours
12.3	the	thes
12.18	restraints	res-/straints

Alterations

11.11   neglected]   *preceded by* are *added interlinearly
in pencil by Channing and overwritten by Thoreau; line
marked marginally by Channing*

11.16   rules]   *written over erased* forms

11.20-21   [ex-/]cess . . . opinion,]   *marked "p" in
margin by Channing; semicolon after* particular *may have
been added or altered from comma*

11.21   long]   *altered from* longue *following
Channing's marginal "sp"*

11.22   sacrifice]   *fourth letter added interlinearly*

11.22-23   candor]   *followed by Channing's pencil
comma overwritten by Thoreau; Channing writes "p" in
margin*

11.27   unluckily]   *fifth letter added interlinearly*

11.27   Oh]   *followed by erased vertical stroke,
perhaps exclamation mark*

11.29   fixed]   *followed by erased* fix

11.30   color]   *followed by erased comma*

12.2   for]   *added interlinearly above cancelled* at

12.3   more]   *added in right margin*

12.16   (aside)]   *added interlinearly*

12.20-21   impertinence . . . from]   *marked "x" in
margin by Channing; no alteration evident*

12.24   wider,]   *comma erased following Channing's
marginal "p"*

12.25   Romans]   *possibly altered from* Roman

12.25   Romans]   *followed by erased* gar
12.35   certain]   *altered from* ceartin
12.35   by]   *cancelled and* in *added interlinearly in pencil by Channing, and overwritten by Thoreau; see next entry*
12.36   considered]   *cancelled following Channing's brackets*

A MAN OF BUSINESS, A MAN OF PLEASURE, A MAN OF THE WORLD

Copy-text: MS, Huntington. Theme, endorsed "D. H. Thoreau"; dated from Channing's Lists.

Emendations

* 13.1	February 28, 1835	*lacking*
13.24	which,	~ ;
13.33	please."	~ ∧ "
14.4	gay—"	*quotation mark above dash*
14.13	Maker's	Makers

Alterations

13.7   energetic]   *followed by erased* , man
13.7   energetic]   *followed by pencil comma, probably Channing's*
13.7   persevering]   *followed by erased comma*
13.15   succeed]   *sixth letter added interlinearly*
13.19   industry]   *first letter written over erased* a
13.20   and a]   and *squeezed into line;* a *added interlinearly*
14.1   That]   T *altered from* t
14.3   mere]   *first letter written over erased* of
14.5   Hence]   *preceded by erased* But save me from the gayety of
14.8   of]   *added interlinearly*
14.12-13   that their]   that *added interlinearly*
14.19   his]   *altered by overwriting and erasure from* he is

MUSINGS

Copy-text: MS, Morgan. A fragment: additional matter has been cut away at the end. In this edition a rule before the paragraph beginning *"Fair Haven"* is deleted. A pencilled endorsement, probably in Thoreau's later hand, reads "April 20 −35".

Emendations

14.24	April	Apr.
14.25	monopolize	monopolise
14.29	in	*on same line as first verse line*
14.30	"the	' ∼
15.1	and the	*on same line as last verse line*
15.8	ethereal	etherial
15.15	premises.	∼ ∧ (*at extreme right margin*)
15.16	dawn ∧	∼ .
16.2	vast	*last two letters illegible*

Alterations

14.29 peal] *written over erased word, perhaps* stroke
14.30 steeple,] *followed by erased* had
14.31 Swinging] *followed by erased vertical stroke*
15.16 *Fair Haven.*] *added in paragraph indentation*
15.16 of the dawn] *added interlinearly; see emendation*
16.12 land.] *followed by line possibly signifying conclusion, and setting off erased note, partly illegible*: The following [*two words, ca. 4 and 3 letters*] 1835
16.13 if] *preceded by flourish, possibly leading to erased note after* land.
16.14 redman] *altered from* red man
16.15 loftier] *added interlinearly; altered from* lofty

KINDS OF ENERGETIC CHARACTER

Copy-text: MS, Huntington. Theme, endorsed "Thoreau"; dated from Channing's Lists.

Emendations

* 16.18	May 23, 1835	*lacking*
17.9	designs	deseigns (*corrected by Channing*)
17.25	design	deseign (*corrected by Channing*)

17.29	Philip Van	~ . ~ .
18.6	descriptions	descrip $_\wedge$ / tions
18.12	carrying	crrying (*corrected by Channing*)
18.18	design	deseign (*corrected by Channing*)
18.22	swollen	swolen (*corrected by Channing*)
18.23	irresistible	irresistable (*corrected by Channing*)

Alterations

17.1   as in] *second letter of* in *written over erased vertical stroke*

17.13   energy] *added in right margin*

17.21   again] *last three letters written over erased letters and followed by erased comma*

17.32   give] *written over erased letters*

18.2   Judgment] *third letter written over erased letter, perhaps* g

18.22   torrent] *added interlinearly*

18.25   so] *squeezed into line*

19.3   attended] *underlined in pencil, probably by Channing*

PRIVILEGES AND PLEASURES OF A LITERARY MAN

Copy-text: MS, Morgan. Theme, endorsed *"Thoreau"*. A pencilled date on the endorsement page in an unidentified hand, "Sept. 18, 1835", agrees with Channing's Lists.

Emendations

* 19.6	September 18, 1835	*lacking*
20.1	mind—	~ —/—
20.19	really	realy
20.28	inheritance.	~ $_\wedge$
20.30	another—	~ —/—
20.35-36	, the proprietor,	$_\wedge$ ~ ~ $_\wedge$
21.1	breathe	breath

Alterations

19.22   fondness for] *last two letters of* for *written over unrecoverable erased letters*

19.30   But this]   *preceded by pencil paragraph sign,*
probably Channing's

20.5   "is]   *preceded by unrecoverable erased letter or*
character

20.7   ourselves]   *second letter written over unrecoverable erased letter*

20.10   Innocent]   *preceded by pencil paragraph sign,*
probably Channing's

20.14   the]   *written over unrecoverable erased word*

20.17-18   dependent]   *third through sixth letters*
written over unrecoverable erased letters

20.18   upon]   *written over unrecoverable erased word*

20.20   look to]   *written over erased* rely upon

20.21   every]   *added interlinearly above cancelled* all

20.21   pursuit]   *altered by erasure from* pursuits

20.22   trust and reliance.]   *added interlinearly above*
cancelled dependance.

20.22   Happy]   *followed by erased* is

20.30-31   —it is . . . man]   *cancelled following*
Channing's brackets

20.33   Reflection]   R *altered from* r

21.1   truth—]   *dash written over erased comma*

21.2-3   thus . . . look]   *marked "X" in margin by*
Channing; no alterations evident although one or both
commas (after thus *and* virtue) *may have been added*

Severe and Mild Punishments

Copy-text: MS, Texas. Forensic, endorsed "Thoreau. No.
2 Sept. 1835", the "2" being pencilled over an unrecoverable erasure.

Emendations

* 21.5	September, 1835	Sept. 1835 (*at end*)
21.13	many	n *lacks one stroke*
22.4	short ∧	~ .
22.5-6	concurred	concured
23.21	may;	~ ,
23.21	erroneous.	~ . . (*see alteration*)

Alterations

21.21   dread]   *altered from* dredd *by erasure*

22.7   capital]   *fourth letter added interlinearly*

22.10   injured]   *followed by erased* comma
22.12   thus]   *added interlinearly*
22.31   vicious are]   *written over erased matter, perhaps* criminal is
22.31   often]   *followed by cancelled* is often
22.35   they act]   *altered from* he acts *by addition of letters and erasure*
23.12-13   not immediately]   *added interlinearly above erased* otherwise un
23.19   are not to]   *added interlinearly*
23.21   this]   *written over unrecoverable erasure*
23.21   erroneous]   *written over erased word ending in* e

POPULAR FEELING

Copy-text: MS, Princeton. Fragment of a theme, endorsed "Thoreau."; dated and titled from Channing's Lists. The topic or subtitle is drawn from Channing's Themes.

Emendations

* 23.22	October 16, 1835	*lacking*
* 23.23	Popular Feeling &c.	*lacking*
* 23.24-28	What . . . with?	*lacking*
23.29	⟨ . . . ⟩	*pages missing*

Alterations

24.1   outdone]   *pencil mark below* td; *no alteration evident*
24.3   Few]   F *written over erased* f
24.7   farther]   *first* r *written over erased* t
24.11   bank]   *altered by erasure from* banks
24.16   contradict]   tra *written over erased* dict
24.21   reason]   *preceded by cancelled* convince or
24.21   host]   *followed by cancelled* who are

STYLE MAY . . . OFFEND AGAINST SIMPLICITY

Copy-text: MS, Morgan. Theme, endorsed "Thoreau"; dated from Channing's Lists.

Emendations

* 24.25	November 27, 1835	*lacking*
25.27	to be	to to be
26.5	alone!	∼ !

| 26.11 | At | *not indented* |
| 26.12 | Resigns | *not indented* |

Alterations

25.2 distinctly] *followed by erased comma*
25.6-7 to render] to *added interlinearly*
25.8 whatever] *second letter written over unrecoverable erased letter*
25.15 which] *followed by erased letter, perhaps* e
25.15 our] *first letter written over erased letter, perhaps* h
25.17 case,] *altered from unrecoverable word by overwriting and erasure*
25.18 rare, and] and *followed by erased comma*
25.19 expression] *followed by erased comma*
26.2 itself.] *followed by unrecoverable erased letter*
26.5 Shakspeare] *altered by erasure from* Shakespeare
26.8 wisdom] *first letter written over erased letter, perhaps* W
26.8 and] *written over unrecovered erased letters*
26.11 *Simplicity*] *followed by erased matter, perhaps* re *or close quotation marks*

THE BOOK OF THE SEASONS

Copy-text: MS, Huntington. Summary-review, in a notebook signed "D. H. Thoreau" on the flyleaf, and labeled below, "Cambridge" and "Index rerum". Immediately after the review appears a notation in darker ink, possibly related to it: "Mather has some where observed, 'July 1st 1724. This day being our *insipid, ill contrived anniversary which we call the commencement.*'"

30.10-11 irresistible: The copy-text follows the source (Philadelphia: Carey & Lea, 1831), p. 51, in a misspelling, "irresastable".

34.34 buoyant: The copy-text reads "boyant". Thoreau may have intended a pun, but his misspelling of this word is characteristic.

Emendations

| 26.13 | March 31, 1836 | March 31st 1836. (*at end*) |
| 27.3 | principal | principle |

27.18	Sees	*not indented*
27.18	him in the	him the
27.22	and	amd
27.35	northern	nothern
28.1	ice,	~ ∧
28.2	crawls	crauls
28.11	loses	looses
28.27	vice	*one stroke of* v *lacking*
29.28	whirling	*stroke of first* i *lacking*
29.32	make	nake
29.35	house,	~ ∧
* 30.10-11	irresistible	irresistable
30.17	elements?	~ .
30.32	Bring	*not indented*
30.33	is . . . sayings	*on same line as preceding word*
31.31	trigger.	~ ,
32.6	motley	motely
32.25	Pour	*not indented*
33.26	instance,	~ .
34.7	the tired	The tired
34.20-21	oculists	occulists
34.26	predominating.	~ ,
34.32	Nature".	~ ",
34.33	Is	Iis
* 34.34	buoyant	boyant
35.12	hither	hther
35.17	to fish	to-fish
35.23	uncivilized	*one stroke of* v *lacking*
35.32	dissipation	disipation
36.1	breathe	breath

Alterations

26.24 miscellaneous] *seventh letter added interlinearly in pencil*

27.24 vale] *written over unrecoverable erased word, ca. 6 letters*

27.26 here] *followed by erased* it

27.27 this] *followed by erased word, probably* is

28.14 to some] *altered from* to the

28.15   most]   *added interlinearly*

28.19-20   were . . . were]   *altered from* are . . . are

29.2   Nightingale]   *second and third letters added interlinearly in pencil*

29.23   storm]   *second letter added interlinearly*

30.16   power]   *written over erased word, probably* sublimity

30.17   elements]   *written over erased word, perhaps* wind

31.6-7   ventures]   *written over erased word, perhaps* happens

31.23   gun-shot]   *altered from* gunshot

31.35   result]   *preceded by erased letter*

31.35   probably]   *fifth letter overwritten*

32.2   startling]   *altered from* strartling

32.3   disturbs]   *altered from* disturbed

32.6   the motley]   the *written over erased word, probably* this

32.19   clouds]   *added interlinearly*

33.22   commencing]   *first through seventh letters written over unrecoverable erased word*

34.6   carolled]   *altered by erasure from* carrolled

34.6   in its branches]   *written over unrecoverable erased matter*

34.7   frisked]   *written over unrecoverable erased word*

34.9   a]   *followed by erased* n

34.18   Oct.]   *written over unrecoverable erased matter*

34.27   the eye]   *added interlinearly in pencil*

35.9   But]   *second and third letters added interlinearly*

35.16   coat-flaps of the]   *added interlinearly*

35.34   can]   *first letter overwritten*

36.3   soil]   *written over erased word, probably* earth

36.7   to wage]   *altered by erasure and overwriting from* in wageing

36.8   to pore]   *altered by erasure and overwriting from* in poring

36.9   stinted]   *written over unrecoverable erased word*

Sir Henry Vane

Copy-text: MS, Huntington. Fragment, endorsed at end, "Concord, April 7th 1836". Not in Channing's Themes or Lists. Title supplied by editor.

Emendations

* 36.17	April 7, 1836	April 7th 1836 (*at end*)
36.18	Sir Henry Vane	*lacking*
36.19	⟨ . . . ⟩	*at least 1/3 page missing*
36.27	were	*last letter trimmed*
36.30	unintelligible	uninteligible
37.7-8	⟨ . . . ⟩	*approximately 8 lines cut away*
37.15-24	"Than . . . "In peace	*lines not indented*
37.24	reckons" . . . "her	∼ ' . . . ' ∼

Alterations

36.28	centre]	*last two letters altered from* er
37.23	firm]	f *altered from* F
37.23	leans]	*followed by erased word, perhaps* in
37.24	In]	*altered from* Iin

LITERARY DIGRESSIONS

Copy-text: MS, Huntington. Fragment, endorsed at end, "Concord   April 14th–36." Not in Channing's Themes or Lists. Title supplied by editor.

Emendations

* 37.29	April 14, 1836	April 14th–36. (*at end*)
37.30	Literary Digressions	*lacking*
37.31	⟨ . . . ⟩	*page or pages missing*
38.2	narrative	narative

Alterations

37.32	out, upon]	*altered from* out, on
38.11	me]	*added interlinearly*

FOREIGN INFLUENCE ON AMERICAN LITERATURE

Copy-text: to 40.34, MS, Morgan; 40.35-41.29, MS, Huntington. Forensic, endorsed "Thoreau   No–7– April 1836". "7" has been pencilled over an erasure.

Emendations

* 38.15	April, 1836	~ ∧ ~ (*at end*)
38.22	become	be come
40.8	Shakspeare	Shak ∧ / speare
40.32	new	mew
41.5	breathe	breath

Alterations

38.25   preceded]   *fourth letter written over erased vertical stroke*

39.2   forms]   *third letter written over erased* l

39.6   concern]   *followed by erased comma*

39.13   ours]   *written over erased word, perhaps* it

39.22   take]   *followed by erased comma*

39.23   is worth]   *followed by erased vertical stroke*

39.27   To]   *written over erased* The

40.3-4   declared]   *written over erased* gained

40.6   Britain]   *altered by erasure from* Brittain

40.8   with]   *preceded by erased vertical stroke*

40.13   prized]   *followed by pencil comma of unknown origin*

40.25   which the]   the *written over erased letters, perhaps* preju

40.30   sustain]   *altered by erasure and overwriting, perhaps from* survive

41.6   things]   *written over erased word, perhaps* subjects

41.7   dreamed]   *altered by erasure and overwriting from* drempt

41.19   literati]   *written over erased word, perhaps* public

41.26   nightingales]   *third and fourth letters added interlinearly*

LIFE AND WORKS OF SIR W. SCOTT

Copy-text: MS, Huntington. Summary-review, endorsed "Cam   May 3d 1836." In this edition rules are deleted after "Cunningham." and "Bloodgood." in the heading.

43.21   25th . . . 1772:   Thus in Thoreau's source, the biographical memoir to Hogg's *Familiar Anecdotes* (New York: Harper & Brothers, 1834), p. 16. Hogg was born in 1770.

44.10   Mador: The copy-text reads "Madoc," following the misprint in the source, p. 106.

44.19   Queen: Thus in the source, p. 107. The copy-text reads "Qeene."

44.21   Women: While the correct title, "The Three Perils of Woman," appears in the list Thoreau copied from pp. 106-107, the variant "Women" occurs elsewhere in the sketch of Hogg (p. 98) and in Hogg's own text (p. 241) to which the sketch is appended.

Emendations

* 42.1	May 3, 1836	May 3d 1836.
		(*at end*)
42.3	Sir ∧	~ .
42.5	Sir ∧	~ .
42.21	genius.	~ ∧
42.28	eighth	eigth
43.1	Sir ∧	~ .
43.2	Sir ∧	~ .
43.9	intimacy	intamacy
43.11	"No	' ~
43.21	Jan'y	Jan^y
43.21	1772,	~ ∧
43.21	Burns'	Burn's
43.34	Poeter.	~ ∧
44.1-2	'catch . . . passed'."	" ~ . . . ~ "."
44.7	Queen's	Qeen's
* 44.10	Mador	Madoc
44.13	Brownie	Brounie
* 44.19	Queen	Qeene
44.21	do.	do ∧
44.25	Queer	Qeer

Alterations

42.5   anecdotes]   *fourth letter followed by erased vertical stroke*

42.22   Scott]   *written over erased word, probably* him

42.29   him]   *followed by erased letter*

42.30   the pages]   the *written over erased letters*

43.22   1759]   *third digit written over erased digit, probably* 7

43.29   Ramsay's]   *preceded by erased quotation marks*

43.31   Muse]   M *altered from* m

44.4   written]   *first three letters altered from* was

44.15 Melodies] M *altered from* m
44.17 Jacobite] *third letter written over erased vertical stroke*
44.20 Perils] P *altered from* p

THE LOVE OF STORIES

Copy-text: MS, Morgan. Theme, endorsed "Thoreau 1836"; "1836" is written in a darker ink, in Thoreau's handwriting, and was apparently added later. Month and day determined from Channing's Lists.

Emendations

* 45.1	September 30, 1836	1836 (*at end*)
46.8	inter-change	inter ∧ / change
46.21	things,	~ ∧

Alterations

45.15 through] *followed by erased letter, perhaps* t
45.20 which] *cancelled and* this *added interlinearly, apparently in another hand*
45.27 goes] *followed by pencil comma, probably Channing's*
46.14 us to] us *followed by unrecoverable erased letter or letters; second letter of* to *written over unrecoverable erased letter*
46.14 friends] *altered by erasure and overwriting from another word, perhaps* selves
46.20 tells] *altered by erasure and overwriting from another word, perhaps* told
46.21 in] *written over unrecoverable erased word*
46.22 sea"] *quotation mark cancelled in pencil, probably by Channing*
46.27 child] *second letter written over unrecoverable erased letter*
47.1 have] *altered from* has; *last letter of* has *written over erased* d
47.3 wonderful,] *altered by erasure and overwriting, perhaps from* wonderfull
47.5 the senses] the *added interlinearly*
47.19 frankness] *first two letters written over false start*
47.23 &] *added interlinearly*
47.23-24 never-failing] *altered from* neverfailing

CULTIVATION OF THE IMAGINATION

Copy-text: MS, Huntington. Forensic, endorsed "No. 10 Sept. 1836 Thoreau." "10" has been added over an erasure, perhaps "12".

Emendations

* 47.25	September, 1836	Sept. 1836 (*at end*)
48.1	conclude	conclde
48.15	Christian's	christian's
48.18	law.	~ ,
48.36	mind takes	mindtakes
49.16	receive	recive

Alterations

48.22   conduct]   *written over erased* actions
48.28   The]   *first letter written over erased letter, perhaps* B
48.36   mind takes]   t *altered from* s ; *see Emendation*
49.2   be placed]   b *written over erased* p
49.14-15   cultivation of the]   *added interlinearly*
49.30   most]   *added interlinearly*
49.33   the old]   t *written over erased* T
49.36   sense.]   *period altered by erasure from semicolon and followed by heavily cancelled* the appetite speedily vanishes before a plentious meal; the organs become blunted by excess.

THE GREEK CLASSIC POETS

Copy-text: MS, Huntington. Summary-review, endorsed "1836 Oct 1st Cambridge" at the end and additionally dated to the right of the title.

The textual editor has compared Thoreau's Greek with that in Coleridge (London: John Murray, 1830), and has emended a few misplaced accents to the correct forms, as they appear in the source. Thoreau's confusing inconsistency in capitalization at 57.4 is emended to the lowercase form occurring in the source. At 57.5, the editor provides μηρός for a partially illegible form in the copy-text, where Thoreau may have tried to transcribe Coleridge's erroneous μῆρος.

53.36   Wolf: Here and at 55.35, 56.15, and 57.10, the copy-text reads "Wolfe." Thoreau duplicates the error from Coleridge, who misspells the last name of the German philologist Friedrich August Wolf (1759-1824). In the second edition (1834) of Coleridge's book Wolf's name is correctly spelled.

54.5 Batrachomyomachia: Thoreau here miscopies from the source, p. 40, as "Batrachomachia." At 57.25, however, he spells the title correctly.

54.33 Epithalamia: "Epithalmia" in the copy-text but thus in Thoreau's source, p. 40, from which he copies the footnote exactly, with this exception.

55.9 many: Thus in Coleridge, p. 49. The copy-text reads "manner."

57.16 Mitford: Thus in Coleridge, p. 63. The copy-text reads "Milford."

Emendations

* 50.1	October 1, 1836	Oct 1st 1836.
50.4	Esq.	*possibly* Esqr.
51.8	heart-stricken	heart-striken
51.19	Northern	Nothern
51.21-22	abundance	aboundance
52.6	eye;	~ ,
52.7	Northern	Nothern
52.20	*feel*	*feell*
53.25-26	the author	theauthor
53.28-29	outlines	outlnes
* 53.36	Wolf	Wolfe
54.1	unconnected	*one stroke in* u *lacking*
* 54.5	Batrachomyo-machia	Batrachomachia
54.7	many	may
54.11	Mr.	Mr ∧
54.19	others'	other's
* 54.21	'ῥάβδον	ῥαβδον
54.27	headquarters	head quarters
54.31	among	Among
* 54.33	Epithalamia	Epithalmia
55.2	many	may
* 55.9	many	manner
55.19	1.	1 ∧
55.22	P.	P ∧
55.34	'Primary . . . Iliad:'	" ~ . . . ~ :"

55.35	Wolf's	Wolfe's
55.36	Dr.	Dr ∧
56.4	many	may
* 56.4	Διορθώσεις	Διορθωσεις
* 56.10	αἱ	ἀι
56.11	different	diffrent
56.12	editors,	∼ .
* 56.12	αἱ	ἀι
* 56.13	αἱ	ἀι
56.15	Wolf's	Wolfe's
56.16	complete	conplete
56.29	or were	ore were
56.30	C.	C ∧
56.35	Aristotle's	Aristotles
* 57.4	ὁμηρεῖν	Ὁμηρεῖν
* 57.5	μηρός	μ͡ηρος (*reading dubious*)
57.10	Wolf	Wolfe
* 57.11	ὁμηρεῖν	ὁμηρεῖν
57.11	together.	∼ ∧
57.12	Mr. C.	Mr ∧ C ∧
* 57.16	Mitford	Milford
57.20	many	may
57.35	and	*small mark beneath* d *may represent comma*
58.4	remain.	∼ ∧

Alterations

50.20   know]   *first letter altered, perhaps from* n

50.24-25   distinction]   *altered from* distintion

51.24   away]   *first and third letters overwritten*

51.27   slaked]   *altered by erasure from* slacked

51.30   sensible]   *preceded by erased* more

52.3   scenery]   *first letter written over erased letter, perhaps* f

52.7   their]   t *altered from* T

52.9   awe and]   *first letter of* and *overwritten*

52.17   fondness]   *fourth through sixth letters overwritten*

52.25   apostrophe]   *written over erased word, ca.* 9 *letters*

52.34   picturesqueness]   *altered from* picturesquness

52.36   bottom by Plato] *written over upside-down*
Introductions

53.15   bareness] *fourth through sixth letters*
overwritten, perhaps from ren

53.16   instinct] *preceded by cancelled* I

53.19   one and] *first letter of* and *overwritten*

53.31-32   compilation] *first letter altered, perhaps*
from m

54.5   Hymns] *fourth letter altered from* s

54.16   Rhapsodist] *first letter altered, perhaps from* r

54.20   like] *third letter overwritten*

54.23   Rhapsodists] *second letter overwritten*

54.28   island] *first letter altered, perhaps from* l

54.28-29   reciters] *last two letters altered, perhaps*
from st

54.29   Homer] *first letter written over erased* The

54.31   whom] *first letter added interlinearly*

54.34   Arachnomachia] *penultimate letter altered*
from a

55.5   arranged] *last letter altered, perhaps from* s

55.19   wrote] *second letter altered from vertical*
stroke

55.23   parts] *last letter overwritten*

56.9   individual] *first letter overwritten*

56.15   Excursus] *sixth letter altered, perhaps from* c

56.16   second] *added interlinearly above cancelled*
first

56.18   and also] and *altered, perhaps from* but

56.19   first] *added interlinearly above cancelled*
second

57.5   derivation] *fifth letter altered, perhaps from* b

57.7   Poet] *first letter overwritten*

57.11   assemble together] gether *added in right*
margin

57.16   about] *last letter overwritten*

57.17   Christ] C *altered from* c

57.32   classed] *second letter overwritten*

57.36   the Greek] the *added interlinearly*

58.2   Little] *first letter written over erasure*

THE MEANING OF "FATE"

Copy-text: MS, Middlebury. Theme, endorsed "Thoreau";
dated from Channing's Lists.

Emendations

* 58.5	October 28, 1836	*lacking*
58.18	Μοῖραι	Μοιραι
58.22	one.	~ —
59.12	spinning	spin ∧ / ning
59.14	Northerns	Notherns
59.30	cui	i *not dotted*
59.31	impellenti	*extra stroke after* m
60.3	Deity.	~ —
60.4	what has been	whas been (*underlined by Channing*)
60.10	whether	Whether
60.11	unavoidable	inavoidable
60.12	ancients.	~ ∧

Alterations

58.9   meagre]   r *written over erased* e

58.11   Fate]   F *written over erased* f

58.15   of fate]   *added interlinearly*

58.16-17   modifications]   *written over erased word, probably* changes

58.22   an]   *altered from* a

58.29   opinion.]   *altered from* opinions.

59.6   wreck]   *altered from* reck

59.12   spinning]   *first four letters written over erased word ca. 6 letters ending* ing

59.15   either regarded]   *originally* regarded either *but marked for transposition by ink underlining and numerals, in a hand and ink consistent with the holograph*

59.24   that]   *followed by cancelled* that

60.4   Fate]   *altered from* fate

60.8   merely]   *added in right margin*

60.8   before]   *written over erased word, probably* what

60.10   agent.]   *followed by erased* and the like

60.15   they.]   y *and period added to* the *followed by erased word filling remainder of line, perhaps* Ancients

WHETHER THE GOVERNMENT OUGHT TO EDUCATE

Copy-text: MS, Library of Congress. Forensic, endorsed "Thoreau No. 11   Oct. 1836." The number "11" has been pencilled over an erasure; and the date, in a smaller hand than the essay, signature, and "No.," may not be in Thoreau's autograph.

Emendations

| * 60.18 | October, 1836 | Oct. 1836. (*at end*) |
| 60.21 | themselves. | ~ —— |

TRAVELLERS & INHABITANTS

Copy-text: MS, Harvard. Fragment of a theme, dated and titled from Channing's Lists. The topic or subtitle is drawn from Channing's Themes. Judging from its contents, this fragment is a response to the "Travellers & Inhabitants" assignment. Sanborn presented it as a portion of the later "Public Influence" theme, dated March 3, 1837 by Thoreau (*The Life of Henry David Thoreau*, 1917, pp. 160-161; see also copy-text note for "Gaining or Exercising Public Influence"). The contents of the two manuscripts aside, the "Travellers & Inhabitants" leaf and the surviving leaf of "Public Influence" are written on paper of different colors. That used for the present piece matches the paper on which Thoreau wrote his other rhetoric assignments in 1836.

Emendations

* 62.1	November 11, 1836	*lacking*
* 62.2	Travellers & Inhabitants	*lacking*
* 62.3-5	State . . . authors.	*lacking*
62.6	⟨. . .⟩	*page or pages missing*
62.22	versts	werzts
62.26	natives in	in *torn away*
62.27	externals	n *torn away*
62.28	or	*torn away; conjectured by editor*
62.29	of	*torn away*
62.29-30	Mississippi	Mississipi
62.31	swindling	*second through fourth letters questionable*

63.6	describes	descibes
63.11	in the eyes	its the eyes
63.19	⟨ . . . ⟩	*page or pages*
		missing

Alterations

62.9   criticise]   *second letter added interlinearly following Channing's marginal mark*

62.19   as]   *altered from* and

62.20   breadth]   *followed by cancelled* l

62.27   (I speak]   *written over ca. 5 erased letters, perhaps the beginning of* duodecimo

62.30   too]   *third letter added following Channing's marginal mark*

62.30   solicitous]   *preceded by cancelled* indulgent is he to his

62.31   swindling bard]   *cancelled following Channing's underlining and marginal mark*

62.31   withhold]   *fifth letter added interlinearly*

63.2-3   expense]   *altered from* expence

HISTORY . . . OF THE ROMAN REPUBLIC

Copy-text: MS, Huntington. A very close paraphrase of the "Advertisement" to Ferguson's *History*, Volume I, pp. v-xxiv in the five-volume Edinburgh edition of 1813. The approximate date of composition is based on Thoreau's record of book borrowing from the Institute of 1770 at Harvard: he checked out Volume I of the Institute's set on September 12, 1836, renewing before October 13 and again before November 17. He borrowed Volume II on October 24 and November 17, Volume III on December 8, and Volumes III, IV, and V later that month. See Kenneth W. Cameron, "Thoreau Discovers Emerson: A College Reading Record," *Bulletin of the New York Public Library*, 57 (1953), 326-329, reprinted in Cameron, *Thoreau and His Harvard Classmates* (Hartford: Transcendental Books, 1965), pp. 109-110. Although adjacent entries in the notebook containing this manuscript would seem to place the composition in April, 1836, the sequence of entries is not strictly chronological.

65.22   Sallust: The copy-text reads "Salust" here, though the name is correctly spelled in the preceding sentence. In every other instance but one Thoreau follows his

source in the spellings of biographical names. The exception occurs at 65.34, "Gellius," where Thoreau miscopies
as "Gettius." Two forms used by Ferguson and copied
exactly by Thoreau deviate from modern standard spellings: "Cataline" and "Xephilinus." That the former was
an accepted spelling of "Catiline" in the early nineteenth
century is indicated by its appearance in Thoreau's own
copy (Abernethy Library, Middlebury College) of William
Scott, *Lessons in Elocution* (Boston, 1820), p. 59, as well
as in three other editions of Ferguson containing the "Advertisement" paraphrased by Thoreau: Philadelphia, 1805
and 1811, and Edinburgh, 1828. All four editions read
"Xephilinus." London editions of 1783, 1825, and 1827,
and Philadelphia editions of 1830 and 1836, all seen by
the editor, have the original short "Advertisement," quite
different from the one that served as Thoreau's source in
this composition, and containing none of the biographical
names.

Emendations

* 63.20	ca. October- November, 1836	*lacking*
63.30	wanting,	∼ ∧
64.28	sovereignty	*fourth letter trimmed*
64.29	yrs.	yrs ∧
64.30	vols.	vols ∧
64.33	Decemvirs	Decem ∧ / virs
65.5	5th	5
65.12	Livy.	∼ ,
* 65.22	Sallust	Salust
* 65.34	Gellius	Gettius
66.1	2nd.	2nd ∧
66.18	may	my

Alterations

63.23   LL. D. F. R. S. E.]   *added after original writing*
64.5   portrait]   *altered by erasure and overwriting
from* picture
64.6   alone]   *first letter overwritten*
64.20   endeavor]   *first two letters overwritten*
64.25-26   and others]   *last letter of* and *followed by
erased stroke*

64.27   Dionysius]   *second letter written over erased* y
64.32   ending]   *first three letters written over erasure*
65.7   580]   *written over erased matter, ca. 5 letters*
65.7   U. C.]   *followed by 3 erased words, ca. 4, 7, and*
7 letters
65.12   Livy]   *altered, perhaps from* he
65.13   Dionysius]   *second letter written over erased* y
65.35   lived]   *second letter added interlinearly*
66.5   though]   *first three letters overwritten*
66.5   with]   *second letter written over vertical stroke*
66.13   Aurelius]   *third letter altered from* l

A WRITER'S NATIONALITY AND INDIVIDUAL GENIUS

Copy-text: MS, Morgan. Theme, endorsed "Thoreau";
dated from Channing's Lists.

Emendations

* 66.23	December 16, 1836	*lacking*
67.29	observatories	obsevatories (*see alteration*)
68.24	conceive	concive
69.23	one's	ones
69.24	ascertained	ascertaind
70.3	this is	this is is
70.8	is,	Is, (*also, on same line as preceding word*)
71.17	Would	*not indented*
71.18	and . . . as	*on same line as preceding word*
72.2	fellows	feltows
72.8	"But . . . might	*on same line as preceding word*
72.9	&c.	&c ∧
72.10	What . . . there	*on same line as preceding word*
72.12	each once	eachonce
72.17	restraint?	∼ .

Alterations

67.4   application]   *followed by erased comma, and
sixth letter followed by erased vertical stroke*

67.5   French,]   *followed by erased dash*

67.5-6   Scotch-men]   *altered from* Scotch men

67.10   third,]   *added interlinearly*

67.19   from mount]   *added interlinearly*

67.24   eye;]   *semicolon perhaps altered from comma (or comma added after* indeed) *following Channing's marginal "p"*

67.25   astronomers;]   *semicolon perhaps altered from comma (or comma added after* glass) *following Channing's marginal "p"*

67.29   observatories]   obsevatories *altered from* obseratories *following Channing's caret*

67.30   It would]   *preceded by pencil paragraph sign, probably Channing's*

67.34   justice]   *followed by erased comma*

67.34   intended]   *fifth letter added interlinearly*

67.36   his]   *altered by erasure from* this

67.36   may]   *written over erased word, perhaps* will

68.9   object]   *written over erased* character

68.10   innkeeper]   *third letter added interlinearly*

68.12   particulars]   *seventh letter written over erased vertical stroke*

68.15-16   ourselves]   our *altered from* are

68.19   possessing]   *followed by* , in a greater or less degree, *added interlinearly apparently in response to Channing's marginal "X"*

68.23   can]   *added interlinearly*

68.27   structure and]   *written over unrecoverable erased words*

69.6   lens]   *followed by erased vertical stroke*

69.12   enter]   *small erasure above this word*

69.15   each]   *written over erased word, perhaps* this

69.17   upon]   *altered by erasure from* upone

69.22   poetry]   *followed by erased comma*

69.27   truly]   *written over erased* justly

70.3   this is]   *first letter of* is *written over erased vertical stroke*

70.12   have]   *written over erased word, perhaps* critical

70.13   rural]   *third letter written over erased vertical stroke*

70.16   mean]   *written over erased* small

71.2-3   is the secret . . . standard—]   *marked "X" in margin by Channing; dash after* standard *may have been added*

71.3   hobby.]   *followed by erased dash*

71.3   was one]   *apparently altered from* is one

71.4   adapted]   *altered from* adapts

71.5   was]   *altered from* is

71.6   His]   *altered by erasure and overwriting, perhaps from* This

71.9   capable]   *preceded by erased* as

71.9   made equally]   *added interlinearly*

71.9-10   manifest,]   *altered by erasure and overwriting from* manifested

71.10   whether]   *first letter written over* in

71.15   Were Antony]   *second letter of* Antony *written over erased vertical stroke*

71.22   asks,]   *written over unrecoverable erased word, ca. 7 letters*

72.16   will]   *written over erased word, perhaps* is

72.17   easy]   *altered by erasure and overwriting from* at ease

72.17   home,]   *followed by erased dash*

72.20   guide-boards,]   -boards, *added interlinearly*

L'ALLEGRO & IL PENSEROSO

Copy-text: MS, Middlebury; Sanborn. Essay (incomplete), endorsed with title and "Jan. 1837"; not in Channing's Themes or Lists. Portions of the manuscript, which has been mutilated, do not survive. Readings for gaps in the manuscript are taken from Sanborn, *The Life of Henry David Thoreau* (1917), pp. 99-101, as recorded in the list of emendations. According to his own account (p. 98), Sanborn saw more of the manuscript than what presently survives. The first extant fragment, pp. [1] and [2] of the holograph before mutilation, is roughly a fourth of a leaf torn horizontally from the middle of a single leaf, lacking about eight lines at the top and nine lines at the bottom on each side. Recto and verso are determined by the milled and rough edges of the paper. The recto text includes "[c]olleg[e]" through "wearied and" (73.3-73.8); the verso text includes "The precise" through "Surely" (73.10-73.14). Fragment 2 consists of a double-leaf folder, the last leaf paginated "5" and "6" by Thoreau. The first leaf of this folder, pp. [3]-[4], is incomplete, about four lines (each side) having been torn away horizontally at the top and about nine lines (each side) missing at the bottom. Page [3] includes "so faithfully" through "<. . .> at" (73.16-73.26); page [4] includes "never been" through "are already" (73.28-74.6). The upper left corner (recto aspect) of the leaf paginated "5" and "6" has been torn away. Pages "5"-"6" include "in every respect" through "not those" (74.8-75.14). Fragment 3 consists of the top third of a single leaf, paginated "7" and "8" by Thoreau. The original whole leaf was probably joined to the now lost leaf on which pages 9 and 10 were written; the right edge of page "7" is milled and the left is rough. Page "7" includes "unreproved" (75.14) through "By wh" (see emendation for 75.23 and textual note for 75.24). Page "8" includes "perhaps" (75.32) through "future–" (see emendation for 76.6). Sanborn declares that the "ninth" page—and thus, necessarily, page 10—was among the fragments he transcribed; unless he fabricated his reading for "The picture" through "Thomson, attri-", he drew it from the bottom of page 10. Yet the material Sanborn provides between the mutilation at page "8" and the text of page "11" is not equivalent to a single whole holograph page, much less two. Thus Sanborn's phrase "fifth and ninth" may be a misprint for "fifth and sixth". Fragment 4 is an intact double-leaf folder, paginated "11," "12," "13," and "14" by Thoreau. The inclusive text on these pages is "butes its sighing" through "exposed" (76.12-78.34). Fragment 5 consists of a single leaf, paginated "15" on the recto, on which the essay text is concluded ("for sale" through "Milton."). The verso bears the endorsement. Matching pinholes and fold-marks for all the fragments confirm the identification of recto and verso sides and show that the manuscript was sewn before mutilation occurred. See also Edwin Moser, "The Order of Fragments of Thoreau's Essay on 'L'Allegro' and 'Il Penseroso,'" *Thoreau Society Bulletin*, 101 (Fall, 1967), 1-2.

73.3-8   college . . . wearied and: Sanborn silently omits this matter from his version of the essay, and Kenneth W. Cameron (*The Transcendentalists and Minerva*, I, p. 170) regards it as probably extraneous. Thoreau used it again in his class book autobiography: see 114.28-33. That Thoreau's remarks about the quasi-religious self-discipline of the student are properly a part of the essay is indicated not only by the physical evidence (on the verso of the same scrap Thoreau is obviously writing about "L'Allegro" and "Il Penseroso"), but by their appropriateness to the subject. The poet's slow, patient, laborious, ascetic, and reverent preparation for his vocation is a persistent theme of Milton's. See particularly Elegy VI, a verse letter in Latin to Charles Diodati written in Milton's twenty-first year, and "Lycidas."

75.24 but: Sanborn, from whom the text is taken from this point to 75.32, reads "But" although the letters "bu" are visible. Also legible immediately below "bu" on a small attached tag of the manuscript is the word "in," which does not occur in Sanborn's text for the mutilated portion.

75.28 Shakspeare: Thoreau's normal spelling of the college period is here substituted for "Shakespeare," the form to which Sanborn regularly changed it.

76.5 were it for but: The first three words are torn away, but Sanborn reads "were it but for" and the size of the torn area would accommodate "were it for."

Emendations

* 73.1	January, 1837	Jan. 1837 (*at end*)
* 73.2	L'Allegro . . . Penseroso	*at end*
73.3	⟨ . . . ⟩ college	*1/3 page missing*
73.3	college	*first and last letters torn away*
73.3	college ⟨ . . . ⟩	*remainder of line torn away*
73.3	student's	*apostrophe torn away*
73.4	a cloud	*first three letters torn away*
73.5	grateful	gratefull
73.8	and	*bottoms of second and third letters torn away*
73.8-9	⟨ . . . ⟩	*about one page missing*

73.14-15	⟨ . . . ⟩	*about 5/6 page missing*
73.16	so faithfully	*tops of letters torn away*
73.21	Handel's	Handels'
73.26	long enough.	*all but tops of 3 letters torn away; Sanborn's reading, p. 99*
73.26	enough. ⟨ . . . ⟩	*remainder of line torn away*
73.26-27	at ⟨ . . . ⟩	*about one page missing*
73.28	Robinhood	*tops of letters torn away*
74.5	Turns them	*all but tops of 3 letters torn away; Sanborn's reading, p. 99*
74.6	⟨ . . . ⟩ to which	*1/2 line torn away*
74.6-7	already ⟨ . . . ⟩	*about 1/3 page missing*
74.8	occupant	*third letter torn away*
74.29	mazes	*last 3 letters torn away; Sanborn's reading, p. 100*
75.23	whispering . . . asleep."	*all but first 2 letters torn away; Sanborn's reading, p. 100*
* 75.24-32	but . . . of her,	*about 1/2 page missing; Sanborn's reading, p. 100*
* 75.28	Shakspeare	Shakespeare (*Sanborn*)
75.33	poem.	~ ∧
* 76.5	were it for but	were it for *torn away*
76.6	mingle as one.	*torn away; Sanborn's reading, p.101*

76.6-7	one. ⟨ . . . ⟩	*about 2 1/2 pages missing;* ought, of, *and* the *visible at edge of tear; Sanborn, p. 101, reads* "[Here a lacuna.]"
76.8-12	The . . . attributes	*all but last five letters Sanborn's reading, p. 101*
76.22	among	anong
77.12	"linked	' ～
77.13	organ",	～ ' ,
77.14	ecstasies.'	ecstacies ∧ '
77.25	mistake;	～ ,
77.30	poet's	poets'
77.34-35	windows"	～ '
78.1	The	the
78.2	Jonson	Johnson
78.5-6	nonconformist	non conformist

Alterations

73.23   Genius]   G *altered from* g

74.10   our architect.]   *first six letters written over erased* Milton.

74.25   a]   *written over erased letters, perhaps* she

74.34   year]   *added interlinearly*

75.3   This]   *first two letters written over unrecoverable erased matter*

75.18   Meat . . . Drink]   *altered from* meat . . . drink

75.19   waits upon]   *altered by erasure, perhaps from* waited on

75.35   that]   *altered from* what

76.17   Æolian]   A *overwritten*

77.14   ecstasies]   ecstacies *altered from* extacies

77.26   us,]   *added interlinearly*

77.27   awhile,]   *added interlinearly*

77.31   an]   *altered from* and

77.33   about]   *written over unrecoverable erased matter*

78.3   are]   *written over unrecoverable erased matter*

78.17   not]   *written over unrecoverable erased matter*

78.17 undertaken] *first four letters written over unrecoverable erased matter*

78.19 blemishes] *altered from* belmishes

78.20-21 pleasing] *preceded by cancelled* striking passage a

78.24 even] *first letter written over erased vertical stroke*

78.24-25 connexion] *third and fourth letters overwritten; sixth letter added interlinearly above unrecoverable erased matter*

ALL MEN ARE MAD

Copy-text: MS, Huntington. Essay of two paragraphs, or conclusion of an essay, endorsed "Cam. January. 15th 1837". Not in Channing's Themes or Lists. Title supplied by editor.

Emendations

* 79.1	January 15, 1837	January. 15th 1837 (*at end*)
* 79.2	All Men Are Mad	*lacking*
79.18	' 'tis	' ₍ tis

Alterations

79.7 folly] *first letter written over erasure*

79.8 the sane] the *followed by erased letter*

79.18 who] *followed by erased word, ca. 4 letters*

THE SPEECHES OF MOLOCH & THE REST

Copy-text: MS, Harvard. Theme, endorsed "Thoreau"; dated from Channing's Lists.

83.21 superior, is: Triangular portions are torn from the bottom of the page, one on either side of the center-fold, creating two lacunae in the last line. Just before the second break is preserved the first letter of a word; just after, preceding "sufficiently", is visible the dot of an i and the better part of the letter s. A tiny fragment of manuscript associated with this essay bears the letter p preceded by a short vertical stroke. The letter just before the lacuna most closely resembles the initial r character-istic of this essay, dropping, perhaps, to the first stroke of a u. It might also be an n, or, more remotely, an s. In terms of the orthography of other words in this crowded final line, the editor judges that the mutilated portion comprises eleven or twelve character spaces, including the initial r (or n or s) and the terminal s. In his 1917 *Life of Henry David Thoreau*, p. 97, Sanborn prints "ruler, is"; Kenneth W. Cameron, in *The Transcendentalists and Minerva*, I, p. 187, prints "sup[erior,] is". The present editor accepts Cameron's reading, which proves more compatible than Sanborn's with the tiny fragment, the spacing of the line, and Thoreau's style ("master and ruler" is conspicuously redundant). Favoring the Sanborn reading, however, is the distinctly r-like appearance of the first word's initial letter, plus the fact that Sanborn might have seen the manuscript prior to the deterioration of the margin.

Emendations

* 79.21	January 20, 1837	*lacking*
81.1	'but perhaps	*on same line as preceding word*
81.2	The way	*not indented*
81.2	scale'.	$\sim$ ' —
81.3	The difficulty	The dif- / *on same line as preceding word*
81.29	policy.	$\sim$. ————
81.30	Beëlzebub	*only slightly indented*
82.12	Here . . . speech,	*on same line as* deep' &c.
82.31	harbinger	harbinber
83.3	Heaven ∧	$\sim$ '
83.4	regain ∧	$\sim$ '
83.6	These words, it is	*on same line as preceding word*
83.16	He . . . followed	*on same line as preceding word*
83.20	to Satan	*second, third, and fourth letters torn away*
* 83.21	superior, is	*all but first and last letters torn away*

Alterations

80.1   First]   *followed by erased comma*

80.7   to restore]   *preceded by cancelled* to restore

80.18   throughout]   *seventh letter added interlinearly following Channing's marginal "sp"*

80.22   retires]   re *written over erased* gives

81.9   his . . . wise]   *written over unrecoverable erased words*

81.15   rebellion]   *cancelled and* a bad cause, *added interlinearly following Channing's underlining*

82.5   of the individual]   *added in right margin*

82.7   of chance]   of *written over unrecoverable erased word, ca. 4 letters*

82.19-20   'My . . . not:'—]   *marked by Channing with a marginal "p"; no alteration apparent*

82.21   evident a]   *cancelled following Channing's underlining and brackets*

83.4   regain]   *followed by erased* &

83.7   not]   *written over erased* of

83.8   self-interest.]   *preceded by erased* a *and written over erased words (only isolated letters recoverable); followed by cancelled* hellish, policy.

83.13   disgrace]   *added interlinearly*

PEOPLE OF DIFFERENT SECTIONS

Copy-text: MS, Middlebury. Theme, endorsed "Thoreau Feb. 17th"; year determined from Channing's Lists. In this edition a rule is deleted after the title.

Emendations

* 83.22	February 17, 1837	Feb. 17th (*at end*)
83.28	aggregate	agre $_\wedge$ / gate
86.2	phrensy	phrenzy
86.7	sober	sobre

Alterations

83.27   A]   *cancelled following Channing's brackets*

83.27   necessarily, nor]   *altered from* necessarily or

84.7-8   individual,]   *altered from* individuality

84.12   far]   *added interlinearly*

84.14   we]   *written over erased word, perhaps* the

84.20   characteristics]   *altered from* characteristis
84.25   probability]   *altered from* probably
84.25   is,]   *added interlinearly*
84.25   so]   *followed by erased hyphen*
84.32   and a]   and *altered from* ang
84.35   called]   *first two letters written over*
unrecoverable erased matter

85.18   the country]   the *written over erased word,*
perhaps our

85.23   prejudice]   p *written over erased* P
85.25   warp or]   *cancelled following Channing's*
underlining of warp

85.36   causes to vibrate all]   *cancelled and* touches
with a master's hand *added interlinearly following*
Channing's marginal "S"

86.2   rapt]   *written over unrecoverable erased word*
86.2   excited]   *written over unrecoverable erased word*
86.11   once]   *written over erased matter, probably* at
first

GAINING OR EXERCISING PUBLIC INFLUENCE

Copy-text: MS, Middlebury; Sanborn. Fragment of a
theme, endorsed in another ink and perhaps another hand
"March 3d 1837" above the title (for 86.15-87.31); plus
Sanborn, *The Life of Henry David Thoreau* (1917), pp.
160-161 for remainder of text. Sanborn confuses the fragment belonging to the essay "Travellers & Inhabitants"
with part of the missing contents of this essay, and includes it in his version of the "Public Influence" exercise,
supplying a transition apparently of his own devising. The
transition is not included here.

Emendations

* 86.15	March 3, 1837	March 3d 1837
87.2	there	*possibly* then
87.31	⟨ . . . ⟩	*remainder of MS* *missing*
* 87.31- 88.16	The thousands . . . qualities.	*Sanborn's reading*

Alterations

86.23   infallible]   *sixth letter added interlinearly*
following Channing's marginal "sp"

87.24   insuperable] *third and fourth letters written over unrecoverable erased letters*

87.29-30   prejudices which . . . attended by] *altered to* prejudices with which . . . attended *following Channing's revision and marginal mark*

TITLES OF BOOKS

Copy-text: positive photocopy, Kenneth W. Cameron, Trinity College, Hartford, Connecticut. In preparation for further reproduction, the prints have been trimmed and mounted, and certain faint autograph strokes have been darkened with ink. A facsimile drawn from these photographs illustrates R. Baird Shuman, "Thoreau's *Of Books and Their Titles*: A New Edition," *Emerson Society Quarterly*, 18 (I Quarter, 1960), 26-34. Shuman's transcription, pp. 26-28, differs from the present editor's in numerous particulars. None of these discrepancies, however, seem to reflect clearer readings by Shuman from the original manuscript, now missing. Theme, dated from Channing's Lists.

89.21   author's: A faint mark above "authors" in the copy-text may be a pencil apostrophe entered by Channing or a subsequent reader.

90.28   Egerton: The copy-text reads "Edgerton," a misspelling.

Emendations

* 88.17	March 17, 1837	*lacking*
89.6	not	mot
89.13	angels'	angels
* 89.21	author's	authors
89.32	Devices"?	$\sim$ " $_\wedge$
90.12	who $_\wedge$	$\sim$,
* 90.28	Egerton	Edgerton
91.17	"the	' $\sim$
91.18	unfortunate	*one stroke of first letter lacking*
91.35	Mr.	Mr $_\wedge$
92.17	Sadī	Sadī̇

Alterations

88.27-28   euphonic]   *altered by erasure from* euphonious

89.4 such as] *cancelled following Channing's brackets*

89.4 Ivanhoe", for instance,] *cancelled following Channing's brackets*

89.9-10 nature of the] *added in right margin*

89.14 seems to] *added interlinearly*

89.14 require] *altered by erasure from* requires *; Channing's pencilled question mark in margin probably postdates this change and the foregoing one*

89.29 allotted] *altered from* alloted

90.20 *dulness*] *apparently altered from* underlined dullness *by erasure and overwriting*

90.33 Looking] L *altered from* l

90.34 Flies] F *altered from* f

91.2 Epitaph] *fifth letter preceded by erased vertical stroke*

91.5 Our] *second letter overwritten*

91.12 have already] *followed by cancelled* have already

91.17 queen] q *written over erased* Q

91.20 grammatical] *fifth letter added interlinearly*

91.25 expletive] *written over erased word, perhaps* cognomen

91.27 it; he] h *written over erased* H

91.30 called] *followed by cancelled* the

91.33 or have] have *added interlinearly*

91.33 moment in] *last letter written over erased letter*

92.1 perhaps] p *written over erased* P

92.1 ill-starred] *altered from* illstarred

92.5 Panegyric] P *written over erased* p

92.13 Prophetarum] *ninth letter written over erasure, ca. 2 letters*

92.27 Old] O *altered from* o

92.34 backs,] *added interlinearly*

93.1 it] *squeezed into line*

SUBLIMITY

Copy-text: MS, Harvard. Theme, endorsed "Thoreau. March. 31st"; year determined from Channing's Lists.

93.8-9 billows': In all editions of Susan Ferrier's novel *The Inheritance* examined by the editor, including the first (1824) and second (1825), the text reads singular "billow's." Whether the form in the topic results from an error in the edition Channing used, or a copying error by Channing, or Thoreau's copying mistake or careless placement of the apostrophe, Thoreau seems to have understood the term as a singular rather than a plural possessive. See 95.25, where, without quotation marks, he writes "the billow's roar."

Emendations

* 93.7	March 31, 1837	March. 31st (*at end*)
94.5	universally	univer ∧ / sally
94.12	sympathize	sympathise
94.25	Nor . . . have	*on same line as preceding word*
94.33	confound."	~ · ∧
95.5	second	sec ∧ / ond
95.15	sublime	*followed by vertical line, apparently meaningless*
96.5	pain.	~ ,
96.13	injures	injurs (*remarked by Channing*)
97.20	philosophers	philo ∧ / sophers
97.22	brute ∧	~ ,

Alterations

93.17   terror] *first three letters altered from* the *by erasure and overwriting*

94.1   that . . . ascribe] *written over erased words, perhaps* which is

94.5   attribute] *written over unrecoverable erased word, ca. 5 letters*

94.6   principles,] *added interlinearly*

94.21   describes] *sixth letter added interlinearly*

95.10   will] *written over unrecoverable erased word, ca. 3 letters*

95.14   indifference] *sixth letter added interlinearly following Channing's marginal "sp"*

95.17   we] *added interlinearly above cancelled* he

95.20   origin] *cancelled and* beginning *added interlinearly following Channing's underlining*

95.33-34   and shaking . . . fall,] *added interlinearly*

96.7 demand] *altered to* command *following Channing's underlining*

96.14 if] *altered from* it

96.16-17 fight . . . calm] *marked "p" in margin by Channing; no alteration apparent*

96.24 our] *followed by cancelled* our

97.3-4 is sublime,] *added interlinearly*

97.5 sublimity] *written over unrecoverable erased word*

97.13 that] *cancelled following Channing's underlining*

97.15 advert to] advert *altered by erasure and overwriting;* to *added interlinearly*

The General Obligation "to Tell the Truth"

Copy-text: MS, Brown University. Forensic, endorsed "16 Thoreau April 28th" and marked in an unidentified hand, "1837". This year agrees with Kenneth W. Cameron's reconstruction of the approximate dates of the forensics in "Thoreau, Edward Tyrrel Channing and College Themes," *Emerson Society Quarterly*, 42 (I Quarter, 1966), 15-34, reprinted in Cameron, *Thoreau's Harvard Years* (Hartford: Transcendental Books, 1966), Part II, pp. 1-19.

Emendations

* 99.6	April 28, 1837	April 28th (*at end*)
99.29	property	properly
100.12	immorality	imorality
100.31	receives	recives
101.7	because	bcause
101.9	because	be cause

Alterations

99.24 inquire] *first letter written over erased letter, perhaps* e

101.5 bring] *first two letters written over erased* wh

"Being Content with Common Reasons"

Copy-text: MS, Middlebury. Theme, endorsed "Thoreau. May 5th"; year drawn from Channing's Lists. A pencilled rule after the topic, apparently not Thoreau's, is deleted in this edition.

Emendations

* 101.12	May 5, 1837	May 5th (*at end*)
101.13	Chap.	Chap ∧
101.27	acquiesced	*followed by small mark, perhaps start of a comma*
102.12	ran	*perhaps* run
102.12	reality?	~ .
102.31	through	throug
103.7	some	Some
103.23	infallibility	infalibility
104.3-4	support.	~ —
104.5	and	and and

Alterations

102.14   things]   *first four letters written over unrecoverable erased letters*

102.22   hill]   *altered by erasure from* hills

102.32   flatness]   *third letter added interlinearly*

103.6-7   a few]   a *written over erased stroke, perhaps* f

103.25   taught]   *first three letters written over erased letters, perhaps* sug

103.33   tie]   *written over erased word, perhaps* bond

THE DUTY, INCONVENIENCE AND DANGERS OF "CONFORMITY"

Copy-text: MS, Middlebury. Theme, endorsed "Thoreau May 19th"; year drawn from Channing's Lists. A rule after the topic is deleted in this edition.

Emendations

* 105.1	May 19, 1837	May 19th (*at end*)
105.6	theirs.	~ ∧
106.7	so	So

Alterations

105.23   the works of creation—]   *cancelled and* Nature — *added interlinearly following Channing's underlining and marginal* "X". *Using pencil, either Channing or (less likely) Thoreau also cancels* their, *interlines* her, *adds an* s *to* operation, *underlines* operation *and* design *and marks them for transposition with numerals* "2" *and* "1"

106.2-4   in a . . . space.]   *cancelled following Channing's brackets*

106.12-14   is never . . . follow as]   *marked "O" in margin by Channing; no alterations evident although comma after* duty *may have been added*

106.17   respect]   *altered by erasure from* respects

106.20   otherwise]   *followed by Channing's pencil comma overwritten in ink by Thoreau; Channing also marks the line in margin*

Moral Excellence

Copy-text: MS, Middlebury. Forensic, endorsed "17   Thoreau. May 26. —37": "—37" is consistent in ink color with the rest of the endorsement, but may be in Channing's handwriting.

Emendations

* 106.22	May 26, 1837	May 26. —37 (*at end*)
106.25	what	What
107.9	of	of of

Alterations

107.1   in]   *written over unrecoverable erased letter or letters*

107.9   faculties]   *fourth letter written over erased vertical stroke*

107.19   lay]   *first letter written over unrecoverable erased letter*

107.21   real]   *first two letters written over unrecoverable erased letters*

108.3   on . . . excellence]   *added interlinearly*

Barbarities of Civilized States

Copy-text: MS, Middlebury. Fragment of a theme, endorsed above the heading, "June 2nd 1837" in another ink and a later, if not a different, hand. A pencil rule after the topic, apparently not Thoreau's, is deleted in this edition.

Emendations

* 108.16	June 2, 1837	June 2nd 1837
109.27	strongholds	strong holds
109.30	than	*lacking*

110.10	beautiful	beautifull
110.32	true, is	true is,
111.8	⟨ . . . ⟩	*remainder of MS missing*

Alterations

108.22-23   The culture . . . term]   *cancelled following Channing's marginal "O"*

108.27   good]   *preceded by unrecoverable erased matter (ca. 3 letters) and written over unrecoverable erased letters*

108.28   bad]   *written over unrecoverable erased word (ca. 6 letters)*

108.28   to]   *second letter perhaps altered from* h

109.7   he may]   *written over erased* man should *or* man shall

109.7   soles]   *altered from* souls *following Channing's marginal "sp"*

109.9   sun]   *added interlinearly*

109.22   embrace]   *first two letters written over erased* see *and remainder added interlinearly*

109.23   in]   *written over erased* at

109.23   single]   *added interlinearly*

109.24   accommodates]   *sixth letter added interlinearly following Channing's marginal "sp"*

109.28   Wales.]   *followed by erased* are familiar instances.

110.13   &]   *added after original writing*

110.17   do]   *added interlinearly*

110.27   Not Me,]   *followed by* that is by life, *added interlinearly in response to Channing's marginal mark and underlining of* Not

T. POMPONIUS ATTICUS

Copy-text: Sanborn, *The Life of Henry David Thoreau* (1917), pp. 183-185. Theme, dated from Channing's Lists and titled from Channing's Themes. The manuscript is missing; Sanborn calls it a "fragment," and says it was endorsed "Thoreau, June 10, 1837".

113.3   fear: Herbert's "Constancie," in *The Temple*, reads "force" at this point (from stanza one), and "calmly" rather than "always" at 113.8 (from stanza three). The possibility of copying errors by Sanborn cannot be dismissed, although Thoreau himself may have misquoted Herbert in the lost manuscript.

Emendations

* 111.9	June 30, 1837	June 10, 1837
* 111.10	T. Pomponius	*Titus Pomponius*
	Atticus as an	*Atticus, as an*
	Example	*Example*

Class Book Autobiography

Copy-text: MS, Harvard. Title supplied by editor. Many of the other entries in the Class of 1837 class book are dated, from May to July, 1837; Thoreau's is undated.

 114.13-14 a page . . . the latter.: Thoreau in fact wrote a page and a half.

 114.28-33 bright . . . wearied and: Thoreau seems to be quoting his own words from an earlier composition: see "L'Allegro & Il Penseroso," 73.3-8.

Emendations

* 113.16	ca. June, 1837	*lacking*
* 113.17	Class Book	*lacking*
	Autobiography	
113.27	12th,	12th ∧
114.8	undone.	*perhaps* undone!
114.12	didn't	did'nt
114.24	Highlands	Higlands
114.36	Memory's	Menory's

Alteration

 114.19 scouring] *written over erasure*

"The Commercial Spirit of Modern Times"

Copy-text: MS, Harvard. Commencement part, dated from the program, *Order of Exercises for Commencement, XXX August, MDCCCXXXVII.* On a cover page, in Thoreau's hand, the topical title is preceded by the heading "A Conference." and followed by the names of the three participants, "Rice. Thoreau. Vose." At the very top of this title-page appear "LIV" in ink, with the first character smudged, and "Thoreau." in pencil, possibly in the author's hand. Page one of the text begins with the signature "Thoreau" and a verbatim repetition of the topic.

Emendations

* 115.12	August 30, 1837	*lacking*
* 115.12	*omitted*	A Conference.
* 115.15	*omitted*	Rice. Thoreau. Vose.
* 115.15	*omitted*	*topic repeated*
116.16-17	Doubtless	Doubtles
117.31	side.	*punctuation obscured by binding*

Alterations

116.2   moves]   *added interlinearly*

116.28-29   cherishes]   *written over erasure, perhaps* sustains

116.29   sustains]   *written over erasure, perhaps* cherishes

117.11   admired and]   *added interlinearly*

Miscellanies

Textual Notes and Tables

DIED . . . MISS ANNA JONES

Copy-text: Concord, Massachusetts *Yeoman's Gazette*, XXII, 3 (November 25, 1837), page 3, column 3; microfilm copy in Concord Free Public Library. Two working drafts survive in the Houghton Library, Harvard University, but the printer's manuscript is lost.

    121.24   her.: In the second draft Thoreau continues the thought as follows: "And who shall say that under much that was conventional there burned not a living and inextinguishable flame?" The sentiment might have been dropped by the printer, the editor, or Thoreau himself on the grounds of unorthodoxy.

Textual Variations

    Variant readings in the right-hand column are from the second working draft in the Houghton Library.

121.2	on the 12th	*Sunday* 12
121.11	amiableness and benevolence	benevolence and amiableness
121.24	*lacking after* her.	And who shall say that under much that was conventional there burned not a living and inextinguishable flame?

AULUS PERSIUS FLACCUS

Copy-text: *The Dial: A Magazine for Literature, Philosophy, and Religion*, I, 1 (July, 1840), 117-121; signed "T.": Thoreau's copy of *The Dial*, with his signature on the fly-leaf of each volume and his pencil corrections and revisions in the text, at Southern Illinois University. The Persius essay was reprinted with twenty-eight further additions, deletions, and other substantive changes in the

"Thursday" chapter of *A Week on the Concord and Merrimack Rivers* (Boston and Cambridge: James Munroe and Company, 1849, pp. 324-329; revised edition, Boston: Ticknor and Fields, 1868, pp. 326-331). All Thoreau's autograph changes in the copy-text are regarded as corrections of the *Dial* text rather than preliminary revisions for the *Week* version.

Emerson's correspondence with Margaret Fuller, who edited the first eight numbers of *The Dial*, suggests that he may have played a part in the text of "Aulus Persius Flaccus." He had lately read Thoreau's manuscript when he first proposed, on March 3, 1840, that Fuller use it in *The Dial*. On April 15 Emerson reported that Thoreau did not care to trouble himself further with the piece, but would, instead, "give us Persius as it is, if we will do the revising" (*The Letters of Ralph Waldo Emerson*, ed. Ralph L. Rusk [New York: Columbia University Press, 1939], II, pp. 259, 280-281). "I have Thoreau's Persius rewritten," he informed Fuller on April 23. Almost immediately Thoreau reclaimed the essay "for re-correction," as Emerson reported about April 27; "it is excellent now" (*Letters*, II, pp. 290, 293). Margaret Fuller was absent from Boston as *The Dial* went through the press; but on July 5, after it had been printed, she protested to Emerson that she had asked for proof copy to be sent Thoreau, "and I understood from Mr. R. [George Ripley] that it was sent, and he did not correct it" (quoted in Thomas Wentworth Higginson, *Margaret Fuller Ossoli* [Boston: Houghton, Mifflin and Company, fourth edition, 1885], p. 155). Emerson was no less distressed than Fuller by the typographical blunders. He called three of them to her attention on July 2 (*Letters*, II, p. 311), asking her to correct "nature" to "satire" by hand in copies of the issue that she might encounter.

122.10   Sibyl: The copy-text reads "Sybil," a misspelling. In Ralph Waldo Emerson's set of *The Dial* at Harvard University, Thoreau's autograph alterations in his own set are duplicated with three exceptions. The first is the correction of "Sybil" to "Sibyl" in the Emerson set but not the Thoreau; the second is the underlining of "vivit" in the Thoreau set but not the Emerson; and the third is the close quotation mark after "vivit," in the Thoreau set but not the Emerson. The corrections in Emerson's *Dial* are made in pencil, probably by Thoreau; most of them have been overwritten in ink, or duplicated in ink, by Emerson. In the 1849 edition of *A Week* "Sybil" becomes "sybil"; the word is corrected to "sibyl" in the 1868 *Week*.

125.11   testâve, lutove: Eighteenth, nineteenth, and twentieth century editions of Persius examined by the editor have "testaque lutoque" in Satire III, 61; but Thoreau might deliberately have taken liberties with his source. In *A Week*, where he provides translations of the Latin lines, he renders this phrase "with pottery or clay."

Emendations

The first and second emended readings are anticipated in the 1868 *Week*; "Marvell" agrees with Thoreau's manuscript practice in the journal and commonplace books. The third is a change in the 1849 *Week* which clarifies an obscure construction. The fourth change likewise originated in the 1849 *Week*.

* 122.10	Sibyl	Sybil
122.23	Marvell	Marvel
124.32	it is	is it
127.14	*omitted at end*	T.

Thoreau's Corrections and Revisions

Readings in the right-hand column are those printed in *The Dial*; those in the left-hand column are Thoreau's autograph revisions.

123.3	satire	nature
124.8	truth	truths
124.21-22	susurros / Tollere	/ Tollere sussuros
125.12	pes	per
125.13	seems not to	seems to
125.29	*vivit*,"	vivit, ∧
126.19	lip	life
126.24	secretam	recretam

THE LAWS OF MENU

Copy-text: Thoreau's copy of *The Dial*, III, 3 (January, 1843), 331-340. The attribution of the piece (which is unsigned) to Thoreau is by George Willis Cooke, in *An Historical and Biographical Introduction to Accompany* THE

DIAL, 2 vols. (Cleveland: The Rowfant Club, 1902). Thoreau's source for the selections is *Institutes of Hindu Law, or the Ordinances of Menu, According to the Gloss of Culluca*, transl. Sir William Jones. Extensive quotations from the *Institutes* appear in a commonplace book of Thoreau's in the Pierpont Morgan Library. Roger C. Mueller, *The Orient in American Transcendental Periodicals* (*1835-1886*), University of Minnesota Ph.D. dissertation, 1968, p. 41, conjectures that Thoreau used a copy of the 1794 Calcutta edition belonging to Emerson in his "discovery" of Menu during the summer of 1841. (Thoreau was, however, aware of the book earlier.) Kenneth W. Cameron, who transcribes and edits the Morgan Library extracts, makes a strong case (*The Transcendentalists and Minerva*, I, p. 310) that the text from which Thoreau copied them was volume three of *The Works of Sir William Jones* (6 vols., London: Robinson and Evans, 1799), a volume which Emerson had borrowed from the Boston Athenaeum the year before. A Thoreau workbook of the early 1840s known as "Paragraphs &c Mostly Original," also in the Morgan Library, contains additional excerpts from Menu and drafts of sentences used in the introductory remarks for *The Dial*. The notebook is facsimiled and transcribed, with commentary, by Cameron in *Transcendental Climate* (Hartford: Transcendental Books, 1963), III, pp. 901-969. See also Thoreau's journal for August 17 and 28, 1840 (the "Lost Journal"), May 31, June 7, September 1, and September 2, 1841, and his letter to Isaiah T. Williams, March 14, 1842, where he quotes one of Menu's aphorisms (*The Correspondence of Henry David Thoreau*, ed. Walter Harding and Carl Bode [New York: New York University Press, 1958], p. 68). A section on Menu appears in the "Monday" chapter of *A Week*, pp. 153-159 in the 1849 edition.

Emerson, who began his editorship of *The Dial* with the July, 1842 issue (Volume III, Number 1), seems to have planned the inclusion of a Menu selection in that number: see his tentative table of contents in a notebook entitled "Dialling," *The Journals and Miscellaneous Notebooks of Ralph Waldo Emerson*, VIII, ed. William H. Gilman and J. E. Parsons (Cambridge, Mass.: The Belknap Press of Harvard University Press, 1970), p. 484. Thoreau's contributions to the July issue, as published, were limited to "Natural History of Massachusetts" and one poem; selections by Emerson from the Veeshnoo Sarma comprised the Orientalia. Emerson acknowledged receiving Margaret Fuller's "extra sheets of Veeshnoo & of Menu —ethnical Scriptures" on December 31, 1842, perhaps referring to excess manuscript copy of the Menu piece and to quotations from the Veeshnoo Sarma that had been excluded from the July number (*The Letters of Ralph Waldo Emerson*, III, p. 108).

130.11-12   the breast: Thoreau's source reads "thy breast"; this passage is not represented in the commonplace-book extracts.

133.21   favor: Thus in the commonplace book as in the copy-text. The source has "valour."

139.21   medicine: The source reads "medicines"; this passage is not represented in the commonplace-book extracts.

Emendations

All emended readings are drawn from Thoreau's commonplace-book extracts, and conform to the source.

131.10	Cavi	Cari
137.7	earthen	earthern
137.26	indifferent	indifference
137.26	pairs	pains

Thoreau's Correction

The reading in the right-hand column is that printed in *The Dial*; the correction, listed in the left-hand column, is Thoreau's only autograph change.

| 139.1 | transcendently | transcendentally |

SAYINGS OF CONFUCIUS

Copy-text: *The Dial*, III, 4 (April, 1843), 493-494, headed "Ethnical Scriptures." Thoreau's copy contains no annotations, and the piece is unsigned; Cooke attributes it to Thoreau. The selections are drawn from Joshua Marshman's translation, *The Works of Confucius* (Serampore, 1809), and an anonymous compilation, *The Phenix; A Collection of Old and Rare Fragments* (New York: Wil-

liam Gowan, 1835). Six extracts from *The Phenix*, including the four with which the *Dial* piece concludes, appear
in a commonplace book of Thoreau's in the Pierpont Morgan Library. These extracts, transcribed and edited by
Kenneth W. Cameron in *The Transcendentalists and
Minerva*, I, p. 274, seem to have been made in 1839. But
Mueller, pp. 57-58, observes that most of the *Dial* Confucius selections from both sources appear in Emerson's
journal before the *Dial* publication, and proposes that if
Emerson did not personally prepare the *Dial* materials, he
may have given Thoreau marked copies of the sources or
lent Thoreau his own journal extracts. Thoreau himself
edited the April number, to which he contributed, over his
initials, translations from Anacreon, three lyrics, and
"Dark Ages." Three Confucian quotations from *The Phenix*
are to be found in Emerson's manuscript notebook T,
along with extracts of Zoroaster from the same source
(*The Journals and Miscellaneous Notebooks of Ralph
Waldo Emerson*, VI, ed. Ralph H. Orth [Cambridge, Mass.:
The Belknap Press, 1966], pp. 387-388, undated entries);
more Zoroaster from *The Phenix* occurs in manuscript
journal E, 1841 (*Journals and Miscellaneous Notebooks*,
VII, ed. A. W. Plumstead and Harrison Hayford [1969],
p. 456). Most of the available and often conflicting evi-
dence for assignment of editorship to the *Dial* "Ethnical
Scriptures" pieces is summarized in Joel Myerson, "An
Annotated List of Contributions to the Boston *Dial*,"
Studies in Bibliography, 26 (1973), 133-166.

Emendations

   The first of these emended readings is an editorial correction of a misspelling that Thoreau copied from Marshman, p. 418. The second is drawn from *The Phenix*, p. 83,
and is made for the sake of clarity; Thoreau's commonplace-book extract is differently phrased. The third is
taken from the commonplace book, which here follows
the source.

141.12	recall	recal
141.20	vain,	~ ;
142.1-3	men? That . . .	men, that . . .
	move.	move?

DARK AGES

Copy-text: *The Dial*, III, 4 (April, 1843), 527-529; signed
"T." With various changes the essay was reprinted in the
"Monday" chapter of *A Week* (1849 edition, pp. 159-163;
1868 edition, pp. 164-167). Since Thoreau's annotated
copy of *The Dial* contains two substantive *revisions* toward the *Week* version, in addition to six *corrections*, the
essay as originally printed serves here as copy-text, with
Thoreau's corrective annotations serving as emendations.
In the *Week* form, the title is dropped and five additional
substantive changes, besides the two abovementioned
manuscript revisions, are introduced.

144.4 *Jabalah Alchátgami*: The copy-text has *"Fabalah Alchâtquarmi."* In *Transcendental Climate*, III, p.
967, Kenneth Cameron identifies the source of the quotation as Simon Ockley, *The History of the Saracens*; but he
cites the third edition, Cambridge, 1757, I, pp. xviii-xix.
More likely Thoreau used the first edition (London, 1708;
Vol. I entitled *The Conquest of Syria, Persia, and Ægypt,
by the Saracens*) or the second (London, 1718). In both
of the earliest editions the quotation appears at I, pp. xxi-
xxii. *"Rephâa,"* the spelling Thoreau gives for another
name in the quotation, is so rendered in the first and second editions, while the third has *"Raphâa"*; there are no
other differences of wording or name-spelling in the quotation between the third edition and its predecessors. The
fourth edition (London, 1847) postdates Thoreau's essay
and introduces a new transliteration of Arabic names.
When Thoreau copied the sentence from Ockley ("Oc-
cleve") in a draft of the "Dark Ages" passage in the Pierpont Morgan Library workbook, MA 608, p. 28, he made
the misspellings that found their way into *The Dial*. The
first error, *"Fabalah,"* may be explained by a very strong
similarity between Thoreau's autograph capital F of this
period and the italic capital J used in all three eighteenth-
century editions of Ockley's *History*.

Emendations

Emended readings followed by (T) are drawn from
Thoreau's annotated copy of *The Dial*. The omission of
the signature "T." first occurs in the 1849 *Week*.

143.24	researcher (T)	reseacher
144.2	*Almatîn* (T)	*Almatĭn*
144.3-4	who had it from (T)	*who had it from*
* 144.4	*Jabalah Alchátgami*	*Fabalah Alchâtquarmi*
144.18	*were* (T)	were
144.19	*are* (T)	are
145.21	art. (T)	∼ ,
146.5	*omitted at end*	T.

Thoreau's Corrections and Revisions

Six are listed as emendations. The remaining two, listed in the right-hand column, are regarded as revisions toward the *Week* version and are not adopted in the present text.

| 144.30 | It | History |
| 144.31 | the modern | novelty |

CHINESE FOUR BOOKS

Copy-text: *The Dial*, IV, 2 (October, 1843), 205-210, headed "Ethnical Scriptures"; unsigned. Thoreau's copy contains no annotations. Cooke attributes the piece to Thoreau, but Mueller (p. 72) thinks it may have been Emerson's work, and Myerson tentatively assigns editorship of the extracts to Emerson, while noting that "Thoreau might have made the selections, using Emerson's copy of the book" (p. 162). A related manuscript is Thoreau's own translation of passages from the French of Jean-Pierre-Guillaume Pauthier, transl., *Confucius et Mencius ou les quatre livres de philosophie morale et politique de la Chine* (Paris, 1841) in a commonplace book of the late 1830s and early 1840s. This notebook, described in the catalogues of the Stephen H. Wakeman Sale (1924) and the 1958 Parke-Bernet Galleries sale of Thoreauviana (number 1825), is now in the Berg Collection of the New York Public Library. None of the notebook passages duplicates the contents of the *Dial* text. But Ralph H. Orth and Alfred R. Ferguson, the editors of *The Journals and Miscellaneous Notebooks of Ralph Waldo Emerson*, IX (1971), p. 8n, observe that Emerson acquired

Collie's translation of *The Four Books* in early 1843, and assign the *Dial* extracts to him; see also Emerson's letter to Margaret Fuller, June 7, 1843 (*Letters*, III, p. 179), enthusiastically reporting his acquisition of the book. A reference to the volume occurs as early as Emerson's manuscript journal J (1841-1842; *Journals and Miscellaneous Notebooks*, VIII, p. 146); manuscript journal R (spring, 1843) contains extracts, one of them duplicating a *Dial* entry (VIII, pp. 354, 356, 366-367, 383, 410, 424). In manuscript journal U, for late 1843, other extracts appear (IX, pp. 7, 8, 32-34).

HOMER. OSSIAN. CHAUCER.

Copy-text: *The Dial*, IV, 3 (January, 1844), 290-305. In Thoreau's copy of *The Dial* the essay is extensively altered in pencil. These changes anticipate *A Week*, where the text, even further revised, occurs on pp. 95-99, 362-367, and 386-396 of the 1849 edition and on pp. 98-102, 364-369, and 387-398 of the 1868 edition. Between the untouched *Dial* form and the 1849 *Week* there are eighty-seven substantive variations, many of them major. Five additional changes of wording appear in the 1868 edition. The essay as originally printed serves here as copy-text, and only those six changes in Thoreau's annotated *Dial* which correct errors are adopted as emendations. A rule is deleted after 171.11.

The November 29 lecture, entitled "Ancient poets," was prepared in response to Emerson's invitation in a letter of October 25, 1843, to Thoreau, then in Staten Island working as tutor to Emerson's nephew (Harding, "A Check List of Thoreau's Lectures," *Bulletin of the New York Public Library*, 52 [1948], 79; *The Correspondence of Henry David Thoreau*, p. 149). Thoreau had discovered Macgregor's edition of Ossian at the New York City Mercantile Library; about November 1 he wrote to Henry S. McKean, the librarian, asking to borrow the volume (*Correspondence*, p. 150). One of his commonplace books contains extensive extracts.

166.33 Boccaccio: The copy-text reads "Boccacio" and a journal draft version of the sentence, January 2, 1842, has "Bocacio." Thoreau's misspelling may reflect the medievalized form "Boccace" employed in notes to the five-volume Tyrwhitt edition of Chaucer's *Canterbury Tales* (London: T. Payne, 1775-1778), the text Thoreau read and copied from during this period.

166.35 Wickliffe: Thus in the copy-text as in the journal draft, January 2, 1842. It is a common, if questionable, spelling of the reformer's name: see *Encyclopaedia Britannica*, eleventh edition, XXVIII, p. 866n. Two paragraphs earlier in the essay Thoreau uses the form "Wicliffe."

169.1 Custance: Thus in the journal draft, December 30, 1841, in a Chaucer extract in Thoreau's Library of Congress commonplace book, and in the Tyrwhitt edition of the *Canterbury Tales*, Vol. I. The copy-text has "Constance."

Emendations

All emended readings except "Boccaccio" and "Custance" are drawn from Thoreau's corrected and revised copy of *The Dial*.

156.27	east	last
163.10	fagots	faggots
164.23	It	He
164.23	it	him
* 166.33	Boccaccio	Boccacio
168.31	are	is
* 169.1	Custance	Constance
173.28	deserts,	~ ∧

Thoreau's Corrections and Revisions

Six are listed as emendations. The remaining 36, recorded in the right-hand column, are revisions for *A Week* and are not adopted in the present text. Words and letters in square brackets in the right-hand column are editorial reconstructions, based on *Week* readings, of illegible manuscript matter.

154.11	is rhymed or measured	is either rhymed or in some way musically measured
154.14	Yet	*marked with paragraph sign*

154.33	It is	*preceded by caret, from which a line leads near a marginal note, second word dubious*: Now merrily?
155.6	that succeeding	that with respect to the simpler features of nature succeeding
157.2	only	*cancelled*
157.7	But man	But after all man
157.14	themselves.	themselves. This raw & gusty day, and the creaking of the oaks & pines on shore— reminded us of more northen climes than Gr[eece] and more wintry seas than [the] AEgean.
157.28-29	rites, don't	rites,—Don't
158.27	want not	do not want
159.26	Normans.	Normans. It is remarkable that there is in Ossian no trace of the influence of Christianity. This is evidence enough, if any were needed, [to] prove the genuineness of these remains, for to omit thi[s in] a modern poem surpasses the cunning of man.

162.26	poetry, but	poetry, it is pastoral & lyric & narrative & dida[ctic,] but
162.26	is for	is of one style & for
162.27	has lost	has in a great measure lost
162.28	office. He	office. Formerly ⟨ . . . ⟩ now it is th[ought] that one m[an sees] as much as an[other.] He
163.10	pleasant	*preceded by parenthesis*
163.11-13	The towering . . . herds.	*circled*
163.13-16	Poetry . . . didactic.	*circled*
164.28-29	We do not . . . class.	*circled*
164.31-33	Through . . . folios.	*circled*
165.1	Wicliffe much	Wicliffe did much
165.7-9	A great . . . sense.	*circled*
166.3-11	It is astonishing . . . load.	*circled*
166.11	He is	But Chaucer is
166.19-28	Only one . . . furrow.	*circled*
166.30-31	expand in	expand at last in
167.18	pleads not	does not plead
168.7-15	The whole . . . cock.	*circled*
169.6-10	His sincere . . . forgotten.	*circled*
169.19-25	Such pure . . . man.	*circled*
170.12	the hearer	*enclosed in parentheses*
170.20-25	Even . . . obeys; and some . . . balanced.	*marked for transposition*
170.22-23	and some	Some
170.25-27	Though . . . lighted.	*circled*

171.5	And surely	Surely
171.17	kernel	breath
173.2	world, but, like	world. Like
173.2	sun, indifferently	sun, he indifferently
173.22	The great	*marked with paragraph sign*

HERMES TRISMEGISTUS . . . FROM THE GULISTAN OF SAADI

Copy-text: *The Dial*, IV, 3 (January, 1844), 402-404, headed "Ethnical Scriptures." Thoreau's copy contains no corrections or revisions. The attribution of the piece to Thoreau is by Cooke, but Myerson (p. 164) tentatively gives it to Emerson: "Thoreau . . . may have made the selections, but the Hermes section was undoubtedly the same as that which A. B. Alcott sent to Emerson in August, 1842 (Alcott, *The Letters*, ed. R. L. Herrnstadt [Ames: Iowa State, 1969], p. 88), and which Emerson promised in the October *Dial* to print in the future (*Dial*, III, 278). . . . See also *The Letters of Ralph Waldo Emerson*, III, p. 248, where Emerson sends Margaret Fuller a 'fair copy' (his own?) of this piece" (*abbreviations expanded*). That last-mentioned letter, however, is dated April 19, 1844, when the issue containing the Hermes extracts was long since in print. Emerson declared that he had previously sent Fuller "an imperfect copy" of "the Hermes"—which must mean either defective printer's copy for the January, 1844 *Dial* or an incomplete set of printed pages after publication. Myerson also notes that Emerson "had a life-long interest in Saadi." The immediate source for the last section of this "Ethnical Scriptures" compilation (the second, "Ascription," is like the first from the *Divine Pymander*) is identified by Mueller, p. 113, as *The Gulistan, or Flower-Garden of Shaikh Sadī of Shiraz*, transl. James Ross (London, 1823). References to and extracts from this translation of *The Gulistan* appear in Thoreau's journal, in his Literary Notebook in the Library of Congress, and in *A Week on the Concord and Merrimack Rivers*, but none of these instances duplicates the *Dial* selections. On the other hand, Emerson's manuscript journal U for late 1843 contains the *Dial* extracts from *The Gulistan* struck through with use marks (*Journals and Miscellaneous Notebooks*, IX, pp. 38-39).

Rules are deleted after 176.2 and 176.28 in the present edition.

175.10   attained: Possibly a compositor's error; the source reads "obtained" (p. 44).

175.24   brute man: "man" may be a compositor's error; the source reads "bruit Beast" (p. 60).

Emendations

The second emended reading is drawn from the source, p. 43.

174.1-2	Hermes Trismegistus ... From the Gulistan of Saadi	*lacking*
175.1	eye ∧	∼ ,
175.17	senses and	senses aud

SIR WALTER RALEIGH

Copy-text: MS, Huntington, a fair copy with pencil revisions, about 1843-1844. Walter Harding in *A Thoreau Handbook* (New York: New York University Press, 1959), p. 46, and Perry Miller in *Consciousness in Concord* (Boston: Houghton Mifflin Company, 1958), pp. 11, 144n., associate "Sir Walter Raleigh" with "The Service" as submitted to *The Dial* but not published there. Thoreau lectured on Raleigh before the Concord Lyceum on February 8, 1843 (Harding, "Check List of Thoreau's Lectures," p. 79); the *Concord Freeman* for February 10 carried a second-hand report, reprinted in Harding's *The Days of Henry Thoreau* (New York: Alfred A. Knopf, 1966), pp. 143-144. A small portion of the essay was used in *A Week on the Concord and Merrimack Rivers*, pp. 108-112 of the 1849 edition.

Thoreau's source for the bulk of his quotations from and about Raleigh is *The Works of Sir Walter Raleigh, Kt.*, with the biographies by William Oldys and Thomas Birch (Oxford: The University Press, 1829). His borrowing "from Lib." of the first volume of this collected edition is recorded without date in a "Memoranda" notebook in the Albert E. Lownes Collection, John Hay Library, Brown

University. On December 10, 1841, he borrowed the eighth and last volume from the Harvard College Library: see Kenneth W. Cameron, *Emerson the Essayist* (Raleigh, N.C.: The Thistle Press, 1945), II, p. 195. Thoreau's commonplace books of the early 1840s contain extended extracts from the *Works* and from, apparently, the 1614 first edition of Raleigh's *History of the World*; and his journal entries of the period include draft versions of many passages that are later used in the fair copy and in a surviving preliminary holograph, also at Huntington.

Edited by Henry A. Metcalf and F. B. Sanborn, "Sir Walter Raleigh" was published in Boston by the Bibliophile Society in 1905. Their edition was based on the fair copy; but Metcalf and Sanborn misread the holograph at several points, omitted occasional words and phrases, ignored some pencil cancellations, and amplified Thoreau's text with passages from the working manuscripts and from the Raleigh *Works*. None of these changes carry authority. The present edition follows exactly Thoreau's fair-copy elaborations on his source material, save in a few instances where he confused references by miscopying. At these points, discussed in textual notes, Thoreau's source is the basis for necessary emendation.

Both Metcalf (p. xiii) and Sanborn (p. 2) claim to have had access to "three drafts" of the Raleigh piece. The "third" is clearly the Huntington Library fair copy. Thoreau's preliminary holograph cannot properly be called a "first draft": rather, it is a body of working papers among which two or more draft versions of various passages may be discovered. If Metcalf and Sanborn meant the term "first draft" to refer exclusively to the known preliminary manuscript, the "second" draft either is an invention or has disappeared without a trace and without confirming documentation for its ever having existed. The greater likelihood is that these editors viewed the single large body of working papers as two isolable draft stages.

Linck Johnson, a Thoreau editor, has proposed that Thoreau's pencil corrections and revisions on the ink fair copy date from ca. 1846-1847 and represent a pre-copy-text state for *A Week*. Several passages from the "Raleigh" essay occur in a surviving two-page working draft in the Houghton Library. The worksheet is probably related to *A Week*. Some alterations in the fair copy are incorporated on the worksheet; others are not, and some altered sentences adjacent to material used on the worksheet are not repeated in that later manuscript. Moreover, Thoreau's pencil changes are scattered throughout the "Raleigh" manuscript; they are not concentrated in the sections corresponding to the worksheet or even in those more extensive sections which found their way into *A Week*. The theory that Thoreau's pencil revisions constitute *Week* draft material is thus not adequately supported by existing evidence. A slender and even playful hypothesis to the effect that Thoreau once intended to include the entire essay in *A Week* would explain the prevalence of pencil changes throughout the ink draft. But such a hypothesis is beside the point since only a few pages of *A Week* as actually published derive from the essay. The "Sir Walter Raleigh" holograph may best be regarded as an independent and integral piece of writing. Thoreau's pencil alterations—whenever they were made—refine the ink draft but do not alter its general character or point toward any larger literary construct to which the "Raleigh" essay would be subordinated.

179.28   King Charles: The copy-text follows the source exactly in this quotation deriving from John Aubrey: "K. Ch." The abbreviation is expanded for clarity.

186.4-18   His enemies . . . trial.:   Faint pencil lines through this paragraph may be use-marks, or may signal deletion. Other passages so treated are 188.7-16 ("Already . . . year of"—pencil line later cancelled), 188.20-36 ("But . . . street?"), 193.1-9 ("We . . . England."), 193.28-195.8 ("Though . . . end."), and 218.1-7 ("For . . . whetstones'.").

188.7   1595:   The copy-text's "1592" is a slip of the pen: Thoreau has the correct date in two drafts of the sentence in the working manuscript.

190.14   Canuri: Thus, correctly, in Raleigh's *Works*, VIII, p. 442 *et seq.* (as in the first edition of *The Discoverie of Guiana*, London, 1596). The copy-text has "Canari."

193.4   "Piratas–piratas":   Thus, correctly, in the source. The copy-text reads " 'Piratos–piratos.' " In the preliminary holograph, the term is misspelled in its first appearance and spelled correctly in its second.

196.6   Commons.:   A pencilled note in the copy-text

at this point, "England has men &c," seems to indicate a continuation from another manuscript. Nothing beginning with this phrase has been found, however, in the working draft or earlier manuscript materials.

196.26-31   on occasion . . . than usual.:   The source, Raleigh, *Works*, I, pp. 176n.-177n., attributes this feat to a Sir Francis Carew, and not to Raleigh.

198.3-4   from . . . church,:   In revising this phrase Thoreau left it garbled. He originally wrote (in ink) "from his natural courtesy to the church," and then made changes in pencil: he cancelled "natural" and added "innate" above; he circled "church", possibly for deletion, and added in the space between the lines on which "natural" and "church" appear, "habit of religious custom". In this last pencil phrase, both the first word and the last are questionable, alternative readings being "a sort" and "courtesy". The various possibilities of Thoreau's intention, beside the reading offered in this text, thus range from "from his habit of innate religious courtesy," (Metcalf's and Sanborn's reading) to "from his innate courtesy to a sort of religious custom,".

201.22   for: The copy-text originally read "on account of." Thoreau interlined "for" and set off "on account of" with parentheses for possible deletion. However, he deleted neither alternative.

203.21   creatures: When Thoreau copied out this passage from the 1614 first edition of *The History of the World* into his commonplace book, he inadvertently omitted the word "creatures." Recopying into the fair manuscript copy-text, he left a blank, intending to supply it from the source.

203.28   Augustine: : So pointed in the source. The copy-text omits punctuation, which is required for clarity.

207.16   true.:   In the copy-text Thoreau adds, in pencil, "V S" ("Vide Scrap" or "Vide Sheet"). The state of the manuscript at present (as, evidently, when Metcalf and Sanborn used it) makes Thoreau's intention unrecoverable.

212.28   which at evening record: Thoreau interlined "when" in pencil above "which" and "this" above "evening record", evidently considering the revision, "when at evening this record". However, he did not cancel "which" and he enclosed the two interlined words in pencil parentheses, his usual doubt-marks.

214.5-6 Sometimes . . . ran.: Thoreau cancelled this sentence by means of a wavy pencil line, but he failed to make a corresponding adjustment in the next sentence. Rather than making an adjustment by emendation (e.g., removal of "But" and capitalization of "for"), the editor restores the original reading.

215.31 with: Inadvertently omitted in the copy-text, but present in a journal draft version of the sentence, January 9, 1842.

Emendations

Emended readings followed by (D) are drawn from the working draft, HM 935. Many emendations are anticipated in the Bibliophile Society edition of the essay.

178.1	Walter	Water
178.2	Perhaps	*not indented*
178.11	enterprise,	~ . (*see alteration*)
178.12	few	Few (*see alteration*)
179.7	Thomas'	Thoma's
179.9	wit."	~ ; " (*see alteration*)
179.12	bred".	~ " —
* 179.28	King Charles	K. Ch.
179.31	mortals".	~ " —
179.36	day."	~ ∧ "
180.3-4	successful	successfull
180.7	Garcilaso	Garcilasso
180.28	a Drake	A ~
180.29	a Halley	A ~
180.29	Galileo	Gallileo
180.31	Spenser	Spencer
180.32	Shakspeare	shakspeare
180.33	inspiration.	~ ∧
180.36	activity ∧	~ , (*see alteration*)
181.14	implied.	~ ∧
181.17	Edward	Ed.
181.19	marched (D)	marches
181.23	end.	~ —
181.28	Spain	spain
182.2	this	of this (*see alteration*)
182.30	equipments—those	~ . Those (*see alteration*)
183.25	affairs.	~ , (*see alteration*)

183.28	treatise.	~ —
184.36	that	That (*see alteration*)
185.18	his	His (*see alteration*)
185.30	canst	cans't
186.11	Scots	scots
186.24	Edward	Ed.
186.28	spent.	~ —
187.10	"with	^ ~
187.17	unrevoked.	~ —
187.33	place.	*trimmed; period not visible*
* 188.7	1595 (D)	1592
188.8	undertaken	*last three letters trimmed*
188.11	recover	reover
188.28	this	*possibly* the
190.12	them.	~ ,
* 190.14	Canuri	Canari (*see alteration*)
190.31	valley.	~ . x x x .
191.13	manurance."	~ " ; —
191.14	preceding	preceeding
191.16	instance,	*perhaps* instance;
191.34	St.	St ^
192.26-27	on the subject	on the subject on the subject
192.31	too	two
* 193.4	"Piratas—piratas"	"Piratos—piratos"
193.4	pirates.	~ —
193.9	England.	~ ^
193.11	when	*last two letters not visible*
193.13	him, after	him. After
193.17	The	the
193.18	scene.	~ ^
193.20	suicide	Suicide
193.21	disgrace.	~ ,
195.5	another (D)	another another
195.8	end. ^	~ . "
195.9	sentence:	~ ^
196.2	prisoner, ^	~ " ,

* 196.6	Commons.	Commons. England has men &c (*interlined in pencil*)
196.16	Savile	Saville
196.19	&c.,	&c ∧ ,
196.21	potato	potatoe
196.21	cherry (D)	Cherry
197.33	it	It (*see alteration*)
* 198.3-4	from . . . church,	*see textual note*
198.11	pavilion.	~ ∧
198.13-14	criticisms	crticisms
199.35	wary	wary wary
200.17	For	*not indented; preceded by vertical space*
200.19	he	He
200.26	experience,	~ ∧ (*see alteration*)
200.35	he	He
201.6	manoeuvring	maneuvering
201.7	vague	vage
201.15	&c.,	&c ∧ ,
* 201.22	for	for on account of (*neither cancelled*)
201.25	to a close	*perhaps* down lower
201.26	exploits.	~ —
201.27	now-a-days	now-a ∧ days
202.5	Spenser	Spencer
202.8	reader's	readers
203.18	bodies. . . .	~ . x x x
* 203.21	creatures	*lacking*
203.22	offices. . . .	~ . x x x
203.27-28	dominion. . . .	~ . x x x
* 203.28	Augustine:	~ ∧
203.30	*above*;	~ ; x x x x
203.34	*soil*.	~ . x x x x
204.1	laws. . . .	~ . x x
204.12	sun's	suns
204.33	universal:	~ : x x x x
205.31	*mens*	*mens* mens (*see alteration*)

206.1	similitude."	~ ." x
206.8	There	*not indented; preceded by vertical space*
207.1	persons.	~ —
* 207.16	true.	true. V S
208.4	deceive	decive
208.7	known.	~ —
208.21	a form	aform
211.10	me.	~ ;
211.34	Indeed	(Indeed) (*see alteration*)
212.2	all,	~ ∧ (*see alteration*)
212.15	Steady	steady (*see alteration*)
* 212.28	which	which (when
* 212.28	evening	evening this)
214.4	A perfectly	*not indented; preceded by vertical space*
* 214.5-6	Sometimes . . . ran.	*cancelled*
214.10-11	attractive	atractive
215.1	Raleigh	*not indented; preceded by vertical space*
* 215.31	with	*lacking*
215.33	course.	~ ,
216.3	the man	*perhaps* this man
216.5	Soul's	Souls
216.6	When	*not indented; preceded by vertical space*
216.32	a revelation	a a revelation
217.8	We	*not indented; preceded by vertical space*
217.12	one's	ones
218.16	not . . . manlike	(~ . . . ~) (*see alteration*)
218.23-24	*Largior . . . Purpureo*	*not indented*
218.25-26	Here . . . With	*not indented*

Alterations

178.1   Raleigh]   *fifth letter added in pencil*

178.2   better]   *added in pencil above cancelled* more
distinctly

178.4   got]   *added in pencil above cancelled* grown

178.5   Raleigh's]   *added in pencil above cancelled* His

178.5   antique & Roman]   *added in pencil above
cancelled* ancient

178.8   and his]   his *added interlinearly in pencil*

178.11   &]   *added in pencil*

178.12-13   which are . . . history]   *added interlinearly
in pencil*

178.14   he]   *added in pencil above cancelled* his were

178.15   possessed]   *added interlinearly in pencil*

178.20   virtue]   *followed by cancelled* and

178.20   as it were]   *added interlinearly in pencil*

178.21   very]   *added interlinearly in pencil*

178.22   who]   *added in pencil above cancelled* and

178.23   the]   *altered in pencil from* those

178.25   the]   *added in pencil*

178.26   profounder or grander]   *added in pencil above
cancelled* deeper

178.26   but]   *followed by cancelled* more

178.28   often]   *added in pencil above cancelled*
frequently

179.9   generally]   *followed by cancelled* such

179.9   wit."]   *followed by* that on one occasion he
beats one of them for making a noise in a tavern, and
"seales up his mouth, his upper and nether beard with
hard wax." *cancelled in pencil*

179.10   heard]   *added interlinearly*

179.23-24   well-compacted]   *followed by cancelled*
body

180.1   this]   *altered in pencil from* his

180.1   suited]   *added in pencil above cancelled*
adapted

180.2   times]   *last letter added in pencil*

180.3   stirring]   *added in pencil above cancelled* active

180.17   than heretofore,]   *added interlinearly in pencil*

180.25   have]   *altered in pencil from* he

180.27   himself,]   *comma added in pencil*

180.36   this]   *added in pencil above cancelled* the

180.36 activity] *followed by* of his life *cancelled in pencil*

180.36 versatility] *preceded by* the *cancelled in pencil*

181.3-4 in the intervals of war] *added interlinearly in pencil*

181.6 proper] *added in pencil above cancelled* truer

181.6 aim] *altered in pencil from* aims

181.8 for] *added in pencil above cancelled* since

181.11 yet] *preceded by cancelled* other

181.13 juster] *altered in pencil from* justest

181.14 implied] *added in pencil above cancelled* he tells of,

181.14 In whatever] *altered in pencil from* and in whatever

181.15 head,] *comma added in pencil*

181.17 that] *added in pencil above cancelled* him

181.18 such] *followed by* an *cancelled in pencil*

181.18 young] *followed by* of the land *cancelled in pencil*

181.18 seeks] *last letter added in pencil*

181.19 he has] *added in pencil above cancelled* having

181.24 in fact] *added interlinearly in pencil*

181.26 All] *altered in pencil from* all *and preceded by* We might say that *cancelled in pencil*

181.26 seems to have been] *added in pencil above cancelled* was

182.1 backward] *preceded by cancelled* slow

182.1-2 to develop] *altered in pencil from* in the development

182.4 especially] *added interlinearly in pencil*

182.5 give] *added in pencil above cancelled* render

182.11 does not] *added in pencil*

182.11 assert] *altered in pencil from* asserts *and followed by* not *cancelled in pencil*

182.25 his] *altered in pencil from* him

182.30 equipments—] *dash added in pencil through period*

183.21 possibly] *followed by cancelled* at

183.25 He] *altered in pencil from* he *and preceded by* for *cancelled in pencil*

184.15 Arcadia.] *followed by* (The Queen walking

one day in the midst of her courtiers came to a mirey place, when Raleigh, who was then unknown to her, taking off his rich plush cloak spread it upon the ground for a foot-cloth.) *cancelled in pencil*

184.36   But] *added interlinearly in pencil*

185.18   Revenge] *altered in pencil from* There is in it the spirit of revenge, which *by capitalization of* revenge *and cancellation of remaining words*

185.18   Also] *added interlinearly in pencil*

185.20   adherents] *altered in pencil from* adherence

185.25   Yet] *added above cancelled* Though

185.28   extent] *added above cancelled* degree

185.29   Jonson] *preceded by cancelled* his contemporary

186.4-18   His enemies . . . trial.] *see textual note*

186.9   exclaimed] *written through* said

186.11-12   increase] *altered in pencil from* introduce

186.20   remembered] *added in pencil above cancelled* said

186.21   ill-] *added in pencil*

187.12   Raleigh] *preceded by cancelled end of a sentence at top of page:* conclusion of the trial.

187.17   with] *preceded by cancelled* f

187.17   unrevoked.] *added in pencil above cancelled* against him—

187.17-21   In . . . confinement.] *cancelled in ink, with cancellation lines erased;* In the meanwhile *added in pencil above cancelled* Where *and* in his imprisonment *added interlinearly in pencil after* himself *followed by* as the world knows *added interlinearly in pencil and cancelled in pencil*

187.28   to him] *added interlinearly in pencil*

187.32   he] *added in pencil*

188.2   interesting] *added above cancelled* singular

188.7-16   Already . . . year of] *see textual note for 186.4-18*

188.8   it will be remembered] *added interlinearly in pencil*

188.15   13th] 3 *reformed in pencil*

188.20-36   But . . . street?] *see textual note for 186.4-18*

189.23   Palace] P *altered from* p

189.28   No one] *altered from* Non

189.32   or]   *preceded by cancelled* ore

189.34   accord.]   *followed by cancelled* And

189.34   That]   *altered in pencil from* that

190.14   the province]   the *added interlinearly*

190.14   Canuri]   Canari *repeated in block letters above*
Canari

190.14   last]   *added interlinearly*

191.6   fresh]   *preceded by cancelled* fres

191.35   the name of himself]   *added in pencil above
cancelled* his own name

192.5   this]   *added interlinearly*

192.9   handle]   *preceded by cancelled* hangl

192.22   military or]   or *added above cancelled* and

192.33   in]   *added in pencil*

193.1-9   We . . . England.]   *see textual note for*
186.4-18

193.8   soon]   *added above cancelled* directly

193.17-18   The reader . . . scene]   *added above
cancelled* But that these sketches of his life may be
complete we will not omit this

193.19   pardon]   *followed by cancelled* him

193.28-195.8   Though . . . end.]   *see textual note for*
186.4-18

193.35   conduct]   *added above cancelled* direction

195.5   another]   *added in pencil above* another

195.6   of]   *altered in pencil from* in

195.17   Hic]   *preceded by cancelled quotation mark*

195.21   valuable]   v *altered from* f

196.1   poetry,]   *followed by cancelled* and

196.6   Commons.]   *followed by* England has men &c
added interlinearly in pencil

196.9   means of]   *followed by cancelled* of

196.16   &]   *added in pencil*

196.22   where his garden was]   *altered in pencil from*
where was his garden

196.29   removed]   *altered from* removing

196.34   effectually]   *added interlinearly in pencil*

197.21   him]   *added in pencil*

197.24   do so]   *added interlinearly in pencil*

197.27   contemplates]   *followed by* the freedom of
cancelled in pencil

197.33   it]   *altered in pencil to* It

197.35   usually]   *followed by* disabled and *cancelled in pencil*

198.3-4   from . . . church,]   *see textual note*

198.5   whenever]   *followed by* an emperor or *cancelled in pencil*

198.5   hero]   *followed by* of his own stamp *cancelled in pencil*

198.12   will]   *added in pencil above cancelled* may

198.16   natural]   *preceded by cancelled* se- *or* re-

198.18   more]   *added interlinearly in pencil*

198.19   English]   *added interlinearly in pencil*

198.20   or rather . . . forest, where]   *added in pencil above cancelled* of stately oaks, where *with pencil* where *added below cancelled pencil* that *and pencil* rather *altered from pencil* is

198.22   on horse back]   *added in pencil above cancelled* freely

199.35   wary]   *repeated interlinearly*

200.16   Greece".]   *written above cancelled upside-down* mander. *at bottom of page*

200.19   A man . . . he]   *added in pencil above cancelled* A man who had acted as he had

200.22   commonly]   *added in pencil above cancelled* often

200.22   by]   *added in pencil above cancelled* when the historian only

200.22   recording]   *altered in pencil from* records

200.22   merely]   *added interlinearly in pencil*

200.25   perhaps]   *added interlinearly in pencil*

200.26   or within his experience]   *added interlinearly in pencil*

200.35-36   he speaks . . . eye-witness, and]   *added interlinearly in pencil; see emendation*

201.4   commonly]   *added interlinearly in pencil*

201.5   to serve]   *added interlinearly in pencil*

201.6   clear]   *added in pencil above cancelled* plain to the reader

201.9   at least]   *altered from unrecovered words*

201.14   sometimes]   *added in pencil above cancelled* he

201.17-20   but in this . . . stage—]   *added interlinearly in pencil*

201.22   for]   *added above* on account of *; see textual
note*

201.24-26   We expect ... exploits]   *added interlinearly
in pencil;* We expect *followed by* So *cancelled in pencil*

201.26   However . . . hardly]   *added in pencil above
cancelled* But consider it as we will, it is not

201.28   author's]   *followed by cancelled* life

201.36   while]   *altered from* which

202.8   his]   *added interlinearly*

202.22   but]   *altered from* that

202.33   beautifie]   *altered from* beautify

203.3   pleased]   *added interlinearly*

203.19   course]   *followed by cancelled* of

203.35   God]   G *altered from* g

204.31   History]   H *altered from* h

205.31   *mens]   repeated above without underscoring
and followed by erased parenthesis*

206.1   But man]   *preceded by cancelled* X And a little
after he adds

206.9   like . . . rivers]   *added interlinearly*

206.14   want]   *added interlinearly*

206.30   counterfeit]   *altered from* counterfeiting *or*
counterfeiter

206.34-35   expands . . . that]   *added in pencil above
cancelled* shows how

207.16   true.]   *followed by pencil* V S (*see textual
note*)

207.23   go on with]   *added above cancelled* complete

208.8   evident]   *added above cancelled* many

209.7   Of]   *followed by cancelled* W

210.12   heroic tone]   *added above cancelled* energy of
feeling which

210.20-21   commencement of]   *followed by cancelled*
his

210.29   body's]   *followed by cancelled* blo

211.29   what]   *added in pencil above cancelled* all

211.34   Indeed]   *set off by pencil parentheses for
possible deletion*

212.2   came . . . spoken at all]   *added in pencil above*
was likeliest not to have been said at all, *set off by pencil
parentheses*

212.4   some]   *added in pencil above cancelled* an

212.8   Raleigh]   *added in pencil above cancelled* our hero

212.15   remembered.]   *followed by* Undoubtedly, *cancelled in pencil*

212.21   at evening]   *added interlinearly in pencil*

212.28   which . . . record]   *see textual note*

212.30   after]   *followed by cancelled* those other *with* those *altered in pencil to* the

212.30   of his axe]   *added interlinearly in pencil*

213.30   they]   *added in pencil above* it were *set off by pencil parentheses*

213.30   only]   *followed by* that they fairly *cancelled in pencil*

214.5-6   Sometimes . . . ran.]   *cancelled in pencil: see textual note*

216.11   our]   *preceded by cancelled* the

216.33   silent,]   *followed by cancelled* yet famo

217.26   men.]   *followed by cancelled* We

217.31   less]   *added above cancelled* less

218.1-7   For . . . whetstones".]   *see textual note for 186.4-18*

218.4   Hood]   H *altered from* h

218.15-16   enterprising]   *added in pencil above* wilfull *set off by pencil parentheses*

218.16   not . . . manlike]   *set off by pencil parentheses for possible deletion*

218.18   creation]   *preceded by* this fair *cancelled in pencil*

THOMAS CARLYLE AND HIS WORKS

Copy-text: *Graham's American Monthly Magazine*, XXX, 3 (March, 1847), 145-152, and 4 (April, 1847), 238-245. Shortened by approximately 4,000 words, the essay was reprinted in *A Yankee in Canada, with Anti-Slavery and Reform Papers* (Boston: Ticknor and Fields, 1866), a posthumous volume probably edited by Sophia Thoreau. For a clue to Sophia's involvement in the *Yankee in Canada* project, see *The Letters of A. Bronson Alcott*, ed. R. L. Herrnstadt (Ames, Iowa: Iowa State University Press, 1969), pp. 362-363; all evidence about the editing of the volume is discussed by Wendell Glick in his edition of Henry D. Thoreau, *Reform Papers* (Princeton: Princeton

University Press, 1973), pp. 219-221. There are sixty-one
substantive and significant accidental differences between
the magazine and book versions. Of these, thirty-nine are
omissions, often of extended passages; one is a word in-
version; fifteen are single-word substitutions, including
corrections of number and changes of spelling where the
difference changes the meaning; three are changes of punctuation affecting the sense; and only three are additions to
Thoreau's original language. Of the additions, one is a
single word, "the," which makes a construction more orderly than in the original but does not alter the meaning;
another is a single word necessary to adjust for a preceding omission of material; the third involves a change from
a rhetorical question to a statement. The present editor
does not regard these sixty-one substantive differences as
arguing strongly for Thoreau's collaboration in the abbreviated *Yankee in Canada* text of "Carlyle." The omissions
are cuts of the sort a copyeditor might make, especially
when faced with space limitations. None of the three additions clearly shows Thoreau's hand; it is in the nature
of additions and their proportional relation to deleted matter that authorial involvement can most readily be ascertained. Most of the single-word substitutions are corrections of obvious errors in the magazine text—as easily
attributable to a copyeditor as to the author. Thoreau's
direct intervention is evident in only one substitution,
"delugeous" for "detergeous," which he may have corrected in his personal copies of the *Graham's* text immediately after publication. Allowing for compositors' misreadings of the original manuscript, then, the *Graham's*
"Carlyle" is indisputably an authorial form, while the
shortened *Yankee in Canada* version is suspect. The present editor therefore adopts from the posthumous text only
those variant readings, chiefly corrections, consistent with
Thoreau's intentions in the *Graham's* version. All substantive differences between the magazine and book forms are
reported in the table of textual variations.

The Carlyle essay was originally a lecture that Thoreau
delivered before the Concord Lyceum on February 4, 1846:
its title was set down in the Lyceum records as "Writings
& style of Thomas Carlysle" (Harding, "Check List of
Thoreau's Lectures," p. 80). Sometime before August 16
of the same year he asked Horace Greeley, editor of the

New York *Tribune*, to seek an outlet for it in print (see Greeley's reply, *The Correspondence of Henry David Thoreau*, p. 169). In this maiden effort as Thoreau's informal literary agent, Greeley offered the essay to George R. Graham of Philadelphia on August 25, praising it lavishly and implying that he would submit it to *Godey's* if it were not accepted for *Graham's Magazine* (letter printed in *Passages from the Correspondence of Rufus W. Griswold* [Cambridge, Mass.: W. M. Griswold, 1898], pp. 206-207). On September 30 Graham informed Greeley through Griswold, his former editor, that he would accept the article. "Of course it is to be paid for at the usual rate," Greeley told Thoreau; his Concord friend should wait for payment until after publication (*Correspondence of Thoreau*, p. 170). Thoreau, whom Greeley had described to Graham as "a scholar, poor of course," seeking publication of the Carlyle piece "to get utterance and bread," did not hear directly from Graham, despite Greeley's expectation that he would. In a letter dated October 26, Greeley tried to set Thoreau's mind at rest about the magazinist's silence, and could report his receipt of an encouraging message from Griswold: " 'The article . . . is in type, and will be paid for liberally' " (*Correspondence of Thoreau*, p. 171). Greeley evidently shared Thoreau's concern, for he had written to Philadelphia three times before Griswold conveyed Graham's assurances. But "Thomas Carlyle" remained in editorial limbo, and Griswold seems not to have acted on Greeley's suggestion, in a letter dated November 21, to "Tell him when his article is to appear in Graham if you can. He will be glad to hear from you" (*Passages from the Correspondence of Griswold*, p. 212). "Why don't Graham publish my friend Thoreau's article on Carlyle," an increasingly impatient Greeley asked Griswold on December 16; "I am disappointed at its non-appearance. Please find out what its prospect is, and advise me" (*Passages*, p. 213). On February 5, 1847, Greeley received and answered a letter in which Thoreau, exasperated, proposed withdrawing the Carlyle essay from *Graham's* for use again as a lecture or for publication elsewhere. "Although your letter only came to hand to-day," he wrote,

I attended to its subject yesterday, when I was in Philadelphia on my way home from Washington. Your ar-

ticle is this moment in type, and will appear about the
20th inst. as *the leading article* in Graham's Mag. for
next month. Now don't object to this, nor be unreason-
ably sensitive at the delay. It is immensely more important to you that the article should appear thus (that
is, if you have any literary aspirations,) than it is that
you should make a few dollars by issuing it in some
other way. As to lecturing, you have been at perfect liberty to deliver it as a lecture a hundred times if you had
chosen—the more the better. It is really a good thing,
and I will see that Graham pays you fairly for it. But its
appearance there is worth far more to you than money.

I know there has been too much delay, and have done
my best to obviate it. But I could not. A Magazine that
pays, and which it is desirable to be known as a con-
tributor to, is always crowded with articles, and has to
postpone some for others of even less merit. I do this myself with good things that I am not required to pay for.

Thoreau, do not think hard of Graham. Do not try to
stop the publication of your article. It is best as it is.
But just set down and write a like article about Emerson, which I will give you $25 for if you cannot do
better with it; then one about Hawthorne at your leisure,
&c. &c. I will pay you the money for each of these
articles on delivery, publish them when and how I
please, leaving to you the copyright expressly. In a year
or two, if you take care not to write faster than you
think, you will have the material of a volume worth
publishing, and then we will see what can be done
(*Correspondence of Thoreau*, pp. 173-174).

Although the article was printed without further difficulties of record, Thoreau waited for payment for more than
a year. When he sent the manuscript of "Ktaadn, and the
Maine Woods" to Greeley on March 31, 1848, after a "long
silence," he reported Graham's delinquency. Replying,
Greeley voiced sorrow and surprise; "since my honor is
involved in the matter," he added, "I will see that you *are*
paid, and that at no distant day" (*Correspondence*, p. 217).
After an interim message about his efforts, April 17, 1848,
Greeley announced success on May 17, sending Thoreau
$50 with an explanation of the mode of collection he had
been forced to adopt: "I finally found the two numbers [of

Graham's Magazine, which he had bought at 'a very out-of-the-way place'] . . . and with these I made out a regular bill for the contribution; drew a draft on G. R. Graham for the amount, gave it to his brother here for collection, and to-day received the money" (*Correspondence*, pp. 222-223).

Within a week of the publication of *Graham's* for March, 1847, Emerson notified Carlyle about Thoreau's article, "which he will send to you as soon as the second part appears in a next number" (February 27, in *The Correspondence of Emerson and Carlyle*, ed. Joseph Slater [New York: Columbia University Press, 1964], p. 415). The piece reached Carlyle, by mail or by the hands of an acquaintance of Thoreau's travelling in England, before May 7, when Carlyle wrote to his sister that "I have got an American Review of me" (*New Letters of Thomas Carlyle*, ed. Alexander Carlyle [London: John Lane, 1904], II, p. 34); and on May 18 Carlyle asked Emerson to "tell Mr Thoreau . . . that his Philadelphia Magazine, with the *Lecture*, in two pieces, was faithfully delivered here, about a fortnight ago; and carefully read, as beseemed, with due entertainment and recognition" (*Correspondence of Emerson and Carlyle*, p. 422). Since the lecture origins of the essay are not mentioned in *Graham's*, Carlyle's choice of words suggests that a covering note by Thoreau—or a conversation with the bearer of Thoreau's parcel if it was hand-delivered—gave him this information.

In the present edition rules are deleted after 222.27, 234.2, 235.17, 245.16, 252.8, and 253.4; and a wide space is provided at 242.12, where the first *Graham's* installment ends.

220.18 Sterling: John Sterling (1806-1844) is the writer designated by the copy-text's "Stirling." The spelling is corrected in *A Yankee in Canada*.

220.31 traveller: Thoreau habitually spelled this word and "travelling" with the double l. In a total of eight instances the copy-text reads "traveler(s)" and "traveling," in conformity with the *Graham's* house style. The authorial spelling is restored in the *Yankee in Canada* version of "Carlyle."

222.30 month to month: Thus in the *Yankee in Canada* form, a more plausible reading than the copy-text's "mouth to mouth." The *Graham's* compositor seems to have misread Thoreau's manuscript here, as he certainly did at 248.3, "Month," for which a journal draft version survives.

222.34   Boones and Crocketts: The copy-text reads "Boons and Crockets"; only the first spelling is corrected in the *Yankee in Canada* printing.

235.20   leaven: Followed in the copy-text by a comma, which the present editor deletes for the sake of intelligibility.

239.3   delugeous: Thus in the *Yankee in Canada* printing; the copy-text has "detergeous." It seems likely that this change was authorial and that "detergeous" resulted from a compositor's misreading of the lost manuscript. Both terms are neologisms, but "delugeous" is a more plausible reading in view of the geological figures and flood references immediately preceding, and the opposition of center and surface in the following sentences. Moreover, Thoreau's lexicons offered the adjectival form "detergent" of the verb "deterge."

240.32   style, [that of his?] remarkable: In the source, Carlyle's *Critical and Miscellaneous Essays* (Boston: James Munroe and Company, 1838-1839), I, p. 272—an essay on Goethe reprinted from the 1828 *Foreign Review*—the passage is punctuated "style—that of his; remarkable". If the pointing in the copy-text is Thoreau's, rather than a compositor's, his intentions are not clear.

242.12   service is rendered.:   The first (March) installment in *Graham's Magazine* ends at this point.

242.15   Dilettantes: At least one instance of the copy-text's misspelling, "Dilettants," occurs in Carlyle. But this locus—the phrase "Pedants, Dilettants" in *Oliver Cromwell's Letters and Speeches* (London: Chapman and Hall, 1845), I, p. 6—is not necessarily the passage Thoreau had in mind. "Dilettantes" is normally spelled correctly in the early editions of Carlyle; see, for instance, the last sentence of chapter ten, *Sartor Resartus*, in the London edition of 1838.

247.24   Sansculottism: Thus in the source, *The French Revolution* (London: James Fraser, 1837), I, p. 296; Carlyle's consistent spelling Anglicizes the French construction, *sans-culottisme*. The copy-text has "Sansculotism."

248.32   Jötuns: Thus corrected in *A Yankee in Canada* from the copy-text's "Iötuns." Thoreau's capitals I and J are often difficult to distinguish. In this paragraph Thoreau refers to "The Hero as Divinity," the first chapter or lecture of Carlyle's *On Heroes, Hero-Worship, & the Heroic in History* (London: Fraser, 1841), where the spelling "Jötuns" is consistently used.

255.9 Teufelsdröckh: Misspelled "Teüfelsdrock" in the copy-text. See *Sartor Resartus, passim.*

255.27 inexpugnable: While the copy-text reading, "inexpungable" (correctly spelled "inexpungible" or "inexpungeable"), might be plausible in this context, Carlyle's word is "inexpugnable," impregnable or invincible, in all early forms of *Sartor Resartus* examined by the present editor. These include the serial text in *Fraser's Magazine*, IX (1834), 443, the private 1834 printing by James Fraser, and the 1838 edition published by Saunders and Otley, London. All Thoreau's lexicons list "inexpugnable"; none have "inexpung(e)able" or "inexpungible," for which the first instance recorded by the *New English Dictionary on Historical Principles* is dated 1888. Whether "inexpungable" is Thoreau's transcription error in the lost printer's copy or a blunder by the compositor cannot be ascertained.

259.22-24 His . . . too.: Thus in the copy-text, part of a long passage omitted from the *Yankee in Canada* version. Even if "Cromwell's" is taken as the contraction of "Cromwell is" the sense of the sentence is not clear; the *Graham's* compositor may have dropped some words. The present editor is unable to confirm the copy-text reading or to recover any different intention on Thoreau's part.

261.4-5 Maidstone: Thus in the copy-text and a journal draft. While Carlyle normally uses the spelling "Maidston" in *Oliver Cromwell's Letters and Speeches*, he has "Maidstone" in the passage (II, p. 32) from which Thoreau drew the quotation that follows.

Emendations

Emended readings followed by (Y) are anticipated in *A Yankee in Canada.*

219.1	*omitted* (Y)	—/By HENRY D. THOREAU/—
* 220.18	Sterling (Y)	Stirling
* 220.31	traveller (Y)	traveler
220.36	workshop (Y)	workship

221.20	travellers (Y)	travelers
* 222.30	month to month (Y)	mouth to mouth
* 222.34	Boones (Y)	Boons
* 222.34	Crocketts	Crockets
223.9	Landor (Y)	Landon
223.33	traveller (Y)	traveler
224.16	eye (Y)	eyes
225.24	transcendent (Y)	transcendant
230.21	tongue,— (Y)	~ ;
230.34	travelling (Y)	traveling
232.2	don't (Y)	do n't
233.32	speak (Y)	speaks
235.3	Past and Present (Y)	past and present
* 235.20	leaven ∧	~ ,
238.5	them ∧ (Y)	~ ,
* 239.3	delugeous (Y)	detergeous
239.27	vein, (Y)	~ . (*perhaps broken comma*)
* 242.15	Dilettantes	Dilettants
247.4	remember	rememember
* 247.24	Sansculottism	Sansculotism
248.3	Month (Y)	Mouth
* 248.32	Jötuns (Y)	Iötuns
249.13	travellers	travelers
249.24	goal (Y)	good
252.13	unfenced (Y)	enfenced
* 255.9	Teufelsdröckh	Teüfelsdrock
* 255.27	inexpugnable	inexpungable
256.5	prophesy (Y)	prophecy
258.12	travellers (Y)	travelers
258.12	traveller (Y)	traveler
261.4	consider	con ∧ / sider
261.23	didn't	did n't
266.32	travellers (Y)	travelers
267.7	discriminating (Y)	discrimi ∧ / nating
267.16	better, (Y)	~ ∧

Textual Variations

Following variant readings in the right-hand column, (G) designates the *Graham's Magazine* copy-text (Harvard

College Library copy P 136.11*) and (Y) the *Yankee in Canada* version of the essay (Harvard copy *AC 85. T 3912. 866y [A], pp. 211-247).

219.16	prizes, &c."—
	        "come
		prizes, ... come
		        (Y)

220.18	Sterling	Stirling (G)
220.36	workshop	workship (G)
221.19	very few	few very (Y)
222.30	month to month	mouth to mouth (G)
223.9	Landor	Landon (G)
223.24-30	Through . . . quarter.	*deleted* (Y)
224.13	As	Since (Y)
224.16	eye	eyes (G)
226.18-25	In the . . . for once.	*deleted* (Y)
227.18	even any of his	even his (Y)
227.19	as a historian	as historian (Y)
228.15	and writer	writer (Y)
230.14-15	Sanscrit; and they	Sanscrit; they (Y)
230.30	about it, with	about, with (Y)
231.28	throws	throw (Y)
233.32	speak	speaks (G)
235.32- 236.4	Every . . . sublime.	*deleted* (Y)
238.5	them ∧	~., (G)
238.14-20	To . . . comparisons.	*deleted* (Y)
239.3	delugeous	detergeous (G)

239.30-
    240.13
	Every . . .
	        prejudice.
		deleted (Y)

241.32-34	The first
	        impression . . .
	        reader.
		deleted (Y)

241.36-
    242.6
	The first faint . . .
	        meridian.
		deleted (Y)

242.8-12	It is . . . rendered.	*deleted* (Y)
242.20-32	Think . . . creatures.	*deleted* (Y)
243.4-22	And this . . . world.	*deleted* (Y)

243.28-
    245.16
	We hear . . .
	        darkness."
		deleted (Y)

246.23-30	And . . . surface.	*deleted* (Y)
247.3-7	But if . . . around.	*deleted* (Y)
247.11-21	There . . . know of.	*deleted* (Y)
247.22	got translated	translated (Y)
248.3	Month	Mouth (G)
248.19-25	The old . . . well.	*deleted* (Y)
249.9-19	There sits . . . more.	*deleted* (Y)
249.24	goal	good (G)
250.5-9	Possibly . . . posterity.	*deleted* (Y)
250.15	unappeasable	most reasonable (journal)
250.22-33	As . . . point to.	*deleted* (Y)
251.5-7	True . . . spring.	*deleted* (Y)
251.22	these	their (Y)
251.30-252.2	There is . . . become.	*deleted* (Y)
252.4	&c.	*deleted* (Y)
252.9	One more	One (Y)
252.13	unfenced	enfenced (G)
252.14-32	He does . . . blue.	*deleted* (Y)
252.33	Carlyle, though	Though (Y)
252.34	lets	he lets (Y)
253.1-4	We have . . . hitherto.	*deleted* (Y)
253.23	from serene	from the serene (Y)
253.35-254.4	its premises . . . around.	*deleted* (Y)
254.25-255.29	We should . . . pacificated."	*deleted* (Y)
256.5	prophesy	prophecy (G)
256.16-32	In this . . . that."	*deleted* (Y)
257.20-27	Homer . . . impressive.	*deleted* (Y)
258.24-262.16	The several . . . see.	*deleted* (Y)
262.17	All of Carlyle's	All his (Y)
263.10-21	The attitude . . . late.	*deleted* (Y)
264.22	even ∧	∼ , (Y)

265.20- 266.6	Simple . . . countenanced.	*deleted* (Y)
266.28-29	Who . . . race?	Carlyle is a critic who . . . race. (Y)
267.16	better,	~ ∧ (G)

LOVE

Copy-text: MS, Texas, for 270.15-271.9 (through "we do not"): fair copy, incomplete. For the remainder of the essay, 268.1-270.14 and 271.9-273.22, the copy-text is *Letters to Various Persons* (Boston: Ticknor and Fields, 1865), pp. 72-75, 76-79. The essay on "Love" and the following one on "Chastity & Sensuality" were enclosures in Thoreau's September 1852 letter to H. G. O. Blake. The rest of the fair copy from which R. W. Emerson—editor of *Letters to Various Persons*—drew the "Love" text has disappeared, but a working manuscript survives in the Huntington Library. The entire text of the printed "Love" is represented in the draft; additional draft matter has been marked for deletion with Thoreau's customary pencil line; the final order of paragraphs is designated by marginal numbers; and the wording of the uncancelled portion conforms, with only four exceptions, to the printed essay. One of those differences is adopted as an emendation in the present edition. The others are changes of the sort which Thoreau might well have made in preparing the fair copy. All substantive differences are recorded in the table of textual variations. It is possible, even likely, that some spelling, punctuation, and capitalization differences between the draft and the printed version are Emerson's improvements of the fair copy; but none of the *Letters* accidentals alters the sense, and in the absence of fair copy it is idle to conjecture which accidentals were imposed by Emerson and which appeared in the lost pages of Thoreau's clean manuscript.

270.7   surely: Thus in the working draft. The less plausible copy-text reading, "rarely," resulted from a copying error. The compositor, who worked either from Thoreau's manuscript as modified by Emerson or from a transcription by Emerson, may have misread his copy. Emerson may have introduced the error if he prepared a transcription for the printer. There is also a slender possibility that Thoreau miscopied his own word in preparing fair manuscript from working draft.

Emendations

The first four emended readings, plus the last one, are drawn from the working draft.

* 270.7	surely	rarely
270.25	sensitive.	~ ∧
270.27	imagination.	~ ;
270.30	still	s *trimmed*
271.4	beloved	*perhaps* Beloved
272.5	Canst	Can'st
272.17	me.	~ ∧

Alterations in the Manuscript

270.17   perceptions]   o *overwritten*
270.26   offence]   c *altered from* s
270.28   its]   *altered from* it
270.28-29   glance . . . eyry]   *added interlinearly*
270.30   still]   *added in left margin; see emendation*
270.32   clipt]   p *overwritten*
271.4   beloved]   *first letter overwritten; see emendation*

Textual Variations

Following variant readings in the right-hand column, (LVP) designates the copy-text, *Letters to Various Persons* (Harvard University Library copy AC 85 T 3912.8651 [B]), and (D) the working draft in the Huntington Library. There are no substantive differences between the fair-copy fragment and the corresponding portion of *Letters to Various Persons*.

269.7	Nevertheless	Nertheless (D)
269.32-33	few marriages such	few such (D)
270.7	surely	rarely (LVP)
271.21	moles	*possibly* the moles (D)
271.35	as to be	as be (D)

CHASTITY & SENSUALITY

Copy-text: MS, Texas. Fair copy, sent by Thoreau to H. G. O. Blake in September, 1852, together with the essay entitled "Love." It was first published in *Letters to Various Persons*, edited by Emerson, pp. 79-84. A working draft survives in the Huntington Library.

276.34 Amoenitates: Thus, correctly, in the draft and in *Letters to Various Persons*; the copy-text reads "Amoenitatas", with the last "a" perhaps changed in the direction of an "e", followed by the cancelled letters "Academ". Under the title *Amoenitates Academicae* were gathered numerous dissertations by students of Linnaeus. Most of these papers are on botanical subjects, "Botanicae" appearing in the subtitle of volumes of the *Amoenitates*. The candidate or "respondent" Isacus J. Biberg presented his thesis, *Specimen Academicum de Oeconomia Naturae*, in March 1749. It was included in volume two of *Amoenitates Academicae*, editions of 1751, 1752, 1762, 1764, and 1787, but the present editor has seen it only in a separate issue (Uppsala, 1749), where the passage translated by Thoreau occurs on page 16. As Terrence Williams writes in his introduction to *A Checklist of Linneana, 1735-1835*, University of Kansas Publications, Library Series, 20 (Lawrence, 1964), "The 185 published academic theses which bear [Linnaeus'] name as praeses are almost certainly his own work; according to the custom at Uppsala, the defendant was responsible only for translating his professor's lecture into passable Latin and for having the essay printed."

Emendations

Emended readings followed by (D) are drawn from the working draft; those followed by (LVP) are anticipated in *Letters to Various Persons*.

275.13	awful (LVP)	aweful
276.14	affection (D, LVP)	*perhaps* affections
276.34	Biberg, (D, LVP)	~ . ,
* 276.34	Amoenitates (D, LVP)	Amoenitatas (*see alteration*)
277.9	pollen." (D, LVP)	~ .".
277.12	flower. (D, LVP)	~ ∧
277.28	ecstasy (LVP)	extacy

Alterations in the Manuscript

274.8 completely] *last three letters written over illegible letters*

274.9   secrecy]   *followed by cancelled comma*

274.12   anxieties]   x *followed by illegible cancelled letter*

274.14   Shakers]   *altered from* shakers

274.23   sight]   s *clarified to prevent misreading as* r

275.1   lusts]   *followed by cancelled* and

275.1   pleasures]   *altered from* plaasures

275.27   than]   h *written over false start*

275.27   man's]   *altered from* mam's

275.35   be]   *altered from* bee

276.34   Amoenitates]   *first written* Amoenitatas *with penultimate letter perhaps later altered toward* e

276.34   Amoenitates]   *followed by cancelled* Academ

277.17   lowlands]   *followed by cancelled* with

277.33   fertile]   *preceded by cancelled* fer

278.4   Beasts]   *indented as paragraph; then run by a line to repetition.*

Textual Variations

Following variant readings in the right-hand column, (LVP) designates *Letters to Various Persons* (University of Texas copy 60-1748), and (D) the working draft manuscript in the Huntington Library.

274.13	affairs	affair (LVP)
274.21	copulation	marriage (LVP)
275.14	than that of	than the presence of (LVP)
276.4	natures, and	natures also, and (D)
276.35-36	Latin) "the	Latin, that "the (D)
277.19	dreamed, is	dreamed to be is (D: *neither cancelled*)
278.7	*lacking after* them.	The ultimate fruit of a tree is not a seed, but much more a flower or rather a truly flourishing tree state. If the earth began with spring —it will end with summer. (D)

Line-end Hyphenation

THE compounds or possible compounds in list A, below, are hyphenated at the end of the line in the copy-texts. On the general grounds discussed in the Introduction, pages 329-330, the editor has resolved each to the form recorded in list A. List B records only those compounds hyphenated at the end of the line in the present edition that should be transcribed with the hyphen in order to duplicate the copy-text forms.

LIST A

18.25	defenceless	99.3	disarm
22.3	other-hand	106.15-16	mankind
23.11	Nevertheless	118.10	earth-born
26.26	bluestockings	122.29	fault-finders
31.22	marksmanship	135.5	disrespect
32.30	meadow-sweet	145.19	outspread
32.32	dragon-fly	155.9	sunlight
33.18	sportsman	157.3	mankind
36.30-37.1	unmeaning	163.10	fireside
		178.10	soldier-like
37.6	cobwebs	179.4	Brampton-Brian
39.30	manhood	179.23-24	well-compacted
40.25	soi-disant	179.27	forehead
41.7	home-bred	179.33	notwithstanding
41.25	mill-wheel	180.8	forefathers
41.26	skylarks	188.35	unexplored
42.29-30	arm-chair	190.22	church-tower
47.14	underpropping	198.2	antediluvian
57.23-24	block-head	199.16	well-ordered
69.29	village-life	202.1	lifelike
77.27	childlike	202.9	childlike
77.31	playhouse	202.34	otherwise
78.15	heavenward	203.33	*husbandman*
83.8	self-interest	206.27-28	speechless
85.17	countrymen	208.6	Recreations
89.27	cast-off	218.16	godlike
96.24	littleness	220.6-7	Craigenputtock
97.28	birthright	221.28	chest-shaking

224.8	booksellers	236.13	ball-room
227.28	endless	236.21	side-light
227.32	unwearied	239.22	summer-heat
228.12	shop-windows	240.6-7	uncommon
230.29-30	blueber-	241.16	stereotyped
	ry-swamps	244.18	Hardly-en-
230.30-31	shad-blossoms		treated
230.33	mail-coach	246.33-34	preoccupied
232.25	peacock's	248.12	background
233.2	naturalness	249.2	shop-work
233.31-32	unexplored	258.7	unfolded
235.22-23	superabundance	270.35	foundationless

LIST B

15.33-34	iron-bound	136.22-23	*north-eastern*
20.32-33	store-house	145.20-21	day-light
27.35-	train-oil	179.23-24	well-compacted
28.1		200.35-36	eye-witness
28.14-15	well-known	201.11-12	eye-witness
29.21-22	door-keeper	230.29-30	blueber-
32.29-30	foam-like		ry-swamps
32.30-31	loose-strife	230.30-31	shad-blossoms
41.27-28	robin-red-breast	231.34-35	half-formed
42.29-30	arm-chair	234.10-11	corn-mill
43.25-26	cow-herd	244.8-9	toil-worn
47.23-24	never-failing	245.1-2	heaven-made
57.23-24	block-head	255.15-16	heaven-written
67.5-6	Scotch-men	262.6-7	top-of-the-morn-
82.8-9	courtier-like		ing
85.11-12	all-embracing	264.23-24	Demi-gods
89.26-27	well-tried		

Checklist of Manuscripts

AN entry for each composition in this volume identifies and describes the relevant surviving manuscripts. The autograph materials listed for Early Essays are in all cases Thoreau's fair copies, the only relevant manuscripts, which serve as copy-texts in the present edition. Only a third of the Miscellanies are based on manuscript (or authorially annotated print) copy-texts, but autograph matter of various sorts exists for most of them. In the checklist entries for Miscellanies, therefore, manuscript copy-texts will be specifically designated as such.

The Seasons: Concord (Mass.) Free Public Library; bound in Henry S. Salt, *Life of Henry David Thoreau* (London: Walter Scott, 1896; bound as two volumes), facing I, p. 23. Brown or faded black ink on both sides of a leaf of off-white paper, trimmed at the right edge. 2 pp.

Anxieties and Delights of a Discoverer: Henry E. Huntington Library and Art Gallery, HM 934. Faded black ink on off-white paper, folded in theme fashion. 3 pp. plus endorsement page, on which appear notations by E. T. Channing ("34") and F. B. Sanborn ("C").

Men Whose Pursuit Is Money: Clifton Waller Barrett Collection, The Alderman Library, University of Virginia. Faded black ink on off-white paper, folded in theme fashion. 3 pp. plus endorsement page, which bears notations by E. T. Channing ("7 T", "34") and F. B. Sanborn (identification of manuscript and presentation note).

Of Keeping a Private Journal: Henry E. Huntington Library and Art Gallery, HM 934. Faded black ink on off-white paper, folded in theme fashion. 3 pp. plus endorsement page, on which appear notations by Channing ("34") and Sanborn ("C"), and the date in an unidentified hand.

"We Are Apt to Become What Others . . . Think Us to Be": Henry E. Huntington Library and Art Gallery, HM 934. Faded black ink on off-white paper, folded in theme fashion. 2 pp. plus endorsement page, on which appear notations by Channing ("9   T", "35"), and Sanborn ("C.").

Forms, Ceremonies, and Restraints of Polite Society: Albert E. Lownes Collection, John Hay Library, Brown University. Faded black ink on cream-colored paper, folded in theme fashion. 3 pp. plus endorsement page, on which appear notations by Channing ("10   T", "35") and Sanborn ("C").

A Man of Business, a Man of Pleasure, a Man of the World: Henry E. Huntington Library and Art Gallery, HM 934. Faded black ink on off-white paper, folded in theme fashion. 3 pp. plus endorsement page, on which appear notations by Channing ("11   T", "35"), and Sanborn ("C").

Musings: Pierpont Morgan Library, MA 920. Faded black ink on off-white paper, folded in theme fashion. The lower half of the second leaf has been cut away, leaving only the tops of a few letters visible. 2½ pp., with typed and ink notations by Sanborn, as well as the pencilled date, on the verso of the partial leaf.

Kinds of Energetic Character: Henry E. Huntington Library and Art Gallery, HM 934. Faded black ink on off-white paper, folded in theme fashion. 3 pp. plus endorsement page, on which appear notations by Channing ("35") and Sanborn ("C–"), and "1834-35" in an unidentified hand.

Privileges and Pleasures of a Literary Man: Pierpont Morgan Library, MA 920. Faded black ink on off-white paper, folded in theme fashion. 3 pp. plus endorsement page, on which appear notations by Channing ("20–   T", "35") and Sanborn ("C"), plus the date "Sept. 18, 1835" in an unidentified hand.

Severe and Mild Punishments: Humanities Research Center Library, University of Texas at Austin, Thoreau MS file. Black ink on off-white paper, folded in theme fashion. 4 pp.

Popular Feeling: Robert H. Taylor Collection, Firestone Library, Princeton University. Faded black ink on off-white paper, folded in theme fashion. 1 p. plus endorsement on verso of leaf, on which appears Channing's notation "35" and early draft matter for *A Week on the Concord and Merrimack Rivers* in Thoreau's hand, apparently ca. 1842.

Style May . . . Offend against Simplicity: Pierpont Morgan Library, MA 920. Faded black ink on off-white paper, folded in theme fashion. 3 pp. plus endorsement page, on which appear notations by Channing ("25   T", "35") and Sanborn ("C"). An "X" before Channing's "35" may be in a third hand.

The Book of the Seasons: Henry E. Huntington Library and Art Gallery, HM 945. Faded black ink on seven leaves of a notebook entitled "Index rerum", paginated "9"-"22" in ink by Thoreau. 14 pp. "Index rerum" is a marbled notebook of ruled white paper, originally seventy-six leaves, of which thirty-six whole and partial original leaves remain in the binding, plus two blue leaves which are pasted in. On the first leaf, recto, appears the inscription "D. H. Thoreau   Cambridge   Index rerum". Thoreau's pagination, beginning with "9" at leaf 22 recto, agrees with neither the original page-count nor the count of surviving pages. The contents of the notebook are various: early journal indexing and lists of topics (leaves 1 verso, 5v, 6r, 10r-v, 19r-v, 20r-v, 21r-v); extracts from Thoreau's reading (2r-5r, 6v-7v, 8v, 9v, 33r, 37r-38v and inside back cover); Thoreau's personal library list (11r-13v, 14r-14v, 15r-15v, 17r-18v); a reading list (34r); notes on an interview with Anna Jones (8r, 8v, 9r, 9v); a Latin composition (33r); a fragmentary draft of a poem (34v); and book reviews and essays (22r-28v, 29r-v, 30r, 30v-32v, 33v, 35r-36v). Three additional manuscript items—one a fragment of a letter by Thoreau—are tipped in at the front.

Sir Henry Vane: Henry E. Huntington Library and Art Gallery, HM 945. Faded black ink on both sides of a leaf in the "Index rerum" notebook (see copy-text note and checklist entry for "The Book of the Seasons," above). The top third of the leaf has been cut away. 2 partial pp.

Literary Digressions: Henry E. Huntington Library and Art Gallery, HM 945. Faded black ink on the recto of a single leaf of the "Index rerum" notebook (see copy-text note and checklist entry for "The Book of the Seasons," above), paginated "33" in ink by Thoreau. The preceding leaf is missing from the notebook. 1 p.

Foreign Influence on American Literature: Pierpont Morgan Library, MA 2392; Henry E. Huntington Library and Art Gallery, HM 934. Each portion is written in faded black ink on off-white paper. 6 pp., with endorsement on the final page, together with Sanborn's pencilled "C". The last page of the Morgan Library portion bears another notation by Sanborn, "XV".

Life and Works of Sir W. Scott: Henry E. Huntington Library and Art Gallery, HM 945. Faded black ink on 4 pages of the "Index rerum" notebook (see copy-text note and checklist entry for "The Book of the Seasons," above), paginated "43"-"46" in ink by Thoreau.

The Love of Stories: Pierpont Morgan Library, MA 920. Faded black ink on off-white paper, folded in theme fashion. Visible in the endorsement beneath Thoreau's "1836" is the erased pencil number "36", presumably in Channing's hand. Nearby is Sanborn's notation "C" and, in an unidentified hand, "39th Theme". Channing's pencilled "T" and perhaps two pencilled numbers, all erased, appear under "39th Theme". 4 pp.

Cultivation of the Imagination: Henry E. Huntington Library and Art Gallery, HM 934. Faded black ink on off-white paper, folded in theme fashion. The last page bears Sanborn's notation, "C", near Thoreau's signature. 4 pp.

The Greek Classic Poets: Henry E. Huntington Library and Art Gallery, HM 934. Faded black ink on off-white paper, folded in theme fashion. 10 pp. A pencilled "C", possibly Sanborn's, appears on the first page beneath Thoreau's date; but this piece, unlike others so marked (presumably for "copied"), is not included in Sanborn's 1917 *Life of Henry David Thoreau*.

The Meaning of "Fate": Abernethy Library of American Literature, Middlebury College (Vermont), Thoreau College Essays. Faded black ink on off-white paper, folded in theme fashion. On the last page are notations by Sanborn, *"Thoreau"* and "XXIV". 4 pp.

Whether the Government Ought to Educate: Manuscript Division, Library of Congress, Henry D. Thoreau collection. Faded black ink on off-white paper, folded in theme fashion. 3 pp. plus endorsement page, on which Sanborn has written "C".

Travellers & Inhabitants: Houghton Library, Harvard University, College Essay fragment; in *AC85. St317, 885 p. Vol. II, Part 1, Edmund Clarence Stedman, *Poets of America*, Extra-Illustrated Edition (Cambridge: Riverside Press, 1885), II, Part 1, between pp. 340-341. Faded black ink on off-white paper, folded for insertion in the Stedman volume. Across the top right of the recto Sanborn has written, "Thoreau 1836 (These are separate fragments)". 2 pp.

History . . . of the Roman Republic: Henry E. Huntington Library and Art Gallery, HM 945. Faded black ink on five pages of the "Index rerum" notebook (see copy-text note and checklist entry for "The Book of the Seasons," above), paginated "34"-"38" in ink by Thoreau.

A Writer's Nationality and Individual Genius: Pierpont Morgan Library, MA 920. Faded black ink on off-white paper, folded in theme fashion. 9 pp. plus endorsement page, on which appear notations by Channing ("44   T", "36") and Sanborn ("C.").

L'Allegro & Il Penseroso: Abernethy Library of American Literature, Middlebury College, Thoreau College Essays. Faded black ink on blue-gray paper, folded in theme fashion. The manuscript is torn and incomplete; where the tops of pages survive, they are paginated "5"-"8" and "11"-"15" in pencil by Thoreau. 13 pp., some partial, plus endorsement page, on which appears Sanborn's notation, "C X".

All Men Are Mad: Henry E. Huntington Library and Art Gallery, HM 945. Faded black ink on a page of the "Index rerum" notebook (see copy-text note and checklist entry for "The Book of the Seasons," above), paginated "40" in ink by Thoreau. Text perhaps incomplete. 1 p.

The Speeches of Moloch & the Rest: Houghton Library, Harvard University, bMS Am 278.5.5. Faded black ink on blue-gray paper, folded in theme fashion. 5 pp. plus endorsement page, on which appear notations by Channing ("45   T", "37") and Sanborn ("C", "IX"). "Jan", in an unidentified hand, is written near "37".

People of Different Sections: Abernethy Library of American Literature, Middlebury College, Thoreau College Essays. Faded black ink on blue-gray paper, folded in theme fashion. On the last page are notations by Channing ("47   T", "37") and Sanborn ("*Thoreau*   C   XIX"). 4 pp.

Gaining or Exercising Public Influence: Abernethy Library of American Literature, Middlebury College, Thoreau College Essays. Faded black ink on blue-gray paper, folded in theme fashion. The manuscript is incomplete. 2 pp.

Titles of Books: Manuscript now missing, but kept at least until 1959 by the Francis Harvey Green Manuscript Collection, the Pennington School (New Jersey). Facsimile: see copy-text note. Described as "six and one-third quarto pages."

Sublimity: Houghton Library, Harvard University, bMS Am 278.5.5. Faded black ink on blue-gray paper, folded in theme fashion. 9 pp. plus endorsement page, on which appear notations by Channing ("50 T", "37") and Sanborn ("C XVII").

The General Obligation to Tell the Truth: Albert E. Lownes Collection, John Hay Library, Brown University. Faded black ink on blue-gray paper, folded in theme fashion. 4 pp. On the last page appears a typed statement, probably by Sanborn, identifying the manuscript and presenting it to a collector.

"Being Content with Common Reasons": Abernethy Library of American Literature, Middlebury College, Thoreau College Essays. Faded black ink on blue-gray paper, folded in theme fashion. 6 pp. plus endorsement page, on which appear notations by Channing ("51 T", "37") and Sanborn ("C. XVI"), and "May 5. 1837" in an unidentified hand.

The Duty, Inconvenience and Dangers of Conformity: Abernethy Library of American Literature, Middlebury College, Thoreau College Essays. Faded black ink on blue-gray paper, folded in theme fashion. 3 pp. plus endorsement page, on which appear notations by Channing ("52 T", "37") and Sanborn ("C XVIII").

Moral Excellence: Abernethy Library of American Literature, Middlebury College, Thoreau College Essays. Faded black ink on blue-gray paper, folded in theme fashion. 3 pp. plus endorsement page.

Barbarities of Civilized States: Abernethy Library of American Literature, Middlebury College, Thoreau College Essays. Faded black ink on blue-gray paper, folded in theme fashion. The manuscript is incomplete. 4 pp., with notations by Sanborn on the first page ("C") and the last ("XXVI").

T. Pomponius Atticus: The manuscript is lost.

Class Book Autobiography: Harvard University Archives, HUD 237.714F, "Class of 1837", pp. 105-106. Faded black ink on white paper. 2 pp.

"The Commercial Spirit of Modern Times": Harvard University Archives, HUC 6836.50, "Exhibition and Commencement Performances 1836-1837". Faded black ink on blue-gray paper. 5 pp. plus titlepage.

DIED . . . Miss Anna Jones: Houghton Library, Harvard University, bMS Am 278.5, folder 3: two pencil drafts on the same sheet of off-white paper. 2 pp. Notes on an interview with Anna Jones occupy two full pages and parts of two others in the "Index rerum" notebook, Henry E. Huntington Library and Art Gallery, HM 945: see checklist entry for "The Book of the Seasons," above.

Aulus Persius Flaccus: Thoreau's annotated copy of *The Dial*, Morris Library, Southern Illinois University, Carbondale (copy-text). Emerson's set of *The Dial*, Houghton Library, Harvard University, *AC85 Em345 Zy841d, also contains autograph corrections, probably by Thoreau: see textual note. Extracts from Persius appear in a commonplace book of Thoreau's, "Miscellaneous Extracts," in the Pierpont Morgan Library, MA 594, pp. 121-122.

The Laws of Menu: Thoreau's annotated copy of *The Dial*, Morris Library, Southern Illinois University (copy-text). Manuscript excerpts from Thoreau's source are included in "Miscellaneous Extracts," Pierpont Morgan Library, MA 594, pp. 124-138 and 156-165: these are transcribed by Kenneth W. Cameron in *The Transcendentalists and Minerva*, I, pp. 310-321. In the workbook "Paragraphs &c Mostly Original," Morgan Library, MA 608, pages 22, 36-40, 42-44, and several later pages, numbered and unnumbered, contain extracts from and passages on Menu: see Cameron, *Transcendental Climate*, III, pp. 901-969 for facsimile and transcription.

Sayings of Confucius: passages from *The Phenix* in "Miscellaneous Extracts," Pierpont Morgan Library, MA 594, pp. 90-91.

Dark Ages: Thoreau's annotated copy of *The Dial*, Morris Library, Southern Illinois University. The entire essay appears in draft form in Thoreau's workbook, Pierpont Morgan Library, MA 608, pp. 24-32 (facsimiled in Kenneth W. Cameron, *Transcendental Climate*, III, pp. 922-930). Earlier versions of several paragraphs occur in the Morgan Library journal, MA 1302, December 27, 1837, October 6, 1840 (in the "Lost Journal"), and August 9, 1841.

Chinese Four Books: Pages 127-149, "Commonplace Book," Berg Collection, New York Public Library: see copy-text note.

Homer. Ossian. Chaucer.: Thoreau's annotated copy of *The Dial* is in the Morris Library, Southern Illinois University. First-draft forms of many *Dial* passages on Homer, Ossian, and Chaucer occur in early journals: Pierpont Morgan Library, MA 1302, entries for September 5, November 30, and December 30, 1841, and January 2, March 11, March 14, and April 2, 1842; Henry E. Huntington Library and Art Gallery, HM 13182, entries for November 7, 9, 19, 20, and 21, 1843. Pages 91-122 of the "Commonplace Book," Berg Collection, New York Public Library, are devoted to extracts from Macgregor's edition of Ossian. Other verse and prose extracts used in the essay, and a draft version of one of Thoreau's paragraphs, appear in a commonplace book of the 1840s, photo-facsimiled and indexed by Kenneth W. Cameron in *Thoreau's Literary Notebook in the Library of Congress* (Hartford: Transcendental Books, 1964).

Hermes Trismegistus . . . From the Gulistan of Saadi: No manuscripts are known to survive.

Sir Walter Raleigh: Henry E. Huntington Library and Art Gallery, HM 943; fair copy in faded black ink, with pencil revisions, on 42 leaves of white paper and 3 of gray, folded and sewed into a fascicle, paginated 1-83 in pencil by Thoreau, with some unpaginated pages blank. This is the copy-text for the present edition. The legend "Final drafts", apparently in Thoreau's hand, appears in pencil on the final page of the fascicle. Pre-copy-text materials include Huntington HM 935, ink draft with pencil revisions, 104 pp. (an early working copy representing several stages of composition); Library of Congress, commonplace book (see Cameron, *Thoreau's Literary Notebook*, index), extracts from Raleigh's works; "Commonplace Book," Berg Collection, New York Public Library, extracts from Raleigh, pp. 50-57, and extract from Sylvester's Dubartas, p. 87; Pierpont Morgan Library, MA 594, "Miscellaneous Extracts," pp. 118-120, extracts from Raleigh; and Morgan MA 1302, journal, entries for March 14, 1838, August 19, 20, and 21, 1840, September 29, 1840 (1840 entries in the "Lost Journal"), April 30, 1841, December 23, 1841, January 5 and 9, 1842, March 16 and 31, 1842.

Houghton bMS Am 278.5 (folder 19), 2 pp., is a fragment of a draft post-dating the copy-text: see copy-text note. A worksheet in the Abernethy Library, Middlebury College, mounted in Volume I of set 490 of the 1906 Manuscript Edition of *The Writings*, 2 pp., is draft matter for the "Night and Moonlight" lecture manuscripts of 1854. Like the Houghton fragment, it post-dates the "Sir Walter Raleigh" copy-text and draws upon it for other purposes.

Thomas Carlyle and His Works: Scattered draft versions of various passages are to be found in Thoreau's manuscript journal, Pierpont Morgan Library, MA 1302: one under date of March 18, 1842, and several others in a notebook numbered "7" in the Morgan Library sequence, ca. 1845-1846, undated entries *ante* February 22. Morgan MA 1303, a volume of drafts, journal entries, and recopied material from earlier journals, August 31, 1839-March 13, 1846, probably written during the Walden period, contains "Carlyle" working drafts on pp. 221 and 225. A separated leaf from this notebook, paginated 232, in the Henry E. Huntington Library and Art Gallery, HM 924, includes another draft fragment. Additional "Carlyle" working materials appear on the pages paginated by Thoreau 24, 25, 28-30, 37, 48, and 67-68 of an 1846 journal-workbook in the Berg Collection, New York Public Library.

Love: Partial copy-text is a leaf (2 pp.) of the fair copy, Humanities Research Center Library, University of Texas at Austin, MS (Thoreau, H. D.) Works: black ink on pale blue paper, physically identical with that of the "Chastity & Sensuality" fair copy and sharing fold marks with it. Pinholes in the left margin, recto, suggest that the complete manuscript was once sewn into a fascicle. The "Love" leaf was removed from set number 487 of the Manuscript Edition (1906) of *The Writings of Henry David Thoreau*. Henry E. Huntington Library and Art Gallery, HM 13196, is a preliminary draft in black ink and pencil on off-white paper in three folders of four pages each and two separate leaves of two pages each. The last page of the final folder is blank; the manuscript thus occupies fifteen pages. Another separate leaf of the same paper, representing a rejected beginning of the essay, is headed "Love & Friendship." In the Huntington arrangement of pages it is followed by a folder of which the opening words are "Considering how few" and which concludes "it was

moles." This entire folder fits physically and textually between pages four and five of the "Love" draft—that is,
between the second loose leaf (ending "will last forever.")
and the full folder beginning "The relation". Sanborn may
be responsible for the disturbed order of leaves, since the
rejected leaf headed "Love & Friendship" bears a notation
in his hand: "These white pages are later than the *blue*.
F. B. S." (The reference to blue pages is obscure.) First-
draft versions of many "Love" passages, plus related and
analogous passages, are scattered among the fragments of
Thoreau's journal of 1848-1850 (Huntington, HM 13182;
also the Abernethy Library, Middlebury College, journal
leaves beginning "I cannot imagine a woman" and numbered 417-[420]).

Chastity & Sensuality: Early draft versions of several
paragraphs appear in the 1846 journal-workbook in the
Berg Collection, New York Public Library, pages 30-32 and
33 in Thoreau's pagination. They date from May, 1846,
and their context is an early form of the passage on reality
ultimately used near the end of *Walden*, chapter two. In
addition, there are two manuscript versions of the essay,
both written on pale blue paper. The earlier, in black ink
with pencil revisions, 10 pp., is located in the Henry E.
Huntington Library and Art Gallery, HM 13196. Page one
bears a notation in Sanborn's hand: "These *may* be from
1849-50". Thoreau brought the essay to almost final form
in this manuscript by designating the order of paragraphs
and revising the diction. The fair manuscript, copy-text
for this edition, is in the Humanities Research Center Library, University of Texas at Austin, Hanley B, MS (Thoreau, H. D.) Works. It is written in black ink on six leaves,
which have been made into a fascicle by a few stitches at
the left edge. 11 pp.